The Great Immigration Scandal

The Great
Immigration Scandal

Steve Moxon

Published in the UK by Imprint Academic
PO Box 200, Exeter EX5 5YX, UK

Published in the USA by Imprint Academic
Philosophy Documentation Center
PO Box 7147, Charlottesville, VA 22906-7147, USA

ISBN 1-84540-011-9

A CIP catalogue record for this book is available from the
British Library and US Library of Congress

Contents

Acknowledgments

It is ironic that the Home Office, by suspending me on full pay for twenty weeks before sacking me, allowed me both the time and the income to write this book; so although they will not want my thanks it is only right and proper that I should offer them. The Home Office also provided ministers and civil servants so spectacularly incompetent and/or deceitful that their efforts helped rather than hindered the exposure of the appalling mess they presided over. A move by the Treasury Solicitor to try to prevent publication of this book provided the oxygen of publicity it needed.

Moving from those who won't want my thanks to those the reader may expect deserve them, I will surprise in the opposite way by not doing the customary hobnobbing. Nobody encouraged or supported me much if at all until the project was well under way. I simply didn't need and didn't seek any, so that is no reflection on anyone or on my feelings towards them.

But of course, I do have some genuine acknowledgments: to my publisher, Keith Sutherland of Imprint Academic, and to David Leppard of the Sunday Times. David has proved invaluable for savvy advice on how to handle all sorts of things, as well as translating complex matters into publicly-consumable fare. Also insisting on a mention are the ever-so-nice staff at Broomhill Library in Sheffield, where I spent much time e-mailing and researching for this book.

I also owe thanks to my ancestors — the line of awkward though meek characters of which I am a recent incarnation (well, all right, I've ditched the meek bit). My Quaker ancestors were imprisoned for their beliefs in 1650, so battling the establishment must run deep within me. John Mokeson and his kin fought against what they saw as the false God of empty worship championed by the state, while today I fight against the false God of universal equality, in His present incarnation as 'Managed Migration', with its inclusive creed that lets in just about anybody and everybody.

Introduction

The Abandoned Line

This book is about the profound failure of Home Office immigration/ asylum policy and the inability to put even the flawed policy into practice. Far from just being a problem of tens of thousands of East Europeans slipping illegally into Britain ahead of Mayday 2004 — as Government apologists would have you believe — I reveal how the systematic abuses of procedure and open invitation to fraud (instigated and allowed by the Home Office at ministerial and top management levels) extend across the whole of Managed Migration. This applies to all of the different types of cases: in particular students, marriage and dependent relatives. There are fundamental problems with both the general ways of working and all the various ways to avoid bothering to apply particular immigration rules. The whole shebang clearly was inspired by what, to most people's minds, is a bizarre attitude to the relation between British citizens and all the other people in the world.

Managed Migration is the main application processing part of the Home Office's Immigration & Nationality Directorate (IND), that also comprises Work Permits UK and the Immigration Service (immigration officers at key points of entry). As I show, from my own research and that of others, and from official reports and news stories cropping up as I was writing *all three* divisions — IND in its entirety — is riven with across-the-board and in-depth failure. One of the most significant aspects of the chaos of Work Permits emerged fully only late in the day (July 2004); while the farce of the immigration and asylum front line has been charted for some time, with recent events only confirming our worst fears.

The disaster — and that is the only way to describe it — is so serious that there are now calls for the Home Office to be relieved of the whole of its immigration and asylum brief. This is such a central feature of public administration that it is no exaggeration to say the present Government has shown itself to be unfit for office.

* * *

Before I started working for the Home Office in Managed Migration I didn't have a clear opinion on immigration other than that a balance between those entering and those leaving Britain would seem to be a normal and healthy aspect of any developed country, and which must have some obvious benefits. I was happy to unthinkingly support net inward migration, assuming that there must be some benefit — otherwise why would it ever have been encouraged or allowed to happen? Before I looked at the research I didn't object in principle even to *mass* net immigration. Not that I supported it either: I just felt indifferent apart from the (demographic and resource implications).

Since my suspension from work, I have had time and reason to have a thorough look at the researched facts. Together with a full realization, in part through working at the Home Office, that Britain is currently sustaining uncontrolled mass net immigration, it is now clear to me that firm opposition to this is the only rational position to adopt. The combination of having very recently worked on the 'front line' and the rare freedom to speak the truth about current practice, plus a good grasp of the research on the various aspects of immigration and a range of related problems, I think leaves me almost uniquely qualified to comment on immigration, albeit that I am not an expert on any aspect. Solid work experience at the coalface surely places me above any general commentator who, no matter how astute, will not have been able to get anything like the perspective and range of information.

The BBC and some other sections of the media mostly refuse to listen, or to not listen seriously, to either experience or research that contradicts the standard political bigotry of the so-called intelligentsia on the subject of immigration, and willful ignorance is smugly paraded under a cloak of supposed public service. The issue is not going to go away and they are going to have to listen, or face the consequences of otherwise fair-minded people being swayed by unsavoury political opportunists, or in vast numbers giving up on the political process altogether.

* * *

I have tried to tell the story of the extraordinary events from my own perspective in the hope of shedding more light and detail on the scandals and cover-ups at the Home Office regarding both policy and implementation in Britain's immigration system. The lengths that the Home Office predictably went to flout the maxim about digging and holes is as comical as it is contemptuous.

The structure of the book is one of storyline chapters alternating with chapters discussing different aspects of the immigration issue (or 'ishoos', as Tony Benn likes to refer to them), the latter including a discussion of the relevant scholarly literature in demography, economics and psychology. Each strand can be read separately if so desired as each chapter is labelled either 'storyline' or 'analysis'. But I wouldn't recommend this approach, because elements of both strands feature in some chapters — it was difficult always to maintain the distinction, which inevitably is forced in places. (I suppose that any structure imposed on writing to make it more coherent is bound to be a heavy compromise.) Anyway, for a sense of neatness, if nothing else, the chapters are symmetrically clustered around a central pivot (Chapter 9) recounting the key event of the visit to Sheffield by the immigration minister Beverley Hughes on December 4 2003, and looking at the general problems I encountered in how the Home Office dealt with immigration applications.

The storyline sections are chronological bar one sharp flip back in time, while the issue sections are placed in some sort of order of importance to the immigration debate and salience to roughly where the storyline has got to. Finally there is the Epilogue, dealing with the Home Office's unsurprisingly convenient contortion of facts to 'find' that actually I had *not* complied with the Public Interest Disclosure Act. So I end up where I started, with another thread of interest: 'whistle- blowing'.

The trouble to which the Government and even the media went to suppress debate is explained by the emptiness of the rhetoric that is all that props up a bankrupt political position, as discussion of the issues shows. The story and the analysis should cross- illuminate and put each other into context. I hope I have done better than just add some 'human interest', so that the book is more than just the sum of its parts.

Perhaps most important of all, I want to introduce readers to the idea that immigration is not an isolated topic but tied up with questions of equal opportunity, men–women relations, the family, the nature of work and many other subjects, all of which are connected in a contemporary (mis)understanding that is set to implode and be replaced with a far more realistic world view. This may sound like out-dated over-optimism, but honesty about immigration looks like the thin end of a highly interesting wedge that could benefit us all.

* * *

The usual slur chucked at anybody talking about immigration needs to be seen off at the outset. It should go without saying that, as a former Lib Dem council candidate in a heavily Muslim ward (with one of the leading members of the recently arrived Bengali community as my running mate), I don't have *any* racist, xenophobic or other irrational feelings towards any individuals or groups either of ethnic minorities or of white people (from Eastern Europe or from anywhere else), or to any religion or the practitioners of any religion. Neither do I seek to encourage racist, xenophobic or other irrational feelings in others. This is anyway a much overblown problem, as I will explain. My contempt is for the *policy*, or lack of it, that allows lax immigration procedures or no procedures at all, and the underlying politics that makes such a bogus and deceitful case.

Individuals can hardly be blamed for taking advantage of an open door to gain personal advantage by successfully relocating to Britain as an economic migrant. Providing that someone's presence here is not by illegal means, including deception, then it would be pointless or counter-productive as well as unfair to attack the person rather than the ill-thought-out law that allowed them to settle and the incompetent, un-democratic and self-serving politicians and mandarins who allow the situation to continue. Even so, it is not possible to say what proportion of recent immigrants have not simply walked through an open door but arrived illegally or by active deception or collusion with criminals or non-bona fide representatives. We know the proportion is very high, and we know that of these a very high proportion are not making a useful contribution to our society. These people do deserve censure and some may feel that it is now reasonable, with the problem so serious, that a 'rule of thumb' perhaps should err on the side of the tarred brush rather than the complacent platitudes currently on offer from the Government and their left-liberal supporters.

* * *

The ethnic or national origins of anyone coming to Britain for permanent settlement would be immaterial if immigration was based only on natural population exchange within the developed world of the skills and experience countries think it is desirable to exchange. It so happens that most of these people would be white, for the simple reason that most of the developed world is white; but there would also be Japanese and Indian sub-continentals, South-East Asians,

Chinese and a few black Africans and South American Indians — some of those from the higher echelons of their societies. It would hardly matter if the colour mix was reversed, with a large majority of non-whites; because all of these people would be socialised in 'Western' ways with excellent English language skills, a higher education and good career prospects. They would be relatively easily assimilated, notwithstanding their individual higher visibility resulting from their skin colour.

However, this is not at all the reality of immigration today. Most people who come to Britain for permanent settlement at present happen to be non-white, because of the ethnic composition of under-developed nations from where unskilled economic migrants come. Again, their non-whiteness would not be an issue, but most of these people tend to behave in a completely different way to nationals from developed countries. They seek out fellow countrymen to live in enclaves because they are not orientated to Western culture, or through peculiarities of their own culture, poor English, or the absence of any skills (let alone higher education) and a lack of knowledge of labour markets. Inevitably such enclaves are likely to be, or seen to be, difficult or a burden for the wider community. Skin colour (together with facial characteristics and maybe dress) merely serves to make it easier to spot individuals from such enclaves — or to make a reasonable guess that someone is likely to be so. Ethnic minority per se is not at all the root of the problem for all it is routinely claimed.

It would be logical to support net inward migration if for some reason the kind of immigration proposed could be shown to provide a lasting benefit to our society. But on the evidence there is no benefit, and no circumstances, either now or in the foreseeable future, where there could be a benefit. As I will explain, mass net immigration is a clear *dis*benefit.

* * *

One of the stances I take in writing this book is that debate should not be hampered by fear of talking about sub-groups within society rather than the individuals that comprise them. It is not excusable to deny debate because of the supposedly overriding need to constantly assert that generalisations cannot be made about groups without unfairly labelling all of the individuals within the group — who may well as individuals not behave like the typical group member. After all, this is precisely what is being done when it is decided that an ethnic minority community is disadvantaged and so for this reason that particular community as a whole must somehow be helped. The politically correct cannot have it both ways and change from one to the other view to suit their position while insisting that others cannot do the same.

In fact the distinction is a red herring, because all people behave much the same if the social group of which they are a member is displaced to a context of a wider or adjacent social group that in some way is very different. Yet the differences between either individuals or groups are not as salient as the simple fact of inter-group dynamics. This is the case with clearly separate enclaves, for example of Pakistanis and Bangladeshis in Northern cities. These are subgroups within society in the true sense, in that they function vis-à-vis the wider society in an 'in-group'–'out-group' relationship. For their predominantly white neighbours the relationship tends to be reciprocal.

There are social dynamics that will always place these communities apart from the wider society, albeit that there will be assimilation into the mainstream culture at the margin. This is not in any way to do down either individual (for example) Pakistani or Bangladeshi men and women, or the groups that comprise them. Indeed, these groups have — or (as we shall see) used to have — some obvious virtues in more successfully retaining social order and values that to some extent have been lost in the wider society. This tends to produce worthy people useful to society, given a more collective and less individualistic orientation; but the question is: useful to the wider society or useful mainly or only to the ethnic sub-group?

If honesty is seen as something between fellow (for example) Pakistanis or fellow Bangladeshis, but not between a Pakistani/ Bangladeshi and a white person, then this is a problem. It is a problem if there is allegiance and a feeling of responsibility to the ethnic community, but not to society as a whole, leading to (for instance) unusually widespread tax evasion that was a matter of indifference or even encouragement by the ethnic community.

It is undeniable that these communities are necessarily divisive in their very presence within the cities where they are located. This is not due to racism by the majority white population but to natural social forces operating both within the enclave and outside it. The strongest forces are actually those within the enclave. It is not helpful to call this racism, just as it is not helpful to use that term to label the wariness of those in the wider community towards the enclave and its members.

These communities are with us and so we have a responsibility to help them to thrive, but we do not have a responsibility to encourage or allow them to expand still further by mass chain immigration of people from the same countries of origin. But this is indeed what is happening, by both legal and illegal means. Neither do we have a responsibility to help the sub-group over and above providing the same help to the individuals within it compared to individuals belonging to the wider society.

These are some of the arguments I will be developing: ones that I draw your attention to at the outset to encourage the reader to pay particular attention when they arise and not to misunderstand them or their context.

* * *

My work in the Managed Migration division was as an in-country 'backroom boy', in common with that of the Work Permits division. This book is about immigration and asylum as a whole but focusing on in-country immigration applications, specifically at Managed Migration. I deal with Work Permits and asylum in sections of the book but, to finish this introduction, as necessary background I think I should give you a picture of the forward troops: the Immigration Service. 'The abandoned front line' (if you forgive the military analogy), although the metaphor even then does not conjure the full extent of the problem. Defensive forward positions in a theatre of war rarely fail to take a considerable toll on an attacking army (providing the defenders don't run away); and even if they do retreat there are fallback positions that can at least check incursions for a time. If that fails then regrouping for counter-attack may well expel the invaders. None of this holds regarding immigration. There is little in the way of a front line of immigration officers to check people on entry and even less once within this super-thin porous membrane to distinguish unwanted newcomers from everybody else. As for the threat of being sent back over no-man's land: this is effectively non-existent apart from relatively rare cases.

This is despite the Immigration Service Union regularly sounding alerts. Their cries have become routine and wrongly presumed by many to be false shouts of 'wolf', for all the evident mounting tally of dead sheep. It is quite amazing that the very people whose careers put them in the most ideal position possible to comment on problems on the ground are the very people whose comments are ignored — and don't I know the feeling. Nobody explains why people who work in immigration would want to exaggerate rather than, if anything, to minimise the chaos they have to confront. After all, it is natural to talk up and to justify your role in life, not to do down your own efforts.

The person who has done most, very recently, to count the piles of ovine corpses and attest to the reality of the wolf at the door is Harriet Sergeant. She put herself among immigration staff at their places of work and talked with their union spokesmen. The resulting book, *Welcome to the Asylum*, published in 2001, remains the only full-length journalistic investigation into the mess; just as her similar work, *No System to Abuse*, charted the impact of uncontrolled immigration on the NHS (see Chapter 14).

Just as I saw for myself in Managed Migration, Sergeant found that nobody within the system actually got shot of people out of the country. This was her main point when I talked with her. 'They just don't deport people', she complained. I should here explain the difference between a 'removal' and a deportation. A deportation order comes from the Home Secretary and should mean that there is no recourse to re-entry until it is lifted — normally after three years. It has to be applied for by an Immigration Service official and applications are rare. A 'removal' on the other hand is just an administrative concept and not a sanction. These are much more numerous than deportations, but they are of little use since they do not prevent someone re-entering the UK, and as soon as they like. This makes the work of the Immigration Service even more futile than it would seem. (I only found out about the distinction myself when I talked to fellow whistle-blower James Cameron, the former British consul to Romania.)

But even 'removal' was not being done. John Tincey of the Immigration Service Union told Sergeant: 'From what our members say I would be very surprised if we were removing more than 12 people a month who really do not want to go home. We really don't have a working method for removing people who don't want to go.' Quite amazing though it is, there are delays of several months to deport even those illegals who are being held in prison after criminal conviction, where deportation forms part of their sentence. Martin Slade, the general secretary of the Immigration Service Union, commenting to the press in 2002, described the shockingly inept removal process: 'In some cases they're simply escorted to an airport and left to decide whether to board the plane themselves'. This is because anyone who is put on a plane must be escorted by two immigration officers and obviously these cannot be spared from other duties given that there are not even sufficient staff to man an initial cursory gateway check (the ISU complained in April 2004 that Dover was completely unmanned at weekends and during unsocial hours). In any case, airlines refuse to board anyone who is distressed or violent. I will return to the question of removal and deportation in Chapter 12 when I consider asylum policy and look at the Government's recent figures, but here I just want to look at general problems on the ground at ports of entry.

The first difficulty British immigration officers face is the sheer lack of numbers and resources, which itself appears to be a deliberate ploy by the Government. This has a dire effect on the ability both to intercept clandestine illegal immigrants and to properly process ostensibly legal ones. Commenting to a newspaper in January 2003, John Tincey (who is himself an immigration officer at Stansted) said that not only were arrival posts 'badly understaffed' but were 'often manned by beginners'. The number of dogs trained to sniff out people has actually been *reduced*. One of Sergeant's immigration officer informants told her: 'They were finding too many people. We think the authorities would prefer just not to know. We have no deterrent. If we catch them, all we do is put them into the benefits system. Why go to the trouble and expense of searching for illegal immigrants if they are allowed to stay anyway?' The 2001–2 Home Office Business Plan targeted immigration interviews for cost-cutting. 'IND funding is tilted in favour of inactivity despite the dramatic increase in abuse', Sergeant concluded. One completely fed-up IO repeated to her the cliché many of them must often have used: 'If you ask no questions, you get told no lies.'

In the week prior to Sergeant's visit to Dover, nearly 300 clandestine illegals were discovered in the course of just three days, despite only a very small percentage of vehicles being checked. Sergeant extrapolated this to arrive at the figure of 300,000 people a year smuggled through the port of Dover alone. As cannot too often be repeated: nobody, not least the Home Secretary — who openly admits it — has even a remote clue as to how many illegal immigrants come into Britain each year, nor how many are here in total. It is not just road vehicles, but trains come across the channel unchecked at the French end and, when illegals are found on any foreign-run train the companies simply refuse to accept their liability to pay fines.

As regards those who are not hiding but do actually present themselves, the situation is severely exacerbated by the operation of the Schengen Convention, to which the UK is not a signatory, whereas our EU partners all are. This legitimates Britain being treated as the EU's dumping ground for unwanted immigrants: a 'third country' within the meaning of the Convention. Although in this case migrants have actually gone to the trouble to get themselves some documentation, obtaining a Schengen area visa is remarkably easy. Alternatively, many come with fake ID. In general, the EU is the 'major means of illegal entry to the UK' by means of forged documents, according to the ISU. Sergeant was once again flabbergasted to find that: 'When immigration officers pointed out the widespread use of forged identity cards to the IND, the Home Office prevaricated. They feared travellers would get upset if they were stopped and questioned. The immigration officers persisted until the Home Office finally sent a note with the simple exhortation: "Do your best".' As we shall see, this (supposed) fear of upsetting people is the standard excuse the Home Office falls back upon to cop out of any responsibility for the failure of their gatekeeping function.

Summarising the whole debacle of the front line immigration chaos, Sergeant could not be clearer:

> Every policeman and immigration officer I interviewed, not to mention immigration lawyers and aid workers, believed (whatever their political convictions, on this they all agreed) that immigration should be removed from the control of the Immigration & Nationality Department of the Home Office. Or, as one policeman remarked, Parliament should send in the audit office and take them apart 'in the public interest'. ... Both the police and the immigration officers to whom I talked believe the Home Office views immigration as a 'problem that can't be solved'. Their energies are directed, rather, towards 'bluffing the British public' that all is well in the wonderland of immigration.

This book is a testament that Managed Migration (and Work Permits) are failing at least as badly, and furthermore that even if any division of IND did work, the whole thinking behind immigration and asylum policy is fundamentally in error.

Chapter 1 — Storyline

Whistle While You Work

'Whistle-blowers', according to the Shadow Home Secretary, David Davis, are not average people but quirky in some way. I am not sure that Katherine Gunn would agree with that. She had a particular point and made no fuss in putting it over — in contrast, some may feel, to David Shayler, who appears regularly — and progressively more eccentrically — as a commentator on spook-related affairs, yet it was unclear to me quite what it was he was complaining about and why we should be interested. But that was before I met him — I now see what he's about.

It has got to help to be inclined to complain about things. Given the likely consequences it must also be a prerequisite that you are not set on a smooth path through life in the manner of most people. That sounds like me: some very strong interests but none too easy to translate into a career.

Just what it is I felt I had to call time on was perfectly clear and just as obviously of major public interest. Realization grew slowly, though with an increasing rate of spikes in my awareness that I was not feeling justified in what I was being asked to do supposedly in the public interest. I even joked with other staff about how much someone could make selling a story to the papers (I hasten to add that I have taken no money whatsoever for the story). This was some time before I ever thought seriously of so burning my bridges.

It's a toss-up whether I have been asked more questions about what I was exposing than why I came forward, but the 'why' questions are where any acrimony lies — though that's from media, not everyday people. Everyone knows that immigration is a taboo subject absolutely guaranteed to boomerang back at you with a charge of racism, so it came as no surprise to me that I am the first named source to spill the beans in this area of government.

After I had made up my mind that my current working life was contributing to a major governmental fiasco and cover-up, quite a number of factors other than the work and work processes contributed, if not to pushing me to the decision to disclose, then to chasing away my inhibitions about so doing. I had joined this particular part of the Civil Service on the prospect of rapid advancement, only to find that this would be considerably delayed. Trapped on a low salary with insignificant annual increments, as an added insult the annual pay round came in at well below inflation.

Even before I started to have concerns about the work, I saw what appeared to me to be a series of abuses of equal opportunities policy, and my complaints about these met with a brick wall and even intimations of disciplinary action. Then Katherine Gunn shopped GCHQ and confirmed that the Official Secrets Act had indeed fallen off the statute book through chronic disuse. It appeared that nobody could remember how to use it. Clare Short delivered the coup de grace in failing to stir the Government even to deprive her of the Labour whip. How now could the Government use the law against a very lowly civil servant disclosing non-classified information when it would not so much as slap the wrists of one of its own members, even concerning 'top secret' documents ? In any case my work had no connection with intelligence or defence agencies.

Until someone pointed it out to me and I found it on the web, I had not come across the Public Interest Disclosure Act — the legislation that the Labour Government had recently introduced. By this time I had been trying for many weeks to bring problems to the attention of the relevant minister and it turned out that this was exactly what you had to do under the terms of the Act before going to the media. I resolved to give it a little longer: three months seemed a good round figure; an entire season. The Clare Short fiasco, together with the discovery of the 'whistle-blower' Act and that I had by chance complied with its conditions, were for me the combined triggers that set in motion a countdown to what I knew I had to do.

Hampered by not feeling able to give details for fear of compromising my anonymity, I tried and failed to get clear advice — both from a (rather overbearing) lawyer working for a charity concerned with 'whistle-blowing' and from my union — on the likely response of the Home Office. Instant dismissal, or suspension? Could I be suspended without pay? Well no: I did establish that this was itself a disciplinary measure so could not be used against me. The problem was that under the Act I could not take any money in return for disclosing, so I would have to gamble that I would not be dismissed for serious misconduct, thereby losing any entitlement to Job Seekers' Allowance for six months.

Suspension with pay may be seen as censure, but to my mind receiving a salary without having to work is one version of nirvana. I survive perfectly well without office politics, and I'm never ever at a loss as to what to do with spare time. Continuing to be paid in effect for causing trouble seemed like a privilege bestowed only upon gods. Though just what would be the public reaction I was somewhat uncertain. I thought overall it would be supportive, so that the usual social disapproval attending being suspended from a job may well invert. Even so, I was not confident that the other staff would see it quite the same way, although I was fairly sure that most would think I had left myself high and dry, and for what?

It helps to be philosophical. Life is about more than work; about more than the particular job you are doing at the time, especially if the job doesn't amount to much. Work, or work of the sort that most other people do, looked at as a necessary experience of life, to do periodically at least — to make sure that you still connect, if you like — I got a sufficient taste of in the six months I was in post at Managed Migration. I had made no real buddies except for the one guy who managed to get himself the sack. Of the folk who could have become friends in time, they were mostly thinking of leaving. It would have taken a long time to have made firm friends. I read a report of some research on work in large offices that found that although over a working life someone could expect to have regular contact with well over 500 co-workers, on average he/she would make just five friendships that could survive one or other party moving to a different workplace. Given that work can kill you energy-wise and so prevents quite a lot of socializing in the evenings, then I make it that work can easily denude your social life more than it helps to create one.

The problem with work today, as I see it, is the same problem with much of life: we have given up a reliable if partly rigid social order in a dubious exchange for an untrusting free-for-all whereby, more than ever before, the few have a good and easy time while the many struggle. The informal side of life at work mirrors life outside, while work itself has also got worse in becoming more constrained, however superficially it may seem more human than it used to be. There is a good case to be made that actually to an extent as never before we are cogs in the machine. Ask anyone who works for a bank; teachers even. The luck may be with those with the spirit to take on board the asocial zeitgeist and to transform their work–life accordingly — if that's possible. Perhaps that is what I was giving myself the chance to do. (Probably that's so much tosh, and I'm just trying to convince myself that I haven't simply dug a great big hole that I won't be able to climb out of.)

* * *

My mind was a jumble. There were so many factors, many interdependent and all of them hard to judge the extent to which they would actually come into play. What kept me from seriously doubting my course of action was the relentlessness of the work; and that many or most decisions I was obliged to make went against my sense of what I should be doing. But how to go about interesting the media in what I had? Immigration had never been an issue that inflamed any passions inside me. It is not an area of politics I had researched. But I guessed there must be some reputable pressure group. Given the sensitivity of the politics then, I reasoned, somebody or some group must have gone to considerable trouble to put forward a balanced and cautious appraisal. Sure enough, searching the web I found the site of Migrationwatch UK. I read all of the findings and press pieces on the site to find that arguments were presented in considerable detail without exaggeration and with caution in using statistics and research. To say the least, the content was highly persuasive and quite apolitical. The organization's chairman, Sir Andrew Green, used to be ambassador to Saudi Arabia and Syria. He was one of the 50 ex-diplomats who were to sign the letter to Downing Street criticizing the PM's support for the Bush position on Palestine and the lack of planning for post-war Iraq. One of what has been dubbed 'the camel brigade' for supposedly doing the time-honoured thing that diplomats do: going native. Hardly a right-wing xenophobe. Migrationwatch is no right-wing think tank as some commentators have claimed. I rang Green and a kindly voice in well-spoken English minus any tang of the 'toff' answered. In a brief conversation it was he who suggested meeting at the place of most mutual convenience: his London flat.

It was a quiet spot, Sir Andrew's compact but period first-floor bolthole overlooking a Pimlico park. Here one midweek afternoon I was to outline at some length the scale of the problem and the sort of documents I had copied and removed from the office. The man who opened the door was slight and delicately featured, looking gently aged with swept grey hair in a suit. I had got there early, so while he finished making phone calls I volunteered to let myself loose in the adjoining kitchen to make tea for us. We sat on opposing sofas waiting for the other to begin. I showed him neither documents from work nor the 6,000 word detailed account I had already written that would be my 'disclosure' I would hand over to whichever newspaper I plumped for. Leaving everything at home, as if I felt in danger of being confronted holding incriminating evidence, I brought with me just a couple of scribbled sheets of flow diagrams as structure for how I would explain everything. He took notes and asked clear pointed questions. I got the impression of a level-headed, intelligent and quite meek man; serious and not given to cracking a joke or responding to one. There was little small talk in getting down to business. He seemed to twig that I knew about key procedures, though I could infer from some of his questions that he was in the dark about quite a lot of the work we did. This was my value: someone who hewed at the very coal face processing applications, who knew in detail what actually were the bases of decisions, rather than what someone outside the organization could research by reading the legislation and assuming that the spirit and the letter of the law were being applied in practice. He was not entirely amazed at the extent of what I revealed. 'Well, we knew there was a problem', he said, regarding students, and other categories. I asked if there had ever been a named source for leaks from the Immigration Service. No, I was the first one. 'I'm surprised no-one has come forward before', he said.

Clearly convinced that I was bona fide and with a powerful story, Sir Andrew suggested some newspapers. The Mail, obviously. He was certain they would jump at the story, but the Mail is maligned as right-wing, and it's tabloid in style as well as format, though with some excellent columns. Then there is the Telegraph, which is probably the best of the papers, if maybe a little staid and identified with the Conservatives. I opted for the Sunday Times, because it's a true broadsheet and perhaps the paper with the strongest reputation for investigation and also the one closest to the political centre (though some may disagree with me on that). Of the papers, bar the Mail and the Express, I thought that the Sunday Times would be the one most interested in running the story as a front page scoop. Katherine Gunn had plumped for the Observer, but I reckoned that there would be too many caveats with that paper's politics. It is 'the Guardian on Sunday' after all; the Guardian being the social worker's rag, I have long thought. I then found out that the Observer's editor was, allegedly, a fervent Blairite — though I would have thought further to the Left. The Sunday Times was the paper with the strongest track record of fearlessly upsetting the Government (on issues other than Iraq, which many of the papers take the Government to task over).

There and then Green rang David Leppard, an award-winning journalist and a key Sunday Times writer (deputy editor for home affairs) whose pieces usually appeared on the front page. Still the same persona of level-headed seriousness, though it was clear they knew each other. Yes, he was indeed very interested. Sir Andrew seemed assured in his confidence of his own assessment. I later talked with Leppard by phone. Not an easy conversation, I did not know what to make of him and I am sure vice-versa. Halting stuff as we each gingerly trod around what we imagined would be the other's stance and reservations, but without much messing about we agreed that he should come up on the train and meet me in Sheffield.

D-day was going to be a Sunday obviously and the Sunday Times, as would any newspaper with a great story, wanted to go sooner rather than later, especially given that the May 1 EU accession date was looming. Sunday February 29, appropriately the leap year day, would be perfect. I would have collected my February paycheck, so I would not put in jeopardy, as I imagined, payment for any days I had worked. Unfortunately David Leppard was away abroad during the last week of February, so I took the opportunity to take remaining annual leave and put the whole thing back seven days to the first Sunday in March. I told nobody at Aspect Court, the building where I worked, though I could not resist dropping the odd hint to one or two folk I used to have covert moan sessions with that I had something up my sleeve and I may not be at work for very much longer.

On his return Leppard came up to Sheffield. We were to meet by the coffee shop in the station foyer. We hadn't bothered with button-holed carnations or a particular magazine under the arm. He hovered; I hovered; ever so briefly before mutual 'recognition'. I guess he looked like a hack and I must have looked like … whatever 'quirky' people are reckoned to look like. I introduced my brother — I had brought him along as a witness, to be on the safe side in case anything was later disputed about what was said. No idea at all, you see, how these things worked. Leppard looked a little wary; not a physically imposing figure, with thin-framed unobtrusive glasses and a boyish face that reminded me of a lad who used to live on our street when I was a teenager. An unsmiling, sharp no-nonsense attitude. We took a taxi ride, during which I diverted the conversation to Sheffield, trying to dance around the awkwardness a little. Leppard ran with this a while but returned to the matter at hand. We arrived outside the grounds of the little block containing my flat, on a steep hill among the stone-built Victorian houses and trees of Broomhill, close to Sheffield's hospital/university quarter. He paid the fare almost before I could think of offering or realizing that he would be on expenses. I suppose I was selling and he was buying, but it struck me that we were both pitching a sale: me my story, and he his paper as the proper custodian for it. Inside, the encounter was a mutually-guarded and strained business. I needed a guarantee of legal cover in the unlikely event that action would be taken against me (though I was in the union). I knew, and we agreed, that I could not be paid any money as a serving civil servant. This was heavily stressed. I had planned to get Leppard to sign a note I had written to the effect that he would not use anything he gleaned from the meeting unless and until we had firmly agreed to go ahead with a full story and that he would not take notes or use a tape recorder. But he would have none of it. I had to trust him, he argued. After all, his reputation was on the line. This threw me quite a bit. I even considered asking him to leave while I thought through how to proceed, but I suppose I simply recoiled from appearing rude and allowed the momentum to carry me along. I was disconcerted.

I read out as clearly and expressively as I could a twelve-page statement containing all the information and argument I wanted to put over; consciously trying to slow down my usual tendency to talk too fast. He took detailed notes in shorthand, only occasionally interrupting with questions. He allowed me to read out the whole thing. I got the impression that I fairly convinced him that I was the source of something better than just a good story. He wanted the statement and supporting documents to take with him. I froze, but my brother stuck his oar in. With experience of contracts from his own work, he reassured me that I wasn't (necessarily) making a big mistake. As a concession to my own worries I said that I would make him copies, but Leppard wanted the originals. OK, I again conceded, but I would have to keep copies. Since most of the documents were just print-outs of e-mails then a photocopy was more or less as good as the print it was taken from. I just didn't want him disappearing into News International to leave me empty-handed while the whole news floor chuckled at such an effortless steal. Could the story have had legs without me to swear by it? I suppose it needed me to give the documents 'provenance', as it were. But I wasn't thinking straight, as well as swimming out of my depth.

We needed a photocopier but it was evening. Leppard asked if I knew of a good hotel: one that was bound to have a business centre within it. We took a taxi to the Novotel near the station and bluffed our way to an office by reception and hurriedly copied the key documents, with help from staff oblivious to the significance of the explosive material. It felt a bit like ransacking a bank — with me as the manager forced to lend a hand. Or crude espionage. 'Where's the miniature camera? ... oh sod it, just use the bloody xerox machine.' Leppard was a little excited, I imagined at least. He reassured me, saying he felt fairly sure he could convince his editor that we had a major story, but he must hit him with everything at once; that's why he needed to take all the stuff with him. Having used the hotel facilities on the grounds that we were having a business conference, I suggested we owed them our patronage of the bar. Winding down over a round of Grolsch the frost was thawing. Leppard joked a little, I recall, jabbing at my fears for my own future. I recall that I even managed a light quip myself. My brother had to go and we wandered down to the station to check train times and then parked ourselves inside a nearby bar until near departure time. Conversation turned a little more philosophical whenever Leppard wasn't lending his ear and craning his neck to the big screen football. I felt that I may be making a big mistake as we shook hands at the railway station. I no longer felt I had any control over events.

Uneasy, I couldn't say what it was I felt might go wrong. Perhaps it was just that I had set the wheels in motion and now I could not turn back. And the driver was no longer myself but a journalist — an allegedly dodgy breed, I was all too aware — I barely knew as an acquaintance, let alone a trusted friend. A secret fear, maybe, that the whole world was about to find me an hilarious joke as my supposed revelations turned out to be just the delusions of a lowly staff member who had simply failed to see the big picture and instead had inflated himself into the hero of a mighty but sham exposé. I seem to have discovered that my long self-proclaimed disinterest to what other people thought of me was shockingly fragile: the truth is I dreaded mockery just as deeply as did everybody else. Though just as chilling was the idea that if I was taken seriously, I would be challenged in terms of 'who are you?' to cry foul when something in my own past might be twisted to show that I could hardly assume the role of some moral arbiter. Instead of a laughing stock, I might be held up for contempt. It would wear off, I supposed, but only to give way to jokes at my expense. All roads, it seemed, ended in 'taking the piss' out of yours truly. Was I — could I be derided as — taking the whatsit out of the Home Office? I hadn't even started looking at all the various ways that simple and obvious practical things could spell disaster. Looking at the worst eventuality, and discounting it in realizing that's what it was, distracted me from appreciating the plethora of more mundane trip-wires and booby-traps I was allowing to be set up ahead of me. Strange, but imagination saved me from a course of just keeping my head down in the face of a realistic assessment of risk. Not that I was brave, or even risk averse; I merely had so little to lose.

Chapter 2 − Timeline

Scandal and Cover-up: A Whistle-Stop Tour

The following is a chronological sequence in diary format of the key events in the unfolding of the immigration scandal, or rather scandals. There are several revelations and cover-ups that were exposed in the news, quite apart from when you pull out the daily news camera lens to reveal overall the biggest scandal of the lot: that there is no case, economic or otherwise, for mass net immigration.

My purpose here is to provide a timeline of initial and main subsequent events that the reader can refer back to when putting into context subsequent sections. I assume no prior knowledge of these episodes, although they were highly newsworthy at the time.

Sunday March 7, 2004

The start of what became the growing scandal concerning the whole of immigration policy and practice, was the Sunday Times front page lead: 'Lid blown on migrant cover-up'. This followed my comprehensive disclosure to the newspaper of my allegations that nationals of those states set to become members of the EU were being allowed into the country supposedly as self- employed tradesmen, first with greatly reduced checking and latterly with no checks whatsoever. The characterization in much of the press and TV coverage was 'fast-tracking', which understated what was a complete failure to apply immigration rules. These applications were under what was known as the European Community Association Agreement (ECAA), latterly processed exclusively at the Sheffield office of Managed Migration, the division of the Home Office where I worked.

I had finally come forward after trying for three months to get a response to my concerns from the immigration minister Beverley Hughes, who was junior to the Home Secretary, David Blunket (the man with ultimate responsibility for immigration policy). I suggested that there was a political motive behind the relaxed and then eliminated procedures: to allow as many people as possible into Britain ahead of the May 1 date of EU accession, so as to minimize the apparent impact on immigration that a flood of arrivals would give. At the very least this was highly convenient to the Government, so even if it began as 'cock up' all the incentive was there to let it run. The Home Office put out a statement simply denying all my claims.

Monday March 8

I showed up for work as normal and was immediately suspended on full pay pending an investigation to ascertain whether my disclosure to the Sunday Times fell within the terms of the Public Interest Disclosure Act (the 'whistle-blower's Act', as it has been dubbed, introduced in 1998 by the Labour Government). In the afternoon immigration minister Beverley Hughes came to the Commons to admit that there was a problem as I had revealed, but that she had not been made aware of my concerns and had no knowledge of the 'fast-track' procedures at Sheffield, which she blamed on junior officials there. She stressed that there was no question of a policy being implemented to hide the scale of an influx from East Europe.

Hughes announced that there would be an investigation, headed by Ken Sutton, a senior official of the Immigration and Nationality Directorate (IND). But the shadow Home Secretary, David Davis, demanded an independent enquiry on the grounds that there would be no confidence in the inquiry's findings if they were conducted by an IND insider, and any investigation needed to have a much broader remit. What Davis did not reveal was that he had just received an anonymous e-mail backing up my claims.

Thursday March 11

Beverley Hughes appears on BBC1's Question Time, having been booked to appear before the furore broke. She is roasted by some of the panel and by the audience. She blames the problem uncovered at Sheffield on the team processing the applications (which is clearly at odds with evidence already out in the open).

Sunday March 14

The second part of my allegations are revealed by the Sunday Times: this time about the failure to apply immigration rules to student and marriage applications — which if taken together make up the bulk of applications to Managed Migration — and resulting abuses. Internal e-mails from senior caseworkers and officials show that there is abuse by bogus students and colleges and by people entering into sham marriages and that the Home Office was fully aware of the problems but was doing nothing about them. This time the Home Office did not dispute my claims.

Tuesday March 16

The first leak, albeit not from a named source, from someone else within IND backing up an aspect of what I had claimed. It was a memo showing that Beverley Hughes personally approved the 'fast-track' processing of 29,000 applications handled by the Home Office at Liverpool. To clear a backlog of settlement applications all passport checks were waived, despite the fact that such checks were necessary to establish no significant absences abroad during the qualifying five-year UK residence, which is a condition under the immigration rules. The memo sent to Hughes stated that there was no reason it should be disclosed outside of the Nationality Group within the Home Office; its author thereby providing the incriminating evidence of improper motive. The Home Office confirmed that Hughes had indeed approved this.

Sunday March 21

Revealed by the Sunday Times: my letter to the senior director of Managed Migration, Paula Higson, telling her of the serious problems in removing all checks on processing applications. This undermines Hughes' claim that neither she nor senior officials had known. Hughes had said previously that under such circumstances she would agree to the calls for her resignation, but it was no surprise that she did not honour this. I had only belatedly realized the importance of the letter earlier in the week, because it was mainly about abuses of the implementation of equal opportunities policy and I had simply forgotten about the other important content relevant to the immigration scandal. Hughes had dismissed my concerns in a brief reply.

Wednesday March 24

David Davis discovers the identity of the person who sent him the anonymous e-mail the day after the immigration scandal first broke.

It was James Cameron: not the film director, but the British consul to Romania, no less. He had been shopped by one of his own colleagues to the Foreign Office. Apart from the corroboration, in the strongest terms, of my allegations; that this was from a senior and long-serving official was extremely damaging to the Government.

Thursday March 25

The Home Office announces that the internal inquiry headed by Ken Sutton has cleared Hughes of involvement in the 'fast-tracking' of EU accession state nationals. Surprise surprise. I had been asked only two substantive questions in the few minutes that Sutton interviewed me just the previous day. The Sutton report is universally regarded as a complete whitewash and was not prominently covered in the media for that reason. Calls for a proper independent and wide-ranging investigation are renewed.

Sunday March 28

The Home Office was turning into a sieve. Another unnamed IND official leaks to the Sunday Times a memo instructing staff to waive all checks on applications more than three months old. The significance of this is that at the time (which is when I was in place) all applications we were dealing with fell into this category because of the backlogs afflicting applications across the board. The Home Office official who leaked the memo said that the backlog clearance exercise: 'resulted in virtually no control on applications... There are now tens or hundreds of thousands of foreign nationals being allowed to stay who do not qualify to be here. This includes drug dealers, other criminals and probably the odd terrorist.' She described this as: 'corruption and abuse on a massive scale.' The memo states: 'This exercise has been agreed by the minister of state Beverley Hughes.' To verify that the memo was genuine the Sunday Times went undercover. The Home Office confirmed that a secret no-checks policy had indeed been introduced the previous August. The Sunday Times front page lead headline got it in a nutshell: 'Memo leak traps migrant row minister.' Ditto Ken Sutton. The memo had been shown to him and this completely destroyed the credibility of Sutton's report, published just three days before. This point is picked up by David Davis, who charged the Home Office yet again with cover-up.

Monday March 29

The identity of the second named source, James Cameron, is revealed in the Commons by David Davis. As an official at the British embassy in Bucharest he worked at the other end of the operation processing the applications of nationals from states set to become new members of the EU: in his case from Romania. Cameron describes my revelations as 'just the tip of the iceberg' and that applicants are invariably granted admission to Britain despite using forged documentation, even after he had informed Managed Migration in Sheffield. His e-mail contained the now famous reference to a 'one-legged roof tiler' and others that by the very nature of their disability could not possibly perform the jobs ostensibly they claimed they could be or were self-employed to do, which was the basis of their applications for UK residence under the ECAA scheme. I had never been in contact with Cameron, nor could I have been (the only communication between British embassies and Managed Migration caseworkers was via impersonal faxes).

David Davis had received the e-mail anonymously the day after my disclosures first appeared in the Sunday Times, but it was not of great use until the identity of the sender was revealed. Then Davis kept it back while he built a dossier to comprehensively demolish the Government's case. Cameron's leak of his own e-mail had not been known by the Government until today and for this disclosure he too is immediately suspended.

As with my original allegations, Beverley Hughes claimed that the Government had not been made aware of Cameron's concerns. But then the Labour deputy chief whip, Bob Ainsworth, saw her denials on the evening Channel 4 News and BBC Newsnight and reminded her of an exchange of letters they had had the previous year on precisely the issues that Cameron had raised.

Tuesday March 30

As if matters could get any worse for the Government, backing up James Cameron, someone in the Foreign Office leaks a letter sent eighteen months before by the senior FO official Sir John Ramsden, warning of a 'massive, organised scam' of ECAA applications generally, and this had been copied to several Home Office officials. This prompts Blunkett to adopt panic measures — immediately suspending all immigration applications from Romania and Bulgaria. Beverley Hughes defends herself in Parliament, insisting that she is 'neither incompetent nor dishonest' and that she has the support both of David Blunkett and of Tony Blair. This smacks of despair, and with leaks now daily and no apparent way around the problem of her letter exchange with Ainsworth, she must have been aware herself that she was unlikely to hold on to her ministerial brief.

The story is partly displaced from being the lead for the day by the arrest of eight suspected terrorists following early morning police raids on twenty-four premises in London, though it transpires that evidence against them was still being gathered, and so the suspicion in some quarters is that it is a 'news sponge' ploy by the Home Office. If this leads in time to the acquittal of suspects when a delayed raid would have given time for the full accumulation of necessary evidence against them, then this could be yet another scandal amongst various scandals in the Government's immigration debacle.

Wednesday March 31

Hughes discusses with Blunkett and Blair the implications of the letters between Ainsworth and herself. Blunkett's staunch defence of her is overruled by Blair who tells Hughes she has to go.

Thursday April 1

Beverley Hughes hands her resignation to Tony Blair and later delivers her resignation speech, defiantly rebutting charges of repeatedly lying; excusing herself by characterizing her errors as: 'however unwittingly, I may have given a misleading impression.' Almost nobody believes her and the following morning's press is scathing. Her replacement is the little known Des Browne who, appropriately, is a battle-hardened former junior minister for Northern Ireland.

Saturday April 3

Trevor Phillips, the chair of the Commission for Racial Equality, declares via a front page lead article in the Times that multiculturalism as an approach must be abandoned. Shortly afterwards the CRE announces that it is to cease funding all projects that in any way promote separatism. This is widely regarded as a monumentally significant political sea change, Phillips being a key advisor to Blair.

Sunday April 4

The Sunday Times details yet more Home Office leaks showing that Immigration Service staff were ordered not to arrest illegal migrants in case they then applied for asylum: to mount raids only when sure that those likely to be caught were failed asylum seekers. No less than four Home Office officials contacted the paper and the paper backed up the story with a letter from an assistant director in the Immigration Service it had received the previous summer. Tellingly the Home Office put out a statement that did not deny the non-arrest policy. The irony is that the Government was lambasting the press for its confusion between asylum and immigration when it was itself in practice confusing the two, merely to doctor figures (regardless of the obvious costs to the country). This is a major scandal on top of that of the complete failure of immigration procedures.

The Sunday Telegraph runs a front page story that the Government has been found to be itself fuelling the immigration scandal as it tried to reduce the asylum figures to fulfil a promise by Tony Blair to halve them. The paper reveals that Blair did a deal with his Romanian opposite number for Britain to let in more migrants by relaxing visa controls in exchange for co-operation in stemming the flood of Romanian asylum seekers. This appears to confirm speculation as to why Romanian and Bulgarian nationals were being treated in the same way as nationals from the other EU accession states, despite Romania and Bulgaria not acceding to the EU until 2007, whereas the others were to join in a matter of weeks (on May 1, 2004).

Tuesday April 6

Tony Blair holds a Downing Street 'summit' on immigration, widely regarded as simply so that he could be shown supposedly to be doing something. It is argued by some that the awkward presentation of this, given nothing new to announce, is partly alleviated by the fortuitous lead news story of that evening of the foiling of a 'terrorist plot' using osmium tetroxide — a chemical so lacking in toxicity that it is not even credible as a terrorist weapon. This would be the second time that a dubious news story emanating from the Home Office has acted as a convenient 'news sponge'.

The restatement of policy is to combat bogus students, bogus colleges and sham marriages, but the measures are either inadequate or unstated and do not address the principal roots of abuse of the system.

Saturday April 17

David Blunkett trumpets raids on massage parlours/saunas (brothels) in Sheffield and Leeds as the successful targeting of traffickers of illegal migrants; the illegals he considers exploited victims (whether or not most of the girls were tricked into coming to Britain — and locals say they gave the definite impression that they were not). This was a transparent attempt to distract the public from the reality of the massive scale of illegal entry and overstay (quite apart from asylum claimants) which the Immigration Service is completely failing to address. This high profile operation took months of work by hundreds of Immigration Service personnel and police. To apply this level of action to tackle the problem overall would require several hundred thousand officers and so in fact highlights the Government's complete inability to deal with the problem.

Sunday April 18

The Immigration Service Union complains that cutbacks have left ports wide open to illegal entry; that all major operations to seek illegals have been abandoned and that there is no cover at all at weekends.

Monday April 19

U-turn number one. Under pressure on the immigration issue, as well as on Europe and Iraq, Tony Blair confirms unattributed leaks (though obviously of Government origin) that appeared in the Sunday newspapers of his decision to allow a referendum on the EU constitution after all. Immigration and Europe (and terrorism) are linked issues that together are a lethal political cocktail, as this capitulation so clearly demonstrates.

Monday April 26

David Blunkett gives some details of the much-heralded proposals for an ID card, announcing the launch of a pilot. The initial publicity was angled towards combatting the terrorist threat, but the main reason, which emerges in the confused presentation, is that it is really about being seen to try to combat illegal immigration and the abuse of access to benefits and the NHS by illegal entrants and overstayers and those with restricted residence conditions; access which is currently uncontrolled. But the card is not expected to be fully introduced until 2013 and even then there is no agreement that it would be made compulsory. There is also serious division within the Cabinet. Generally welcomed, the proposal for the scheme is for Blunkett a useful diversion from the immediate immigration crisis to which it contributes nothing at all.

Tuesday April 27

U-turn number two. At the last minute Tony Blair changes the subject of his speech to the CBI in London to that of immigration. This is widely reported as a U-turn, following the EU constitution U-turn of the previous week. On policy it is yet again restatement with no new initiatives, but what is new is the general admission of a serious problem. It is 'crunch time' for immigration, he says, and a 'top-to-bottom' review of the whole of policy is needed. Blair also affirms that those who comment on immigration policy are not racists, though he does not also point out the unfairness of a charge of incitement to racism — which, for example, he had himself lodged against Michael Howard in a Prime Minister's Question Time session.

It is announced that there will be restriction of benefits to EU accession state nationals after May 1, but no detail of how this is to be achieved when currently there is no system in place for routine checks on eligibility to benefits either at Job Centres and Benefit Agency offices or within the IND.

Saturday May 1

D-day for eight of the ten EU accession states. From today, citizens of all of the countries that had been destined to become part of the EU — all except Romania and Bulgaria, which do not join until 2007 — are free to travel unimpeded throughout the EU, Britain included; but are allowed to work *only* in Britain and Ireland. A confidential Home Office memo orders frontline immigration officers not to check EU passports for fear of upsetting nationals of the newly acceded states, contravening promises to tighten up on what had been the 'light touch' approach to European visitors to take account of the terrorist threat. Severe staff shortages are confirmed, as is the abandonment of checks at Calais of coaches heading for the UK, despite the fact that no checks at all are carried out at Dover on the assumption that checks have been made on the other side of the Channel. David Blunkett had promised a register of all EU accession state migrants arriving from May 1, but the Home Office was now saying that it was not even going to count them.

Either side of May 1, various stories surfaced about the ease with which forged passports and immigration documents could be obtained in Eastern Europe; the porosity of the new EU border — leading to other nationals posing as those of newly-acceded EU states; the poor economic conditions and discrimination against minorities motivating migration; etc.

Sunday May 23

A row between the Government and civil servants over the spinning of immigration and asylum issues is exposed by the Sunday Times. The leaked 14-page Home Office Marketing and Media Strategy, written jointly by Blunkett's political advisers and civil servants, is designed to 'neutralize' the issue of asylum ahead of the general election, starting in July; but calls into question Whitehall independence and would appear to be an abuse of public funds. The intention is to reduce bulletins on immigration — notably from the National Audit Office — because 'no-one believes any of the statistics', and to use supposedly independent 'third party endorsers'. Giving a pat on the back to the BBC for its attitude, it promises to give the corporation stories with 'human faces' to show the positive impact of immigration, and to use advertising. The report seems to be leading to an own-goal in trumpeting new signs and posters at ports, and (possibly) new uniforms for staff to advertise controls at ports, and a 'refugee integration strategy' to help people settle in Britain.

Tuesday May 25

An attempt to get the Government off the hook backfires. A National Audit Office report claiming that there is no evidence to link falls in asylum figures with increases for those in immigration categories turns out simply to have failed to look for the evidence it purports does not exist. Government figures on asylum are shown only to be 'mostly reliable', with significant sources of under-counting. On the same day, separate Home Office figures show that 'removals' are falling far short of even the reduced levels of newly-arriving asylum seekers, and that what had been a rising rate of 'removals' had now reached a plateau.

Sunday May 30

Comparing the problem to that of pre-1980s Northern Ireland, the Government's serious alarm about widespread active support for al-Qaeda amongst British Muslims is revealed in yet another Home Office leak to the Sunday Times. That 15,000 young British Muslims actively support al-Qaeda is admitted by Home Office supremo John Gieve in his Project Contest paper — a wide-ranging plan that includes pumping money into Muslim enclaves in a bid to tackle serious alienation and massive economic inactivity, and intervention to train imams from abroad. There is also an explosive proposal to amend the Race Relations Act specifically to outlaw anti-Muslim comments and discrimination.

Wednesday June 9

A window on the extent of immigration/asylum chaos was opened by Home Office expert, Robert Owen, when he gave 'highly classified' evidence on oath at Swansea Crown Court. He revealed that between 40,000 and 50,000 was the actual number of Chinese nationals living in Manchester, not 8,000 as officially recorded. Owen admitted he could not even 'guesstimate' the total number of illegal migrants living in the country, though it was 'considerably higher' than the official figure. The current controls both on immigration and asylum could not cope, he said, the variety of routes into Britain was 'unbelievable', and that 'we have no serious removal arrangements'. Owen explained that illegals no longer bothered with asylum and hiding in lorries, and instead simply posed as students using forged documents provided by gangs.

Sunday June 13

It emerges (in the Sunday Times) that there are trumped-up charges of 'criminal misconduct' against the other whistle-blower, James Cameron. Staff at the Bucharest embassy are furious about Foreign Office allegations of improper dealings with a travel agency, with suggestions of kickbacks and even sexual favours. This was seen as a way of getting round the 'whistle-blower's Act' to remove Cameron and his wife from their posts. The charges were exactly the same as those, now dropped, against the British ambassador to Uzbekistan, Craig Murray, who exposed systematic torture by the Uzbek regime to the chagrin of the Government. It seems that 'sex for visas' is the stock charge the Foreign Office resorts to, to try to get back at renegades and to discourage others.

Monday June 14

James Cameron faced his disciplinary hearing at the Foreign Office and though not sacked was removed from his post in Romania, given a 'final warning', and had his pay and promotion prospects frozen: everything in fact just short of sanction that would transgress the Public Interest Disclosure Act. Cameron's bosses told him that they were not competent to hear his case under the Act. The question of the charges of criminal behaviour would be dealt with later, he was told.

Wednesday June 16

A token, but well-publicised, police operation in London against a gang using fake immigration stamps and documents to get overseas nationals registered at colleges, including two bogus colleges in Tooting. Police suspected the fraud had been going on for years. This operation was the only one against bogus colleges/students reported in the whole of 2004 (at the time of going to press), and the Home Office put out a statement emphasizing that the great majority of student applications were genuine. The spin here is that there is not really a big problem and what problem exists the authorities are on top of: quite the reverse of the reality.

Thursday June 17

Re-igniting the whole immigration scandal, a National Audit Office report that nine out of ten Bulgarian and Romanian ECAA applicants that were accepted should instead have been refused, provided easy headlines. The Home Office had repeatedly overruled British embassy visa section staff. David Clarke, the principal author of the report, put it bluntly: 'The suspicion there is clear. They weren't really coming across to set up a business. They were coming across to take up jobs and therefore displace potential jobs here.' The astonishing mindset at the Home Office was also exposed: 'Home Office staff believed that they were not able to make it any more onerous for Bulgarian and Romanian nationals to set up business in the United Kingdom than for British nationals.'

Sunday June 20

The BBC exposes a Zimbabwean asylum racket whereby supporters of Robert Mugabe's Zanu-PF party — including the notorious Stalin Mau Mau — have been granted asylum in the UK after being coached to pose as members of the opposition party by a group of exiled Zimbabweans living in Birmingham, which also provides fraudulent Home Office immigration letters and passports. It is thought that thousands of people have come into the UK in this way, to swell an expat Zimbabwean British population already in excess of one million.

Sunday June 27

Even after she resigned, Beverley Hughes comes under renewed fire as new revelations surface of a cock-up when she was in post. 25,000 houses earmarked for asylum applicants are empty because of the falling asylum numbers, but the contracts do not allow use of the homes by anybody other than asylum seekers. All of the houses have to be fully furnished to boot. The blunder is costing £100 million annually.

Monday June 28

'Health tourism', and the wide abuse of the NHS by recent immigrants to the UK ineligible to use it, was raised as a serious issue by doctors at the BMA's annual conference. Estimates of the proportion of patients seen by GPs who were not legally registered ranged from 10–40 percent, yet no guidance was given to doctors in how to cope. Proof of address was all that was needed to register with a GP. Visiting relatives from Africa, Eastern Europe and the Indian subcontinent were a particular problem. However, the BMA's GP committee said that doctors would refuse to report cases of abuse; the responsibility being that of the Home Office.

Wednesday June 30

My disciplinary hearing at the Home Office before the HR supremo, Steve Barnett, who insisted that no decision about my dismissal had been made. As expected, no decision was announced on the day. After the meeting a TV crew claimed they overheard a Home Office official talking about my sacking (or so they inferred): that it would be 'unacceptable in the current climate'.

Thursday July 1

A Government-inspired pressure group is launched: the Migration Alliance — clearly one of the 'third-party endorsers' planned in the Home Office report leaked to the Sunday Times. It is headed by the ex-immigration minister, Barbara Roche, and the launch comes ahead of a vaunted attempt by the Government to announce measures to tackle immigration problems starting later in the month. The idea of the MA is to try to rubbish the Migrationwatch think-tank, but from a source that can be portrayed to be at arm's length from the Government. With Orwellian truth-inversion it is the genuinely independent Migrationwatch (MW) that MA brands as 'masquerading as independent'. Headed by a former UK ambassador and a leading economist, MW presents data with caution and in detail, but the organization is routinely branded 'right-wing'. MA allies the TUC, three major unions and the Joint Council for the Welfare of Immigrants. As usual, the idea seems to be to counter attacks on Government immigration policy and practice by falsely portraying opponents as anti-immigrant.

Wednesday July 7

A proposal to introduce a new criminal offence of incitement to religious hatred was resurrected by David Blunkett, despite what many see as a sop to the Muslim community having been defeated by the Lords in 2001. Widely regarded as an affront to free speech that would stifle debate and may even affect comedians, the Labour Asian peer, Lord Desai, spoke out against the idea. Tough penalties already exist for conspiracy to commit violence and for religiously-aggravated assault. Assurances by Blunkett of sensible and un-biased application confirmed in many minds that over-zealous and pro-Muslim application would indeed be the result. With unfortunate timing characteristic of the Home Secretary, coinciding with the announcement was a visit to the UK by the Quatar-based imam Yusuf al-Quaradawi, who is banned from the USA for openly advocating suicide bombing against Jews by Muslim children — which he justifies by a misreading of the Koran. Blunkett's own deputy, Home Office junior minister Fiona McTaggart, withdrew her support from a conference supported by the Metropolitan Police in protest at the cleric's headline involvement. Muslim leaders, on the other hand, queued up to proclaim that criticising al-Quaradawi was an insult to Islam and that he was a moderate, supported by mainstream British Muslims.

Wednesday July 14

Major abuse of the Work Permits system was uncovered with a written answer by the new immigration minister, Des Browne, to a parliamentary question. Of the 145,351 Work Permits issued in 2003, 73,866 were 'permissions' given to foreign nationals already in the UK in another immigration category: they had 'switched' from short-term tourist or student visas, despite the regulations forbidding this. Employers and would-be foreign employees were being allowed to flout the system en masse.

Saturday July 17

After trying and failing to pass off the Work Permits abuse as renewals, the Home Office is forced to admit that it did not know the extent of the problem. This led to calls from the Liberal Democrats that the entire immigration caseload should be taken away from the Home Office and handed over to an independent agency. At long last the sleeping giant in the immigration debacle stirred. Unions started to complain about abuses undercutting indigenous workers: according to Unison, student nurses were being made to work full-time despite supposedly being allowed to work part-time only.

Wednesday July 21

Economic migration to London 'cannot be open-ended for all-comers', was 'a clear challenge', and necessitated a strategy to protect the economy: this was the conclusion of a report by the Number 10 (Downing Street) Strategy Unit, citing an annual influx of 200,000 foreigners and a 'London exodus' of 150,000 middle-class families. Major stresses on health, education and police services are conceded (with half of all schools enrolling more than 40 percent of students for whom English is not their first language), as is the finding that the city scores poorly on measures of neighbourliness and social trust. Even so, the report sticks with the erroneous line that there are 'overall benefits' even if there are 'losses to some', and recommends 'continued development of a strategy for managed international economic migration and tackling illegal immigration, building on current programmes'. The seriousness of the problem seems to be dawning but the need for radical action is not.

Monday July 26

Sacked, I am. For 'gross misconduct'. A courier sent by the Home Office arrived late at night with a dismissal notice after twenty weeks of suspension. Five pages of refusal to consider evidence and untenable reasons supposedly why the Public Interest Disclosure Act did not apply in my case confirmed that the Home Office had no intention other than to sack me from the outset.

Chapter 3 — Storyline

For the Last Time

Making sure the passport, if indeed that is what it was (i.e. a real one), was together with the other documents inside the standard clear plastic pouch, I snapped shut the stud that held the closing flap in place and headed from my place in a spacious cluster of workstations for the despatch shelves in the middle of our office floor. I tossed this, my very last piece of work, fairly carelessly on top of the others, but not so nonchalantly that I didn't ensure that it stayed there on the pile instead of sliding off and taking half the pile with it.

A ramshackle pyramid, it could collapse either from the bottom or from the top — the pile of casework, or the division of the Home Office for which I worked. Like the trick of whipping the tablecloth from under the crockery, I could fly out of my lowly job and nobody would notice. But as if I was carefully assembling a tower of cards — when one card clumsily placed might bring the whole lot crashing down — I could slip away seemingly quietly but leaving a legacy that our political overlords might choke on.

I could have thrown this very last completed case, frisbee style, right across the room. A parting gesture inviting some reprimand to which I could insultingly shrug my shoulders. But this would have been quite outside my character. Nevertheless, I was trying to work out why I was bothering to take any care at all. Really though, it would have been more effort to have done any different. The job was routine but relaxed. Not quite boring. Not quite a lot of things, and a million miles from being good and rewarding employment, but it was far from torture. Don't get me wrong, I was hardly damp-eyed with premature nostalgia for a pretty short time in my life which was to be, within minutes, history. It was best not to think much: I had already daydreamed of an arm suddenly placed on mine and a frog-march to some manager's office and a 'we know what you're up to' interview.

I could pull some stunt if I wanted to. But that would detract from what I was going to do. I was starting to feel the responsibility I was about to take on, as if the attention to which I was shortly to expose myself could act retrospectively — and it could, if I did anything outlandish or particularly contemptuous. Any daft stunt, however trivial and innocuous, would be unwise. Besides, there was nobody to 'get my own back' on. One or two I did not care for, and one nasty if ineffectual older woman whose anti-male prejudices had led her to take an instant dislike to me the minute I was installed at my desk, but apart from that a decent and varied lot of people you could do a lot worse to find yourself spending your working day alongside. Some really pleasant folk amongst them, and more than one or two I would have liked to get to know well. One or two women I liked and was attracted to but I suppose I was too old for. No, I should act the part of someone who was not leaving the office for the very last time; though not too determinedly so, in case the acting could be seen as just that.

For over six months I had showed up daily at the unprepossessing modern six-storey Aspect Court, one of the buildings temporarily housing the Home Office in the centre of Sheffield next to the bus station and directly opposite the oldest building in town (the half-timbered Queens Head pub). Stationed at one end of the third floor, I surveyed a scene indistinguishable from many other standard bland office environments. Seated amongst neutral colours, strip lights and large plain dark carpet tiles, like everybody else I would click my computer mouse to get into a database (called CID) to record what I did with the documents I processed and to access a 'knowledge base' of legislation and guidance notes to remind me of what I was supposed to be doing. Or to go into a thing called 'Warehouse' to find histories of applicants — whether they were still appealing their failed asylum application, for example.

You would not know, simply by looking over this scene, that we were not insurance clerks or in the council housing department, unless you read print-outs of instructions I had pinned to the neck-height dark green partition boards on two sides of my desk. The office is entirely open-plan, with even the overall boss not in so much as a cubicle to distance him from us, but with his back to everyone in one corner, sat in his high-backed throne alongside his secretary. The rest of the staff, including team leaders and even line managers, are grouped in clusters of four, hardly separated from each other by the aforementioned screens. We were able to glance at each other over them, or swivel round in the chair to talk to those seated in the adjacent foursome of workstations. Across the space down the centre of the floor by the windows on the other side of the building, the arrangement is duplicated. Like all modern buildings it is designed so that you are hardly aware of the environment, with no opening windows and air conditioning circulating and recirculating viruses giving you serial colds and sore throats, but almost noiseless, as are the dozens upon dozens of computers, apart from the slightly annoying regular bleeps. You can hear a general circulation e-mail arrive as in fast succession the computers bleep their acknowledgment of its receipt. Each individual computer seems to occasionally bleep for no reason as if waking itself up.

Today, at the end of a seven-hour stint, when I hit the green metal knob to activate the heavy door on the third storey exit, I was, as I said, almost in acting mode. The lift seemed to take a little longer than usual, which was long enough. There was nobody else in it to distract me, or to make me worry slightly about what I might say to them. Then it was out with the swipe card to … no, that's what I do to get in! Another reminder that although I may be good at sorting challenging problems, I am pretty dumb when it comes to remembering the mundane. You had to hit another button on the side door to leave the building. My swipe card would never be usable again. Out in the fresh air, I did not get a 'what the hell have I done' feeling, but I had my mouth firmly shut, as if unconsciously I might blurt out the secret. One or two heavy sighs, but I barely felt any weight on my shoulders. Relief that I was out of harm's way: nobody now could haul me into a manager's office and confront me with a list of the recent e-mail print-outs betraying my intentions.

* * *

That clear plastic pouch I had just despatched — the final case of my caseworking existence — was another all-too-easy ticket to a secure life of permanent UK residence on the basis of the flimsiest evidence that such a rite of passage was deserved. It was a marriage settlement case. Bangladeshi, Pakistani … I can't recall. (And of course, I did not want to be able to recall the actual identity of any individual. Divulging the names of any applicant would have been a serious breach of confidentiality and I was never tempted to make copies of individual case histories by way of proof of what was happening. I had nothing against the applicants we were dealing with: it was the system of non-procedure or ultra lax procedure that was the issue.)

Whoever it was had arrived as a husband with a visa certifying his married status and had been living, he claimed, as such for the past year. It may well be that what he stated on the multi-paged black-and-white 'SET(M)' application form (that's the one for UK settlement on the basis of marriage) was perfectly true. A gas bill in his name and for the address he shared with the woman he claimed to be his wife was his ticket to a new life. And it made me wearily dispirited that this entirely inadequate supposed proof of the continued existence of a marriage was all that was required — all that he needed to have enclosed with the application — to guarantee my complicity in a widespread fraud against the UK citizenry of which he was himself now about to become a part. (At this stage we were not supposed to be interested in the marriage certificate: that had been OK-ed previously — by staff with no recourse to anyone with the requisite language skills, nor with any knowledge of such certificates other than what had been picked up on the job. As I explain in Chapter 11, many marriages in Britain are bogus and most marriage certificates from abroad are thought to be likewise. And this is quite apart from the contracting of marriage which though 'genuine' is purely to get round immigration rules.)

The time I spent processing this application was a matter of a few minutes. After opening the clear plastic pouch and finding and taking out the passport, the first thing was to look at the stamps and/or visas inside the applicant's passport. The passport looked likely to be what it purported to be, but I could have no idea whether or not it was, because not only had I had no training in detecting forgery, I had had no training whatsoever concerning the passports of different countries. I had found out what, for example, a Pakistani or Bangladeshi passport looked like, simply 'on the job'. If I did not know the main features of a genuine passport then how on earth could I spot a fake one? With hardly any training even in our own immigration stamps, then how could I spot a forged one of these? Clearly they would be very easy to do. So easy, in fact, that it would be almost child's play by the standards of forgers to produce a perfect replica of a Home Office stamp. The secret would be to apply it so carelessly that it looked like the fast and casual work of the Immigration Service. Visas again I took on trust: no training about those either. If I felt suspicious — though this would be merely an irrational hunch — occasionally I might quickly show a passport to a near neighbour for their take on it, for what that was worth; but I never found a dud this way.

I checked the name in the passport, and the date on the marriage visa being in-date; I next went on to the computer to check in a database called 'Warehouse' that there was nothing adverse recorded in the guy's immigration history. I could then switch to the main database ready to start to record my brief notes. Back to the pouch, I filched for what was termed the sponsor's passport — the one belonging to the woman 'present and settled in the UK' (or so we hoped) the applicant had married — to see if that name tallied, before another rummage among the documents in the pouch to find some sort of evidence of a 'subsisting relationship' and income such that he would not require 'recourse to public funds' (but how could we know?). I was now supposed to put a red tick near the end of the application form in a box labelled 'VALID', and sign my name. This was the official approval that the application could at least be considered: that at least it had the bare minimum of information so as to make a decision. And the bare minimum was usually perfectly sufficient.

The computer notes would be a fairly set formula to some extent customized by the caseworker. In my case: 'SET(M) application in-time and valid'. Glancing over stuff like the gas bill and a wage slip or two — and again these could be fakes: how would I know? — I would then succinctly list the evidence supplied: 'Evidence of subsisting relationship: minimum five documents supplied, including gas bill from applicant to shared address. Evidence of funds: last three months' wage slips from applicant'. I might qualify this with something like: 'very low income but not insufficient to justify refusal under the rules.' Then the magic word: 'granted'. A space would separate these decision notes from those the despatch department would read: 'Despatch: please endorse passport with ILR ('indefinite leave to remain') vignette and return with sponsor's passport and all documents to applicant.' (Vignettes — fancy small colourful things complete with photo, stuck into passports — had only just been introduced, belatedly, to try to combat the fraud of the all-too-easy-to-forge immigration stamps.)

The only thing the Home Office wanted to keep hold of was the application form; so all the evidence was returned, leaving no opportunity to check it at a later date. I keyed in a standard line about 'retained documents' and some internal cryptic gobbledegook about a store known as 'Layby' where the pouch had to end up, having been united with its parent file en route at the Documents Management Centre, wherever that was — Poona for all we knew. I had another screen to fill which gave the basic info about the case outcome, and then I was ready to print out all the guff that was on the computer: the stuff on the case that was already inputted plus what I had added. After a delay while the printer decided if it could be bothered to cope with the workload, three sheets spewed out and I laid a particular coloured paper 'flag' on top to show that it was a 'grant' and stapled the lot together.

How many thousands of times had I done this? Hang on: have I actually done a thousand, or is it still just many hundreds? I remembered: I can't have done ten tons, because the procedures kept changing. There is a Home Office law, you see, that any new procedure is a complete cock-up, and several remedial changes later but before everything is quite ironed out, some committee makes us adopt an altogether new procedure and the same trouble-shooting process starts over. Whether this is to keep us from going stark-staring, or to provide exercise for managers by getting them to walk to committee rooms more often, nobody bothers to guess. Anyway, with everything else stuffed back in the pouch, I sauntered over to the above-mentioned central shelves to slip the flagged 'CID notes' on the bottom shelf and, as I said, toss the pouch on the shelf marked 'despatch'.

End of job. End of a job not at all well done if you ask me, but done in the way that I was obliged to do by Home Office management, who I imagine in turn were under orders from Home Office mandarins, who I also imagine themselves had had a meeting with Home Office ministers which went something like this:

'Sir Humphrey?'

'Yes, Minister?'

'Er, can you do that rather awkward thing I mentioned yesterday, but without using any more staff; and on the ... er ... quiet?'

'Well ... yes Minister ... but you will not want to be told how the, erm ... awkward thing you mentioned yesterday ... actually did get done. Minister.'

There is a pause.

'Yes, Humphrey. I ... will leave it in your ever capable hands.'

More than once I had drifted into fantasy. There was daydream time in the Home Office factory. (I dare say that if you didn't drift off every so often, or didn't take enough tea, fag or chat breaks, then some health & safety team would come and drag you away from the screen and remind you of your responsibility not to sue the Home Office for the effects of computer overuse.) My daydream or 'daymare' was a scenario where instead of spilling the beans I had stayed put and kept mum like everybody else. Cue tacky aftermath-of-war movie; retribution scene:

'I was only obeying orders.'

'But you pulled the trigger … over and over again … how can you not be responsible? Did it never occur to you that what you were doing was wrong?'

'Yes … of course it did. But if I had tried to stop what was going on, then I would have been shot. It would not have made any difference.'

Silent stare. Eyes glance up but immediately cast down in shame.

Earlier in the week I had been across the road in the ancient Queens Head pub during a lunch break. Under the fat oak beams with two of the women from my team, I said that I had 'something up my sleeve'. 'Don't jump off a cliff!', one of them had quipped, amused. This was a mutual light moaning session about what we were being asked to do. Management was the problem, they decided; the managers were a bit of a joke. I said it was higher up; at the political level. A couple of days before that, I had been leaning over the desk of another one of the underground disgruntled, really wanting to share the secret with her. 'I might not be here after the end of the week'. 'Why?', she asked. 'I can't tell you, but you'll find out'. Daft thing to do, in the office, where we could be overheard. I had a similar conversation with a more senior staff member but I was a little more revealing, if cryptically. People knew of my criticism of equal opportunities implementation and most would think I was talking about that, but perhaps this more senior staffer realized I was referring to something bolder. 'Don't trust anybody', I was reminded: he insisted. I knew from a third party what he really thought about the work. I had never got any impression from him — which showed that he must not have trusted me — that he actually felt if anything stronger than I did. Apparently the guy in the Romanian embassy who shopped James Cameron to the Foreign Office felt stronger than Cameron did about the scams they were obliged to ignore. It can be one of those you least expect who turns traitor. Someone who seems to like you could actually be very ambivalent. They could admire what you do but not you yourself when it could have been themselves getting the credit.

So how many other people harboured a secret disgust? How many administrative officers, executive officers, higher executive officers, senior caseworkers and even higher-up line managers thought that

the systems we were a part of could be accurately described to out-
siders and not raise eyebrows or be met with consternation? Were
even senior staff reconciled to what they were doing and making
others do? The place was kept in check by natural human conformity
but also by a spiral of silence.

* * *

On my last day I recalled my first. I was still none the wiser about
what sort of work I would be doing; in common, it seemed, with
everyone else. Despite enquiries I couldn't get anyone to tell me anything. The only Home Office work I had heard of based in Sheffield
was dealing with work permit applications (Work Permits UK), so I
assumed this is what it would be; not that I knew much about them,
or had much interest in finding out. When we were enlightened that
the work would be dealing with the full range of applications in
immigration, it occurred to me that keeping new recruits in the dark
was deliberate, to cut down the chance of getting staff with a political agenda. Your political views were of no consequence, supposedly, as long as you did not fall foul of the equal opportunities
rules — though I dare say that these rules, being so zealous, effectively eliminated the very sort of people the Home Office would dis-
agree with politically. And if immigration per se was a serious
problem for anyone, then a day or two of willy-nilly granting all
applications would send them into apoplexy and out of the building
never to return.

I should take this opportunity to address suspicions regarding my
motivation. At the time I 'joined up' I had no political axe to grind on
the issue of immigration. Having never been politically excited
about it one way or the other, I had not researched the facts or opinions; not even the policy of the Liberal Democrats, despite having
until recently been an activist for that party (though I knew their policy must be liberal and welcoming). My 'no axe' attitude remained
for most of my brief tenure, right until my doubts had seriously esca-
lated and I had half made up my mind to bring what was going on
out into the open. It was only then that I went on the web and found
some research. I certainly had no problem at all with immigration in
regard to the presence in the country of ethnic minorities, having
lived in Leicester — the city with the highest proportion of ethnic
minorities in the whole of Britain — for 20 years, and in the centre of
the city in an area where I was in a small minority of white people. I
had set up and run community campaigns with Asian immigrants,

and had stood as a Liberal Democrat councillor with one of the leading members of the recently arrived Bengali community as my running mate. My credentials in this regard were pretty impeccable.

Neither can it be argued that I returned to Sheffield because I had become disenchanted with life in a city 'overrun' with ethnic minorities. If that were true then how come it took me 20 years to realize I felt this way? It's true that I had become fed up with corruption in local politics, but that was as much to do with the usual workings of the Labour Party (who were then always in control) as much as machinations within Asian communities. It's also true that the arts scene I was involved with was not supported by ethnic minority people and in many respects the presence of such a large proportion of culturally non-English people made the city effectively function in some ways, including the arts, as a much smaller place. But if I felt any problem with non-whites then why should I move to a part of Sheffield where there are a considerable number of ethnic minority students? I moved back to Sheffield because near there is where I was brought up and I wanted to return to my roots, have closer contact with my extended family and be back among the hills, stone-built houses and extensive woodlands: the kind of countryside I had been missing. I knew I could enjoy a better quality of life here and open up a new chapter in my life. There was nothing to hold me in Leicester — my closest friends had moved away — and if I did return to my old researching job I could do it more easily in the 'virgin territory', in this respect, of Sheffield.

I have also been accused of being a 'media plant' (an extraordinarily lazy media animal?) or even a Conservative Party stooge. I assure you that I am/was neither of the above. I have been a part-time journalist, but writing only on the arts. And I have never even voted Tory, let alone supported them in any more active way. I take the charges as a compliment — testament to the effectiveness of how I went about 'blowing the whistle', and I have to smile.

Chapter 4 — Analysis

Uneconomics

It is a mystery why any Government, least of all one that purports to be Left of centre — even New Labour — could initiate or support a policy of mass net immigration or allow it to continue. Powerful arguments that would be better characterized as being from the political Left, rather than from the Right, doom any policy of overt or covert mass immigration. The research shows that the brunt of the overall economic *dis*-benefit is sustained by the poorest — including ethnic minorities and recent migrants. Moreover, there are serious problems of both principle and practice even in regard to the minority of the highly skilled. Why the Left and New Labour hold the position they do appears to be at root down to a psychological peculiarity, rather than just a throwing of hands in the air at an intractable problem. I will address the psychopathology issue in Chapter 6, but here I will go into the economics.

There are two very different kinds of mass inward migration we are currently experiencing. One is the supposedly- (but, as it turns out, usually not) skilled Work Permit holder — approaching 200,000 grants to non- EU citizens annually, handled by the Work Permits UK division of the Home Office. The other is the well in excess of 500,000 mostly unskilled and overwhelmingly non-working (at least officially) applicants under the rules (supposedly) for marriage, students, dependent relatives, etc — handled where I used to work in the Managed Migration division. The majority of the latter could be characterized as family reunion for permanent settlement: marriage partners, parents, grandparents and children; notably of Pakistani, Bangladeshi, Indian and various African nationals.

Although on the face of it you would expect a net contribution from Work Permit holders (but see below) the threefold outnumbering by the Managed Migration caseload provides a heavy net drain. And this is even before you take into account that across-the-board, in-depth failure to implement immigration rules — as I have exposed — will mean that very many of these will be bogus applications. Overall, migrants in general are less likely to be in employment than the general population, so this destroys any justification in terms of the 'pensions gap'.

Plugging the 'pensions gap' is one of the new myths about immigration, yet the support ratio of taxpayers to pensioners is actually adversely affected by immigration. Even if the mix of migrants could be altered, the vast numbers required would lead to an unsustainable population growth. Number crunching shows we would need to double the UK population to 120 million in a few decades and eventually require more than the entire population of the earth today! Short of this but still vastly increasing immigration would make little real difference. 'Madness', is how the leading pensions expert, Professor David Miles, describes the idea.

In any case, the decline in the birth rate — that has worried commentators and governments about how tax income can be boosted sufficiently to pay growing numbers of pensioners — is more apparent than real, owing to this being a time of changing patterns in childbirth. Demographers dispute the significance of the decline in fertility over the past two decades. The headline figure (the Total Fertility Rate) is misleading in understating fertility levels in times of changing behaviour. The TFR is a snapshot in time which extrapolates what is found at that instant across the whole reproductive lifespan of a woman. As we live at a time when women are tending to move from having children when young to having them when they are significantly older, a different measure is required to accurately show fertility. This statistic is known as Cohort Fertility, and the figures across Europe come in at around 2.0: pretty much replacement level. The transition period of delaying childbirth accentuates the undershooting of fertility rates because women end up childless through procrastination over when is the right time to have a child and do not realize how quickly their natural fertility falls away during their 30s. They end up childless by accident, but in their wake other women will learn not to make the same error.

So demographers are agreed that there is unlikely to be any population decline beyond a small drop for a few decades. The only remaining problem then is the increasing number of older people that the tax base has to be able to support — a problem that progressively increases through the two or three decades that the 'baby boom' generation become of pension age. But this too is a problem much more apparent than it is real. There is no difficulty for societies to handle a transition to an older average age, because there is an enormous slack to be taken up of under-employed and unemployed older workers. At the moment employers allow themselves the luxury of discounting applications from anyone who has reached the age of fifty, or even forty. Yet all the evidence shows that this is irrational: older people are just as good at learning new skills as someone in their twenties, but with the added assets of experience, greater reliability and stability. Age discrimination is shortly to be outlawed so companies will find themselves being in a position to fully understand this. Worries that employers have about the health of older workers are also misplaced. Health, certainly up to the age of sixty-five, has consistently improved, to the point that significant problems are likely to arise only with those in their seventies and eighties; not those in their sixties. Most people are more than capable of continuing work past the age of sixty-five but currently they are compelled to cease, however much they may resent it. A retirement age of seventy would still leave many years of active life to enjoy, in marked contrast to the experience of people several decades ago when most men could expect to suffer ill health if not death shortly after receiving their gold watch, if indeed they survived to retire at all. Short of raising the retirement age across the board, the abolition of enforced retirement at sixty-five may alone do the trick. This has been a suggestion for a long time. Norman Pannell, in his book *Immigration, What is the Answer?*, published in 1965, pointed out that: 'If this rule were relaxed many thousands of men and women would be available to perform the tasks now undertaken by immigrants.' A leaked Government memo (yet again to the Sunday Times) in June 2004 shows that raising to seventy or even abolishing the retirement age is exactly what the Government intends to do.

The very large numbers of older as well as relatively young men in economically depressed areas on long-term Incapacity Benefit is a reflection more of the area in which they live than on their health. Long-term Incapacity Benefit has multiplied several-fold over the same period that health has progressively generally improved, so that now there are 2.7 million people in this category, mainly in the North. This has been a longstanding problem that began in the Thatcher years, recognized to be a transfer of people from the unemployment figures to a less politically sensitive statistic. Convenient for authorities, there is collusion on the ground. If local doctors know that their patients have little chance of getting work, then they are often likely to support claims for a benefit that pays more than

Income Support or Job Seeker's Allowance and frees people from official harassment. Back pain and depression are self-diagnosed by the patient, and medical staff have little scope to dismiss such cases as clear malingering. If there were the jobs available and they paid a living wage, then this 'scrapheap' would miraculously disappear.

Putting together age discrimination reform, a five-year raising of the retirement age, a comprehensive regional economic development programme for economically depressed areas, and with a tightening of Incapacity Benefit provision — such a collection of reforms would solve the 'pensions gap' problem, not easily but successfully if there is the political will to press them home.

* * *

What should more seriously alarm the political Left is the finding that, in EU countries, for every hundred migrants eighty-three indigenous workers eventually lose their jobs. This is the most recent research (June 2003) and mirrors disturbing results of US studies (November 2002) showing labour at the bottom of the market experiencing pay cuts of 20 percent through migrant competition. A 2003 report by Professor George Borjas of Harvard, the world's leading economist regarding immigration, puts it at about 10 percent, still a substantial effect. Although our economy differs from both the continental European model and that of the USA — falling somewhere in between the two — it is highly unlikely that there is something peculiar to the UK situation that protects us from this adverse impact on both jobs and pay.

> There is a huge amount of evidence that any increase in the number of unskilled workers lowers unskilled wages and increases the unskilled unemployment rate. If we are concerned about fairness, we ought not to ignore these facts. Employers gain from unskilled immigration. But the unskilled do not.

These are the words of the LSE's Professor Richard Layard, the UK's pre-eminent labour economist and a key figure in putting together the 'welfare to work' policy of New Labour.

Compounding the problem of job loss and pay erosion, added stress to the infrastructure (housing, transport, healthcare, social services, etc) raises the cost of living, which is never offset by corresponding pay increases for lower-paid workers, again leaving the indigenous workforce to suffer. In the case of housing, the Council for Mortgage Lenders blames immigration for the consistent increase in house prices above the level of earnings, and immigration is the reason for Government-sponsored mass house-building programmes. The combination of shrinking household size, as people desire to live alone, and natural population growth is outstripped by immigration as the reason for household creation. Infrastructural overload is made more acute in Britain because the great majority of migration (two-thirds) is into London and the South-East. But it is not only employees in this part of the country who carry the consequences, earlier research established that immigration prevents intra-UK mobility. People in the North stay put because of insufficient pay vis-à-vis high costs in the South, both caused by inward migration.

The heavy distribution in favour of London leads to another major expense: the preponderance of the unemployed or under-employed amongst migrants requires a huge sum in Housing Benefit/Council Tax rebates to cover the rents, which are multiples of those in other parts of the country; not to mention the larger benefits, both in-work and out, paid in respect of the larger families on average of third-world migrants, albeit that many migrants are lone males. But in the case of the latter (many Indian subcontinent, East European and African migrants in particular), where there is income surplus to basic needs, remittances are sent to their home countries rather than earnings being spent in the UK. In this way many migrants fail to contribute to our economy in the same way that an indigenous worker would.

The most optimistic overview of studies — which includes Work Permit holders and 'highly skilled migrants' — shows at very best a small negative overall economic tally. But that is before the additional costs discussed above are factored in, plus the costs of administering immigration, congestion and the extra strain on services (the costs provided out of tax revenues, in addition to the extra costs to individuals out of taxed income already cited), and the lost tax revenues and benefit costs through the resulting unemployment or under-employment. Then there is the negative contributions made by bogus applicants that projections have been wrongly putting on the plus side. Even more of a massive distortion of the economic picture is made by figures often not including the dependents of immigrants. Even if the lead applicant is in full-time work, the in-work benefits claimable in respect of dependents can turn an income tax contribution in effect into the net receipt of benefits.

* * *

Still more expenditure is required to try to offset the effects of any consequent damage to social cohesion. Has anyone even tried to count the cumulative costs of our divided Northern towns and cities? The situation in West Yorkshire and Lancashire former mill towns, together with Bradford (and to a lesser extent in Leeds and Manchester, being administrative centres with wider economic bases) came about because of a short-sighted mass immigration policy to bring in third-world people to take relatively low-paid work in textile mills in an obviously doomed attempt to try to beat competition from third-world production. The result was the opposite to that intended: mill owners failed to put in the investment in more efficient machinery that may have allowed them to continue to compete, because the cheaper workforce gave them a breathing space. The migrant workforce gave them the option to carry on as before and then to cut their losses, rather than follow the bolder strategy of the true entrepreneur. The result is that now we have almost no textile industry left whereas we could have retained a top flight of high-tech efficient manufacturers. Even in Sheffield, where there was a long-acknowledged serious problem of overmanning in the steel industry, significant numbers of Indian subcontinent migrants came in, albeit not on the scale experienced in West Yorkshire and Lancashire. Yet it could not have escaped anyone's attention that the near future for all manufacturing was towards high-tech investment, massive cuts in the numbers of workers and a higher proportion of the jobs that remained being for the semi- or fully skilled. Unskilled migrant workers were the very last thing that was required.

The wave of immigration into our Northern cities actually exacerbated industrial decline as well as making much worse the subsequent unemployment: a double hit of massive cost to the taxpayer. Now these same people are trapped in their unemployment because of new waves of immigration into the South-East making it even more difficult for these people — the previous waves of migrants and the native white workers they had displaced — to relocate. And still the costs mount with large-scale secondary migration continuing completely unchecked into these same depressed areas.

There is a school of thought — and not just Charles Murray — that there is a swathe of the former white working class who will not respond to any inducements to retrain, and prefer to work the system, claiming benefit, possibly supplementing with black economy earnings. On this model, mass net immigration could dilute this rump and help to offset the cost of it. But even if such immigration made a net economic contribution — which most certainly it does not — this would ignore the dynamic aspect: that the migrants would force down wages at the bottom of the market and serve to increase the size of the white underclass as more people come to realize that work is fruitless. It is one thing to give up on the underclass and cut your losses, as it were, and just cough up to keep them off the streets; but quite another to enact measures — or to allow situations to continue — that convert ever-wider successive sections of working people into new members of the very same group of non-participants in society. This is the sure route to eventual complete social breakdown.

* * *

Scraping the bottom of the barrel for justification of large-scale net immigration leads away from economics to the 'sexy' end of politics. There is an intuition that immigration somehow means more equality. The zeitgeist at the end of the '60s was encapsulated in one of the very biggest pop hits of the era: a song by Blue Mink called 'Melting Pot'. The vocal duo who fronted were a white man and a black woman, singing in harmony: 'What we need is a great big melting pot/Big enough to take the world and all its got.' Unfortunately, the laudable notion of a benign cauldron where everyone comes out not whiter than white but more equal turns out not to be. Immigration increases inequality within the host country. This is what has been found in various countries and is easily explained. While the people already towards the bottom of society lose out through job and wage competition from migrants, those towards the top, who can make use of the cheaper and more abundant labour force swelled by migrants — both large employers and middle-class individuals (either directly, for example as employers of home helps, or indirectly as diners at foreign cuisine restaurants) — make a gain because of the lower costs of employing people. Accentuating this, the immigrants themselves polarize wealth distribution. Some of those who enter as Work Permit holders tend to earn more (and often considerably more) than the average across the population, but the majority coming here under Managed Migration don't work at all and those who do tend to earn considerably less than the average. In a nutshell: the rich get richer and the poor get poorer.

Other supposed upsides of net immigration also turn out to be chimeras. 'Big is beautiful' is still widely believed but quite untrue for economies. The increased size of the domestic market swelled by immigrants is of no consequence in a open economy such as that of Britain. Whether the market for a company is in the UK, on the European continent, over in the US or far away in the Far East, is largely immaterial. There is a difference, however, between the effects of immigration on countries according to their geographical size, but it is one that works against Britain. Large countries can benefit because they acquire the critical mass of population to make feasible the building of roads and other infrastructure that can open up areas to development. But in a small country like ours the opposite is the case. When there are too many people, too many goods trying to navigate the transport arteries, and other infrastructure is stretched, then what worked before works no longer and sometimes expensive radical solutions are required out of all proportion to the relatively marginal extra load that caused the breakdown. We have diseconomies of scale.

The evidence regarding the failure of immigration as an economic policy is overwhelming and presented in detail by University of Cambridge economics professor, Robert Rowthorn (*The Economic Impact of Immigration*, 2004 — a web publication); by the Oxford University demographer, David Coleman ('Demographic, Economic and Social Consequences of UK Migration', in *Work In Progress: Migration, Integration and the European Labour Market*, edited by Helen Disney, 2003), and by the former BBC economics reporter and Times Europe correspondent, Anthony Browne (*Do We Need Mass Immigration?*, 2002).

There is no economic case for mass inward migration, for all that Blunkett and Blair repeat the much criticised figure pulled out of some earlier Home Office research that we were better off to the tune of two or three billion pounds annually compared to being without (recent) immigrants. By all accounts, a couple of billion pounds is a drop in the ocean of the economy as a whole; quite insignificant. But as critics of this figure have widely observed, if you apply all of the caveats actually mentioned alongside the figure, it becomes heavily negative, even before the neglected costs listed above are put on the balance sheet.

Even the Home Office itself accepts that there is a problem. In 2001 the Home Office published its own research paper, *Migration: an Economic and Social Analysis*. Anthony Browne, in his excellent book, *Do*

We Need Mass Immigration?, picks out the telling paragraphs (here shortened):

> In general, migration increases the supply of labour: this is likely, in theory, to reduce wages for workers competing with migrants, and increase returns to capital and other factors complementary to migrant labour. ...

> If native workers are not prepared to accept a wage below a given floor, and migration leads to the market wage for some native workers falling below that floor, then migration could in theory lead to an increase in native unemployment.

Browne points out in his book that the Home Office has made no attempt to answer the question of whether the standard economic theory has actually come to pass in the real economy. But in a recent article for the Spectator, Browne brings us up-to-date:

> The Home Office commissioned an economic study on the impact of immigration, which found that an increase in immigration amounting to 1 per cent of the non-immigrant population would lead to an increase of 0.18 percentage points in the non-immigrant unemployment rate. However, in an extraordinary act of politically correct immigration denial, the immigration minister Beverley Hughes issued a press release saying, 'The research shows that it is simply not true that migrants 'take the jobs' of the existing work force'.

In Britain, an increase in immigration equivalent to one percent of the non-immigrant population is roughly half a million. On the above formula this would lead to about a hundred thousand white unemployed. On top of this would be disproportionately high numbers of extra unemployed among immigrants, not least those very recent arrivals who have produced the unemployment effect. Then there is all of the hidden unemployment of full-time jobs turning into part-time ones, permanent work becoming temporary or short-time, and unemployment itself being replaced by supposed disability, early retirement, forced re-training, or withdrawal from the labour market to become economically dependent.

It's not just jobs but wages as well. As everybody knows only too well, wages at the lower end of the market have fallen dramatically in real terms and for many even in absolute terms. (For example, as I write, Sheffield bus drivers have been on strike for a week. They were paid more fifteen years ago than today — in pounds not in real terms.) The leading economist regarding immigration, Professor George Borjas of Harvard, concludes that: "immigration lowers the wage of competing workers: a 10% increase in supply reduces wages by 3 to 4%". In his Spectator article, Browne cites an amazing fact:

> There is such a large pool of cheap labour that, for the first time ever, national chains such as McDonalds and Burger King are no longer paying their highest rates in central London. Shop shelf-fillers now earn 10 per cent less in London than the average for the rest of the country.

The problem is such that many men can no longer even think of starting a family or owning a home — even supposing that women would be attracted in the first place to men who demonstrably can barely support themselves. Is it any wonder that unemployment — now 7 percent in London — under-employment and crime are so intractable?

Browne puts it this way:

> … unskilled British youth too often conclude that rather than work for such paltry wages, it is far more attractive to get involved in crime or deal drugs. The destruction of unskilled jobs and the importation of unskilled labour means that we have undermined unskilled workers in Britain to such an extent that it can seem a rational choice to stay out of the labour market and get involved in crime.

Although the Government does not dare to commission research in this country, there is abundant evidence from the USA, where nothing less than a disaster has been experienced by low-paid workers, and black workers have sustained the worst impact of all (see Browne's book for a detailed presentation of the evidence).

Not all of the chasm that is opening up between the well-paid middle-class and the once tolerably-paid but now impoverished major sections of the working class is down to immigration, of course. And that point should be stressed because of the natural tendency of people to blame an 'out-group' for anything they feel is going wrong. This is why the intelligentsia considers it so irresponsible to even discuss these matters, and this is understandable; but enough is, as they say, enough. While the Government can justifiably duck responsibility for the workings of the global economy, it has to own up to its miserable failure in social policy that has made things immeasurably worse. More than that, it is responsible for deliberately harming the most vulnerable sections of society and therefore of harming society as a whole. The sustained attack on various fronts against men and the family on entirely cod-political grounds is astonishing and damning enough and this has directly contributed to massive social breakdown amongst lower earners; but with pro-net mass immigration policy as well, politicians will soon rue their pursuit of self-aggrandising 'sexy' political stances at the expense of the lives of the mass of the people they are supposed to represent. For a Labour Government and the Labour Party this is bound to amount to something greater than a mere major setback.

Sticking purely with the question of immigration, what is needed from government on the economic front is clearly expressed by Robert Rowthorn:

> It is often said that immigrants are needed to do the jobs that locals will not do. This may be true in a few cases, but in general it is false. In most parts of the country there are relatively few unskilled immigrants and it is the locals who do most of the jobs which British workers supposedly will not do. The problem in the end boils down to wages and conditions. When employers in the South of the country say that they cannot get workers to perform menial tasks, what they often mean is that local workers will not accept, or stay in, jobs at the kind of wages and conditions that they are offering. In this case, the problem is not an absolute shortage of labour, but a shortage of cheap labour. The most effective way to raise the wages of low paid workers is to maintain an artificial shortage of labour so that employers have no option but to pay more. This is inconsistent with the mass importation of cheap labour from abroad.

Whether or not the Government is finally getting wind of the economic arguments or not, more and more spokesmen are retreating to the line that we need immigrants because we have all these jobs going begging: half a million that we cannot fill. Patricia Hewitt harps on about this but Does Gordon Brown subscribe to this economic illiteracy? Any labour economist will tell you that all employment markets need 'churn', a level of job vacancies consistent with the flux of people moving between jobs. If the ratio of vacancies to filled posts falls below a certain, albeit low, proportion then the economy seizes up. With only half a million vacancies, which is less than 2.5 per 100 employees, there is in fact no slack at all in the form of long-term vacancies over and above normal 'churn', either for immigrants or for anyone else to take up.

But what about specific jobs or job sectors where (supposedly) we experience recruitment difficulties? Focusing just on Work Permits, this territory is not much more hospitable to the Left. That we apparently require so many is testament to the failure of 'Education! Education! Education!' as regards vocational training. Britain is alone in all Europe for failing to train/retrain/retain enough health care professionals and teachers. Where is the 'joined up thinking' here? The Government has set a well-publicized target of fifty percent of all young people to go to university, yet young people cannot find places on the vocational courses they want and most of those leaving university cannot find graduate-level employment. The number of jobs requiring a degree at entry level is actually declining and was never high. Current estimates put the number at 70,000 or 80,000 annually, but each year there are 400,000 new graduates chasing them — plus all of those who missed out in previous years. The 'milk round', as it was called, of firms turning up to universities to recruit, amounted only to a few thousand positions. The lack of a need for people with degrees would be even starker if it was not for some employers using degrees to filter out possibly poorer candidates for want of other ways to whittle down a crowded field. There is widespread complaint of poor-quality tuition, students unequipped to begin a university education — unable to decently write or do maths — worthless courses (extreme relativism in social science; media studies, surf technology, golf science, etc) and inflated final grades; not to mention the scary escalation of student debt that will tend to discourage post-graduate vocational training and even a career track at all given the sliding scale of student loan repayments. Many students don't make it to graduation; the drop-out rate even approaching 50 percent in some institutions. Career earnings are not greater for most graduates than for their non-graduate counterparts for all that the Government repeatedly insists otherwise. A civil engineer, for example, can train either by the degree route or through an apprenticeship; the skills gained are comparable as are the rewards. Why not, instead of paying for the university route, divert money away from senseless university expansion to help firms train in those skills they would otherwise have to outsource from abroad?

A particular qualm of the Left, with a concern for the third world, is that we are draining countries that can ill afford to export their home-trained talent. For example, almost all nursing staff with Work Permits come from third world countries and no less than two-thirds of all Work Permit holders are now third-world nationals — more than a complete reversal of the situation until very recently indeed. Third-world Work Permit holders are far more likely to apply for settlement than those from the developed world, and the refusal rate for applications is just 5 percent. This shows that the Work Permits scheme has major loopholes exploited by economic migrants. Furthermore, concern for the individuals (rather than for their countries of origin) also serves to make it more problematic to return these migrants after a spell of work. So it is that Work Permit holders — and their dependents — qualify for UK residence after just four years, simply by remaining in work. (Of course, a strong argument could be made that most people would be happier if they returned to their home culture in their home land and would have been happier still had they never left.) What happens when the types of occupations for which there is a shortage changes? This happened with IT professionals. A 'shortage' category until 2002, IT is so sharply cyclical that within a short space of time the demand can turn negative. It makes no sense whatsoever to attract migrants into such a field when indigenous workers can expect to experience imminent redundancy.

Like all other areas of immigration, Work Permits is open to abuse on a massive scale. There is little or no checking up on what people actually do after arrival; whether they take up the job on offer or change from the job they are supposed to be doing to something entirely different. This is a green light for milking the system in the same way that bogus colleges have been set up to take advantage of the lax implementation of immigration rules regarding students. As in the abuse of the ECAA rules by Eastern Europeans that was evident when their dependent relatives made piggy-back applications, the abuse of the Work Permit system can be found indirectly. In her trawl through abuses of the NHS, Harriet Sergeant (see Chapter 14) found that very many of those with Work Permits coming from countries with endemic TB were written to but the letters returned as 'address unknown'. People were changing their names and moving on.

Where there are rules these have been on the slide: yet again implementation is in an appalling state, under the self-imposed ridiculous stricture of turning around 90 percent of applications inside a day of receipt. How can this do other than to completely undermine checking? Supposedly all Work Permit applications must be in respect of a job for which there are no suitable resident workers available, but this is now ignored regarding all of the supposed 'shortage' occupations: engineers (for whom there is serious unemployment in the Sheffield area) actuaries, teachers, vets and healthcare professionals and, until 2002, IT professionals. There is also supposed to be the condition of a genuine vacancy in the UK, but nobody checks. The overseas national must be qualified or experienced to NVQ level three or above, but this hardly counts as highly skilled. About 5,000 Work Permits granted annually are for chefs, and 2,000 are for other workers in hotel catering. Is the Government really saying that we need to import such workers? Have we a shortage of restaurants, and if we had, who cares? Indian restaurants have long since reached saturation point and there is no guarantee that they will remain in vogue with the general population (if indeed in many places most people will be able to afford to eat out at all).

There is no ceiling for the annual granting of Work Permits: the whole thing is driven by demand from employers, no matter how inappropriate their requests may be. Employers love a supply of relatively cheap and compliant foreign labour, and the condition that Work Permits must be in respect of jobs paying the going rate for the job can easily be circumvented in spirit if not by the letter; and again, nobody is doing any checking. The Work Permits system is an abuse three times over: it absolves employers from bothering to train people and so leaves British workers unskilled; it repeats across the economy the fatal error made in colluding with textile mill owners to forever forestall needed investment, thereby perpetuating low-skilled work at ever lower wages and in ever decreasing numbers; and it is an open door to yet another permanent settlement route for those less interested in contributing skills we need than in accepting the economic security of the UK taxpayer.

A new major area of abuse was uncovered in mid-July 2004 after the new immigration minister, Des Browne, told Parliament that about half (73,866) of the total number of Work Permits issued in 2003 (145,351) were what he described as 'permissions' from other immigration categories (written answer to a Parliamentary question, *Hansard*, July 12 2004). In other words, these people had 'switched'. But the regulations are that this is not allowed. Those on a Work Permit must apply from abroad. Foreigners were arriving ostensibly as students or simply as tourists and then colluding with employers to abuse the Work Permits system. The Home Office tried to pass off the figures as renewals, but this is not what Browne had said; when pressed the Home Office accepted that it could not give a breakdown.

The response from opposition parties went beyond the usual condemnation from David Davis: Mark Oaten, the Lib Dem Home Affairs spokesman, said that an independent agency should be set up to process the whole of immigration casework: 'The Home Office track record in managing immigration is appalling and it's time to look at a complete upheaval which may include taking these functions away from the Home Office'.

* * *

With the overwhelming tally of economic woes, not least those on the Left side of the political equation, who would have thought that a Labour Home Secretary would be the one to put the case for the political Right? David Blunkett said that the message he got at his posh London dinner parties (now there's a representative form of vox pop) was that there were nowhere near enough cheap lackeys preferring to come here to work for low wages rather than stay home in Eastern Europe or wherever. This is an argument from the Right, David, that you cite in favour of immigration! Keeping the bosses happy by undercutting the locals. Perhaps the Home Secretary should nip down the pub for beer & sandwiches and see if he can rustle up just one point in favour of net mass immigration from his own side.

The Story Breaks

Rarely have I been so self-conscious as when I walked into work the day after the story broke. Do I walk the same as other people? I remember a long time back someone saying that I didn't. Various TV cameras were at the entrance to Aspect Court and one of the crews had asked me to go back and walk down the street towards the front entrance. How best to make you feel self-conscious. I would have felt even more so if I had known how often that footage would be shown as each development in the story required a reminder of who started the ball rolling. The business with the swipe card and the entrance door was not staged. It was not a reconstruction for the cameras. When a few increasingly less clumsy passes of the clearly now useless card would not unlock the main entrance door, I put my hand over my eyes, salute-style, to peer in to see if I could catch someone's attention. Nobody seemed to be there or paying attention. They were probably hiding behind the silly water feature in the foyer, thinking they might just be picked up in the background by the cameras. I may have looked like a prize pillock here, I was thinking; but I was fairly sure that it would be the Home Office that was put in a worse light, with the concrete visual image of a physical obstruction to me getting into the place where I worked.

I muttered something back at a cameraman about the card not working and that I would try round the back. The sight of the train of cameras swinging round behind me as I turned the corner into the rear car park scattered a clutch of staff on a quick smoking break. I'm starting to feel a bit lonely already here. I'm the only person who doesn't mind the cameras. They had been leaning nonchalantly against the wall by the door but bounced their behinds off it and exited sideways very sharpish. The fastest movement of anybody I had ever witnessed at the Home Office. Not that they had anything to hide; people were free to take fag breaks or any kind of break whenever and as often as they wanted, so long as they churned out sufficient work. I can't remember if the swipe card worked on this door; perhaps someone opened the door for me.

Just inside the door, for a second or so I wondered if I should bolt up the stairs which were immediately to my left and rush on to the third floor where I worked and catch everyone unawares. (I was later told that people were disappointed that I didn't make it to my workstation. Perhaps they would have liked the drama of the frog-march out with meagre odds and sods in a black bin liner.) But what the point of that would be I hadn't the remotest idea. You might have believed I would have put in some thinking about possible situations and gone over them several times in my mind, especially if like me you are usually at fault in thinking about things too much rather than too little. Well, we all surprise ourselves, and fairly regularly. I shut down considering options and strode over to the reception desk and the man there was on the phone before I asked for anyone. Standing well to one side, near the glass front door where the cameras might have been taking a peek, I stared at an upright steel slab permanently dribbled over with a thin sheet of water. The foyer water feature was a statement of the bland: featureless in its quest to be inoffensive. No 'floozie-in-the-jacuzzi' here. I had less than a minute to wait before the Sheffield chief with my team leader in tow arrived. They were not going to pose by the dread water feature where they could be filmed; I was ushered through a security door into a small room on the ground floor.

I said a warm rather than casual 'Hi' to both, and my team leader muttered something, looking sheepish, though for no reason that struck me why he should. A straightforward, quite friendly and non-pushy mature lad really (in his mid-twenties), with hair loss that had prompted him to go all the way, as is the fashion, and shave off the lot. He could go into civil servant manager mode in a flash, but although I think he was wary of me, he had never bullshitted me, or not in an obvious, insulting way. He had me moved on to his table cluster on our work floor where, presumably, he thought he could keep an eye on me. A good-natured minor battle under the surface had gone on between us. The boss — the chief boss — was a kindly, well-respected middle-aged, or late middle-aged, man with a pleasing mild Scottish accent. I never saw him in a suit and I never saw him over-assert himself. Always approachable and up for banter, you would never know that he was the chief unless someone pointed him out as such.

My team leader stayed wordless, avoiding a glance; all was left to the chief. He simply read out, in a quiet and as friendly a way as he could have done given the circumstances, the first paragraph of the letter which announced my suspension from duty. Something about the Sunday Times and that I was the source. Suspension, yes …then an investigation. Now I got this bit: the Public Interest Disclosure Act. Well they knew what I was about and were up to speed with the law; no waffle about the Official Secrets Act. I was not to attempt to communicate with anyone on the staff. I said that I thought that was a perfectly reasonable request and thanked them. A quite amicable if brief exchange. My swipe card was politely requested and confiscated. A formality given it had already proved itself useless. I suppose it was so I couldn't wave it at someone to show I had a right to be in the building if somehow I subsequently managed to get in. They couldn't be stripping me of my Home Office identity because, as they had just explained to me, there was to be an investigation — however just going through the motions it may turn out to be — to see if I had done anything wrong. I said my goodbyes to each before the security guy ushered me out.

* * *

It had been something of a struggle to get all the TV crews to show up. Yes, it was arranged; they didn't just happen to be there guessing roughly when I'd show for work. The TV media sleeps on Sunday, I had discovered, and nobody had got back to me from ansaphone messages I had left on Sunday night — if there was an ansaphone to leave a message on. I would have to arrange my own photo (that is, video) opportunity first thing tomorrow. David Leppard rang me and told me to go and buy a mobile phone courtesy of the Sunday Times, because I wouldn't be able to survive without one.

Starting very early I rang round and got to talk with journalists, producers, call-centre operatives … who knows who they were. Some were clueless. After trying to explain, I asked: 'Did you see the Sunday Times yesterday?' … 'Well don't you think that you ought to have a crew there?' Then people started ringing back. They had wiped the dried gooey stuff out of the corners of their eyes and actually expressed interest. Yes, they knew what I was talking about; somebody must have given them a shufty of the Sunday Times. I was going to meet with Channel 4 first, just up the road from work, away from where the other TV crews might be.

I put my suit on, which is far too dressed-up for work normally. The dress code was smart casual, so if you turned up with a tie on people would assume you were either going to an interview or doing some sort of presentation for management. But today I wanted to look like I was a civil servant, and I supposed most people still think of bowler hats and brollies. I drew the line there. I did not want references to the Monty Python Ministry of Silly Walks. A suit and tie would suffice. I often walked or cycled in but I went by bus so I wouldn't risk getting a bit sweaty. Anyway it was early and chilly, because I first had to go to BBC Radio Sheffield to be on the Radio 4 Today programme.

Shut in a tiny room with headphones and a microphone and no staff in sight, I was listening to how the programme was shaping and the occasional over-spoken apologies from the producer about how long I'd have to wait. Just a few seconds is all I got. Humphries ended by asking me: 'But you can't actually prove it can you?'. Very un-politician-like I answered, a simple: 'No'. Luckily they had David Davis, the Conservative shadow Home Secretary, lined up, and he successfully made the points I should have made myself. Nobody then said anything else over the headphones; nobody came into the room. I slipped out on to the street and made my way back to the shopping centre to wait for a phone shop to open.

I got a cheap pay-as-you-go mobile when the shop opened at half past nine and straightaway rang the TV guys who were en route, to check they knew where they were going; and also a friend who was taking calls while I was incommunicado. I was making calls on the hoof as I'd said I'd be turning up for work just before ten, and it was already pushing twenty-to and I had a five-minute walk to get to where I would meet the Channel 4 crew. They wanted a quick pave-ment interview away from other crews prior to me going in; I sup-pose just in case the experience of turning up for work turned me into a jibbering clutz for the rest of the morning. No problem with nerves here. In fact I never had that problem at any interview I did. Put me in front of an audience I can see and I may well get stage fright of varying severity, but never just looking at a camera lens or an interviewer. The BBC collared me, and recorded a piece that went out later on bulletins and on Newsnight. I know what I said, because friends were taping the TV for me, and this is transcribed from the video:

> It's a political exercise. To admit people before May the first so that they don't become part of the figures for after May the first. Clearly they are

part-and-parcel of the same influx; it's just a laundering exercise, basi-
cally. And I don't see why, as a civil servant, I should be partaking in this.
I don't work for the current Government; I work for the civil service on
behalf of everyone in the country.

Ten o'clock was the end of the flexi-time window; the latest time you
were supposed to show up. Not that it would make any difference,
because I knew they wouldn't let me do any work. The thing was
that I didn't want to give them anything, however minor, they could
discipline me over.

After the shortest working day ever, I came out of the front
entrance to explain what had gone on. 'What do you think of your
suspension?', one interviewer prodded me. 'I agree with my suspension', I wrong-footed them. 'It's normal procedure in these sort of
circumstances. The Home Office could not have done anything else'.
This caused some mirth back at the Sunday Times, Leppard later
told me.

Channel 4 and the other crews wanted me to do a live feed but
their satellite truck had been stuck north of Sheffield on the M1. To
save time I would have to go with them in their van to a rendezvous
at some lay-by just off the motorway. Channel 4, the BBC, ITV, Channel 5, Sky … lord knows who; we all set off in convoy and got to a
godforsaken parking spot near a pub by a scrubby wood where all
the vans parked up like trailers in Wagon Train.

I had gone first with Channel 4 because of the C4 evening news: it
was the best on TV, I thought; albeit that apparently nobody is
allowed to present it who is not either female or of an ethnic minority
unless they're called Jon Snow. I gave them first shot. The unseen
studio presenter, whose voice I recognized, asked me: 'Do you
believe that ministers, like Beverley Hughes, knew about this, or
not?' I replied:

> Well, it's not for me to say. I can't know that. Either she's incompetent
> and didn't know what was going on; or she's not telling us the truth. I
> find it hard to believe that she didn't know what was going on over so
> long a time in her own department. What is puzzling as well is that I first
> tried to raise these issues on December the fourth, more than three
> months ago, and I was blocked by management.

C4 got their ITN buddies up next. The interviewer chatted after the
take, asking me if there was anything in my recent past that could be
used against me. It seemed like concern to tell me to watch my back,
but was it also the journalist looking for an angle to bring me down?
When afterwards he had a long mobile phone chat with his base, I

guessed he was arranging a check-up on my past. I was now feeling distracted as well as tired with the focus required to answer every question fluidly. I apologized to the BBC in case they felt left out, and did a long feed for them. I think there was Channel 5 and BBC News 24 … I was getting a touch addled, and my throat was getting beyond cups of water thoughtful journalists handed me. Why do they do such long interviews when they will only use a few seconds? To get something inadvertently juicy they can tar you with, I suspected. But stuck in the March morning chill in an unprepossessing car park by the M1 trying to keep sharply focused was rapidly becoming not my idea of fun. This was work. I knew that if I eased up my concentration I might dry up or even make some gaff.

Channel 4 whisked me back to Sheffield, and after all the hullabaloo a peculiar non-lonely aloneness grabbed me back at my flat as I waited for the taxi laid on to take me to local TV land up in Leeds and a shuffle between ITV and BBC studios, where I was also to do a feed to the Richard Littlejohn show on Sky. That one was weird, because the studio monitor displayed me and not Littlejohn. Quite off-putting. The BBC Look North interview went as well as the rest earlier in the day. 'Obviously, it's not up to me to accuse the minister of lying', I guardedly said. 'I would suggest to look at the reasonableness of it. It's not just [the changed procedures]; you've got to factor in the other probability: is it reasonable that it took her three months to realize I'd written to her?' Perhaps I was being a little ambitious in expecting a local TV audience to grasp straight away the idea of multiplied probability!

'Well you're famous all of a sudden', one of the presenters, Christa Ackroyd, had quipped before the show started. Hell, I *was* famous, albeit maybe just for a few days. I have lost count of the number of times since that I have heard the 'you've had (more than) your fifteen minutes of fame' quip. And there was no tangible benefit at all as far as I could see. By the end of the day I was pooped. No food and far too much coffee. I had a good chat with the taxi driver on the way back and that was good for perspective. He was in part putting the case for a few recent immigrants he knew about, and I agreed with him. He could tell that I was no racist, he said. Well that's comforting to know! Although he could have been saying that to try to persuade himself against other inklings he might have had.

It was long after eight by now as I headed for my front door and standing nearby was a syndication photographer for various newspapers. About a hundred shots later — in my lounge, in the garden

— I stuck on the telly to find out if I'd had a good news day. A not too unflattering photo of me was the backdrop to Kirsty Wark, who introduced a report that began: 'The Government must be cursing whistle-blowers …'. Good use of interview clips illustrated what Wark referred to as 'the Moxon affair'. For the story to be graced with such a tag confirmed that it had really taken off.

* * *

Seeing how I was going down in the news was also how I had started the previous day; the morning the Sunday Times first splashed the scoop on the front page. I couldn't sleep much and kept getting up in the very small hours to check the TV teletext for anything registering in the news. Then, at about three or four in the morning the story suddenly popped up immediately below the top headline on ITV Oracle. Nothing on the Beeb's Ceefax though. Having got some sleep I woke to find the ITV Sunday programme with Joan Bakewell flicking through the papers. She read out the Sunday Times' main headline — 'Lid Blown on Migrant Cover-up' — and mentioned my name. I had finally arrived in the news. This felt like the point of no return. The first concrete evidence that the news was out. The Sunday Times hadn't pulled the story after some injunction, or because they got cold feet after deciding I was a low-quality source. No sudden breaking big story had blown me into next week.

No guest on either the ITV or BBC early morning shows picked up on the story; the one good hard news story of the day. Inconsequential showbiz gossip or pointless and boring speculation was all that was on offer, despite an uneventful Saturday to report on and no big-running news saga. If ever there was an illustration of the denial surrounding the whole subject of immigration, this was it. Frost didn't even pick out the headline when he meandered in his creaking style through the press. It's hard to believe this was the same David Frost who spat satire at the establishment when he fronted 'That Was the Week that Was'? I rang my cousin and before I said anything he made the same observation. His other half also could hardly believe it.

Then the reporters started ringing. I was in the phone book, so even the most lazy journalist should have been able to track me down. 'Are you the Steve Moxon …?' They started turning up at the door; some without bothering to ring first. I don't think it was even nine o'clock. If my memory serves me correctly, the Mail was first, with the Express not far behind. At one time I had reporters from three different papers together in my lounge scribbling in their note-books, while one or two snappers twisted their cameras and clicked. Outside on the lawn and on the steps by the shrubbery were for some reason where they wanted me to pose. After they went away, when I thought of something I needed advice on, I rang Leppard. The TV people were all asleep, as I said. All day I tried. My ansaphone had been on and was stuffed with dozens of messages I hadn't time to lis-ten to. Amongst them, I discovered on Tuesday morning when I first had time to try to unblock all my communication channels, were two quite friendly sounding brief messages from the Sheffield Home Office chief asking me to ring him. I imagine that his seniors had been having the heeby-geebies about the sight of me on TV coming into work, and were keen to deprive the story of the extra momen-tum it would gain through such an obvious photo opportunity. This was to be the first in a long line of failed attempts at damage limita-tion.

Chapter 6 — Analysis
Extreme Denial

So far the Government and the political Left has ignored all of the economic arguments that are clearly fatal to any policy of mass net immigration and the political Right has been mostly mute, unclear that it could successfully take on the plethora of 'sexy' political shibboleths. While the Left sees immigration as a positive form of 'diversity' and does not want to give ground now it has had to swallow what it used to see as the negative variety of 'diversity' in market individualism; the Right sees it the other way round. Having always championed the market (or at least since 1979) the Right has an uphill task persuading electors that they have inadvertently swallowed the 'diversity' thing in its other forms.

'Diversity', as those of you hitherto unfamiliar with the term now will have gathered, is a trendy catch-all term for politically-salient group differences. It was imported from the USA and unknown on these shores until about a decade ago — and who would give it as much as another decade before it will be widely used as a euphemism for many things pretentious or sordid? David Goodhart's article, 'Too Diverse?', in the influential Prospect magazine, looked at the 'progressive dilemma' of diversity versus solidarity (another catch-all term used in the sense of politically-salient within- or between-groups tendency to agreement) that underlies many areas of policy. This is the problem that if we accept and promote ever-more different values and lifestyles — a trend that is due to immigration in particular — then inevitably there is a reduction in the feeling of shared commonality and a consequent withdrawal of the tacit agreement by members of the public en masse regarding payment of tax and the welfare state. Goodhart sparked a debate with his article in February 2004, just a month before the immigration furore took off. Then when that was in full swing, the chair of the Commission for Racial Equality, Trevor Phillips, after initially lambasting Goodhart's article performed a volte face and called for the abandonment of the concept of multiculturalism. Phillips' comments are so seismic because he is a close advisor to Tony Blair. Within days the CRE announced that it would no longer fund projects based on the idea of separatism. Perhaps after all there is a growing realisation on the Left that all is not well with an unthinking pro stance on immigration.

There seems to be a retreat from the virulent anti-racism by which the debate about immigration has been successfully stymied for so long. Condescendingly the population is regarded as ineradicably racist at the same time that commentators on the Left are somehow immune to the condition. The reality — which appears to be dawning on them — is that we are, in this respect, all the same. Research shows that far from there being a minority, large or small, of xenophobes, we are all individually psychologically identical in perceiving ourselves in terms of our 'in-group' as opposed to 'out-groups' of any other collection of people showing dissimilarity to ours. Conversely, it is clear that the notion that only 'deviants' could be what we could term 'racist' is plain false. ('In-group'/'out-group' is a phenomenon readily observable in the real world, which can be manipulated in social psychology experiments; it is not 'psychobabble'.) The good news is that in any situation, such as in the school playground, the majority social grouping readily accommodates small numbers of highly dissimilar individuals and these individuals readily assimilate in return. It is only when the minority becomes substantial to the point of assuming the status of a rival 'in-group' that mutual hostility may begin.

A major problem is that for too long the predominantly Left intelligentsia has seen itself as an 'in-group' implacably hostile to the 'out-group' of the general population, in a dangerous pathological development of the mindset of a group of people who perceive themselves as society's leaders. The psychology behind this, however conscious or unconscious, appears to have two related components beyond the normal arrogance of a group claiming leadership status. First, there is the protracted frustration and humiliation of witnessing the progressive discrediting of the favoured Marxist philosophy as succeeding vaunted vanguards — the working class, students — failed to deliver. The grating discord between a social elite and its increasingly marginalized and obviously nonsensical belief system, is hardly the trajectory of a group destined to remain dominant for long. Second, and more important, is the extreme denial of the corollary of the mass solidarity of the ordinary people the political Left supposedly champion, which under charismatic leadership is transformed from a benign and normal aspect of human life into a pathological totalitarian hostility to 'out-groups', leading both to Stalin and to Hitler.

As is now being more fully understood, Hitler may have been to the Right of the communists but he was to the Left of everybody else; he was in fact a socialist, in common with Mussolini and Mosley. The difference between fascism and socialism is one more of perception than reality after the internecine conflict on the Left between internationalism and nationalism — an even falser distinction when you consider that fascism was pan-European and extended to the Argentina of Peron. The deeply unwelcome truth is that all of the evil demagogues of the last century, from Stalin to Pol Pot, were drawn from the political Left. Hitler and Stalin were indeed cut from the same cloth. Nationalism and, indeed, racism and eugenics were until recently hallmarks of the Left. This is now a matter of embarrassment verging on physical trauma, so it has become a fundamental denial. It is a denial that has a deeper root in the irreconcilable conflict between equality and leadership, and a refusal to countenance the reality of the 'in-group'/'out-group' dynamic.

I would imagine that most readers would be resistant to this analysis, so although something of a detour, because the conclusion is so important, rather than just leave those who are interested to consult authorities on the subject and the rest to dismiss out of hand, I will now expand on the notion of internationalism. Actually this issue is a good route into the Left's mindset, because if you challenge someone with socialist leanings about the extent to which immigration policy is irrational, then internationalism is sometimes volunteered as an explanation. Prospect's editor David Goodhart proffered this when I chatted to him while discussing the publication of an article in his magazine.

Many will have heard of claims that Hitler was really a socialist, but only through facile rebuffs that Hitler's Nazis were 'national socialists' in name only, as if this was the only evidence put forward. On the contrary, it is the defence of the received view and not the challenge to it that relies on semantics. The received view is that Italy, Germany, Spain and Japan in the early/mid-twentieth century were all regimes united in an extreme nationalistic far-Right revolutionary politics called fascism, after Mussolini's term for the movement he headed in Italy. In fact, Spain under Franco was an attempt to stay put or to turn back in time to a Catholic monarchical state, while Japan remained a feudal system run by warlords but now globally militaristic through a modernist veneer that procured competitive weaponry. So Spain and Japan at this time had ultra-conservative regimes. Italy and Germany by contrast were in the throes of popular revolutions to completely overthrow their establishments. The only thing that all four regimes had in common was antipathy towards Lenin, not least because of the appalling economic disaster in Russia in the wake of the Bolshevik revolution. What is the point of revolution by or on behalf of the masses if the masses thereby starve? But even so, some forms of fascism were not particularly anti-communist.

Mussolini's fascism was pragmatic socialism and akin to the Third Reich minus the anti-Semitism and its ruthlessness. Both Hitler and Mussolini were true socialists. Hitler's slogan, 'common use before private use', he shared with the German Left, and his other key rallying cry, 'one state, one people, one leader' is his demand for a fully classless society. What they rejected of the Left — the only thing they rejected of the Left — was Marxist class war, but they were fully on-board the Marxist revolutionary levelling of their societies in favour of ordinary working people and against the establishment. The conventional view is that fascism was simply a conservative revolt against the decadence of the ruling elite, but it was much more than that. It was not conservative at all. The objective was the same as the rest of the Left but they saw Marx's analysis as an abstraction that did not translate into physical factions that could and should go to civil war. Instead of everyone being either a member of the proletariat or of the bourgeoisie, everyone was simply a worker against the establishment. Instead of pretending that the workers could rule collectively, both Mussolini and Hitler realized that strong leadership was necessary — just as Lenin and Stalin had come to understand. This did not have to come from the 'proletariat', and could not be the many governing the many, for the obvious reason that this was not government at all, but chaos. Pragmatically all that was needed was for the few with vision, regardless of where they had come from, to grasp and exercise power in favour of the many. This still produced demagogues though; power without checks always does. As we know only too well, both fascists and (pseudo)-socialists made this same mistake.

Many members of both Italy's and Germany's socialist parties voted with the respective tyrants, and indeed Mussolini had been a member of Italy's socialists (and only broke with them because of their neutrality in World War I: Mussolini wanted to side with the allies against the obviously doomed Austro-Hungarian empire). What is especially telling is that for many years the Left internationally cited Mussolini's regime as worthy of praise, before veneration was transferred to Stalin's Russia.

That what is considered 'far-Right' was actually socialist can be demonstrated by a scholarly examination of Mussolini and Hitler in their own words and actions. John J. Ray has done this in considerable depth, in his on-line article, 'Modern Leftism as Recycled Fascism'. Several authors have produced similar analyses, notably the Israeli historian, Zeev Sternhell. James Gregor (*The Faces of Janus: Marxism and Fascism in the Twentieth Century*) argues that the notion of fascism (including Nazism) as being of the ultra-Right is an old Soviet lie taken up by intellectual apologists in the West. Both Hitler and Mussolini got their methods from Lenin and Stalin, but then Stalin and Mao returned the favour in taking up Hitler and Mussolini's powerful hybrid of socialism and nationalism (in Stalin's case, this was the difference between him and Trotsky who, of course, was murdered for his dissent along these very lines — before Stalin adopted the same position himself). Even the quintessential Maoist stance of permanent revolution was pioneered by fascism.

As John Ray puts it:

> in the end fascism and communism were two very similar Leftist sects … The fascist origins of modern-day Leftist ideas should then help to alert us to the authoritarianism and potential for tyranny that lurks beneath their supposedly 'compassionate' surface.

This includes Tony Blair, who in taking up the catch-phase 'the third way' is directly stealing from Mussolini: it was the latter's description of the alternative to capitalism and communism! But as Ray points out, Blair is further to the Right than Mussolini. 'Third Way fascism', according to Roger Eatwell:

> sees capitalism as too individualistic, and ultimately not loyal to the community. It sees socialism as too internationalist and based on false views of equality … (it attempts to combine) the best of capitalism (the naturalness of private property; its dynamism) and socialism (its concern for the community and welfare).

All of the stances taken by the modern-day Left have their precursors in Mussolini, the first socialist despot to try to square the circle of economic success and socialist doctrine. His making a virtue of pragmatism has been followed by rulers in Russia and China, as well as by Blair.

One reason that fascism became a bete noir is its association with racism, but this is a red herring. Quite obviously antisemitism was a feature of the Third Reich (though Hitler clearly denounced it in his younger days), but Mussolini certainly was against this, and together with Hitler's generally inhuman personality it was the antisemitism which made Mussolini recoil from Hitler. There was a greater proportion of Jews in Mussolini's fascist party than in any other social grouping in Italy for which there were statistics. Sir Oswald Mosley's British Union of Fascists actually threw out anyone who made antisemitic remarks — the recent four-part Channel 4 series on Mosley portrayed the leader himself as an opponent of antisemitism. In fact it was in part identification of Jews with the Left (that was by now attacking fascist movements' internecine style) that led to fascists in other countries toeing Hitler's line in this regard, but even then only reluctantly. History reveals that in fact antisemitism was if anything more rife in Left circles, especially in Soviet Russia, and is evident in the writings of Karl Marx himself. If truth be known it was present in many if not most places you looked. As for eugenics: this clearly originated from the Left — most vigorously advocated by 'progressives' in the USA. Racist eugenic theorizing as advocated by the Left abounded throughout Europe. Hitler boarded as a passenger a train that had long been running. (Evidence on this is widely available: space precludes a detour within a detour here.)

A root of the internationalism–nationalism polarity is the principle of equality that is fundamentally what the political Left is all about. Equality is the Left's religion. If all men are equal then are not all nations also equal? Well yes, but nations do work and 'if it ain't broke, don't fix it'. They are robust 'in-groups'. So, pragmatically it is best to move towards the tough but at least realistic goal of ensuring that all men within a nation are equal. Napoleon Bonaparte asserted equality; he being the heir to the very first revolution of the Left: the French Revolution. As John Ray shows, Mussolini may have invented the term, but Napoleon was in spirit the first fascist. Just as all who followed — from Hitler and Stalin, through Mao and Peron, to Kim Il Sung, Pol Pot and the Shining Path — Napoleon's words were of equality, but his deeds were to build a cult of the leader. Attempting to make a nation of equals seems to have led to war with other nations to 'spread the word'.

John Ray concludes:

> So what Hitler, Mussolini and Peron all show is what most modern-day Leftist intellectuals passionately deny: that you can be an extreme Leftist and an extreme nationalist too. And it shows something very troubling too: that the combination of Leftism and nationalism is popular!

The problem with internationalism is that it is completely impractical. Asserting the rights of others outside the nation inevitably introduces the free-rider problem on a massive scale, the more so that economic disparities prevail across the world. Instead of exporting war, as both the extreme nationalist and pseudo-socialist nations had done, those nations that deny the reality of nationhood leave themselves open to importing their own exploitation. However the economic upper hand (or alleviation of subordination, actual or merely perceived) is achieved, exploitation is exploitation, whether it is by means of warfare or via something more subtle. The problem of the free-rider invading a host society from outside is a problem only too apparent in the issue of immigration and asylum.

* * *

The legacy of the great denial regarding fascism and the Left in the mindset of the class of would-be leaders — the Left intelligentsia — and its deeper root in the irreconcilability of equality and leadership, and failure to understand 'in-group'/'out-group' dynamics, is a near equal and opposite reaction of totalitarian morality, which is the movement generally known as political correctness, where any and every minority is held up to be more worthy than the 'fallen' mass of ordinary people. It is as if the deep-seated Christian notion of 'the fall from grace' — the original purity soiled by contact with the world — has been revived for a secular age. It is, if you like, the secular religion. (It is also a hopeless and inappropriate cause, as brilliantly argued in Matt Cavanagh's book, *Against Equality of Opportunity*. But this is beyond the scope of the present book.) It shows that the notion is probably much deeper than Christianity; a psychological invariable that never went away. The sad truth is that the political Left is still indulging in pathological hatred, but instead of directing it outwards, it is directed closer to home: at the very people in whose name it is supposed to be working. This is the ultimate example of the emergence in a social group (our society as a whole) of a leadership that is so full of itself that it actually splits off to form not a sub-group but what it perceives to be its own completely autonomous social group. The political Left is in effect a society on top of a society; a self-sufficient splinter social group that sees as its principal enemy the very group from which it sprang. This makes sense for a social group based on an idea of justice well past its sell-by date. It is one thing to practice corruption at the top of the tree, but being in the tree at all requires some degree of accountability; whereas no accountability at all is required if you fly away 'off your tree' altogether. As was famously said and oft repeated: power corrupts, and absolute power corrupts absolutely.

The combination of the utter failure of the socialist vision and the extreme denial of 'in-group'/'out-group' hostility leaves the Left in a mammoth sulk that shows through in the ludicrous abstract irrelevant theorizing of post-modernity and deconstruction that inexcusably has been allowed to dominate universities; from the 1980s on in the sneering nihilism of one pole of popular culture exemplified by the then new 'stand-up' comedy; and by a supremely arrogant dismissal of any other view by the great majority of commentators — not least by journalists en masse at the BBC, both enabled and shackled as they are by a corporate hypersensitivity to the moral totalitarianism of the equal opportunities and diversity lobby.

The migrant is the most championed minority figure of all. In the (let's call it a) semi-conscious view of the Left, he is both an ideal peg for extreme denial and yet another class of saviour for the cause, being the disadvantaged person from outside the core of the capitalist world, untainted through never having declined to grasp the chance when offered of 'rising up' against the bosses, as it were. The migrant is the innocent child of the global village. This is the basis of the strong version of human rights that governments have saddled themselves with. As Harriet Sergeant summed up in her book, *Welcome to the Asylum*:

> Western immigration law has moved away from excluding anyone it considered undesirable to believing that individuals are invested with inalienable human rights that must be protected by the Government who, as an anonymous writer in the Harvard Law Review stated, 'owes legal duties to all individuals who reach America's shores, even to strangers whom it has never undertaken, and has no wish, to protect.'

By contrast, the ordinary indigenous UK citizen is, in ways masked by bogus constructs from politics, derided. By this 'logic', especially reviled is the person originally supposed to have been at the vanguard: the working class *male*. He is the victim of 'the last acceptable prejudice', according to Michael Collins in his new book, *The Likes of Us: a Biography of the White Working Class*. Denounced by pseudo-Marxist feminism (the great booby prize of the failure of socialism), his offspring are urged to forgo ordinary vocation for a university soaking in the now discredited standard social science model and 'political correctness' (though no longer in the vain hope of fulfilling Marcuse's notion of student revolutionaries). Or, if he still chooses the 'previous' life, to endure the punishment of competition from those supposedly more worthy, such as the migrant and the 'liberated female'; and taxation to fund non-family families — the family being thought of not as a natural human grouping but as an institution of the old order to be replaced. The EU, by contrast, has been rehabilitated; from an alien 'capitalist club' to an ally in helping to force through ways of further denuding the ordinary man of political power. (The EU Commission is impregnable to democracy and formulates all of the proposed legislation without any input from the EU Parliament: a dream engine of the intelligentsia for social engineering. The 2004 Euro elections showed that many or even most people are realizing this.)

Reinforcing all this is the transparent 'I'm better than you' self-advertisement in championing those apparently we make no gain in supporting. This is the familiar psychology of the liberal, clearly as biologically rooted in mating strategy as the peacock's fanned tail, and high time it was regarded as somewhat risible.

Or perhaps there is some gain? These are votes for Labour. Sergeant has an interesting take on all this:

> Kindness to strangers is always more attractive than concern for the majority. ... here is our modern day version of the medieval priest – enjoying the reverence of the public while profiting from the sale of indulgences.

There is too, of course, the steady decline in trust that marks social relations generally, but the feelings of the public for politicians especially; so politicians bounce this back on to those who demand to be better served, creating a vicious spiral of mistrust.

Aside from simply not knowing what to do about a longstanding mess, for the Left to support a policy — uncontrolled mass net immigration — that is so plainly and plurally anti-progressive indicates that non-rational emotion must indeed be at the root of their slipshod economics and incoherent stance. This goes too for the soft centre apologists for those who hold this position (or how they are so masked) in New Labour, and fits alongside the other silly notions I have touched on to make up the unpleasant side of the Left long overdue for outing. An unrelenting contempt for ordinary people and a determination to view all social developments as an inevitable part of the road to eventual socialism (Marxist historicism); a combination of disdain and *que sera sera* escalating in direct proportion to mounting evidence and common sense that individuals and society are being seriously damaged by what are really social aberrations.

Immigration may be the stalking horse by which a truer and far less flattering picture of political divides emerges; the Left taking over from the Right as the main focus of loathing. Locating all politics along a Left–Right continuum may soon come to be seen as outdated as in reality it has long been, leaving the general public with a still deeper attitude of 'a plague on both your houses'.

Or ...it might just reinvigorate politics.

The mass of ordinary people who Blair, Blunkett, Labour both New and old, and the political Left ostensibly speak for, are actually the very people they despise. New Labour is perhaps a curious combination of the beginnings of a repudiation of this as well as an even stronger exemplification of it by still more devious means — as in their pre-eminence in the art of spin. Yes, the out-of-date confrontational policies have been amputated: wholesale nationalization, the closed shop, anti-NATO unilateral nuclear disarmament and the dominance of the union block vote were all dropped. But the knife did not get anywhere near to the tumour itself. Tony Blair's clearly genuine Christian fervour has served to blind him to the problem. He is convinced there is nothing fundamentally wrong: just a bit too much ideology getting in the way of good management; thus Blair's key platform of the need for extensive restructuring of public services for greater efficiency, with the rest being just a matter of presentation. He is barely half right. He is right that ideology is getting in the way, but wrong that mere pragmatism is all that is needed to clear the path ahead. Our Tony appears honestly clueless that it might be something about the ideology itself that is what really needs changing. But I think people are (or soon will be) starting to wake up to the general truth.

There will be a big score to settle.

The One-Legged Romanian Roof Tiler

One of the key 'dos and don'ts' we were told in the first few days, during 'induction' sessions, was that we were not to talk to anyone outside work about what we did here, because our work was sensitive and newsworthy. The person asking questions might be a journalist or a political activist. Then after induction we were introduced to two young personable people who were to be our initial trainers: a woman and a man, the latter being of an ethnic minority. (Not that I gave any thought to these aspects at the time, but in training (outside computing), the caricature of the white male being not easy to spot turned out to be quite true.) The so-called training was tedious almost beyond endurance. To stay awake, I asked questions to try to put things in context; to make connections and suss common threads; and got regular long stares from one youngish woman determined to convey to me her authoritarian streak. Without any context to help make sense of it, we were not taught but simply read to, by caseworkers themselves evidently untrained in how to lecture. The endless volumes of guidance notes, which were supposed not to obscure but to illuminate the immigration legislation, were read out verbatim, including the lines of gobbledegook reference numbers of all the sections, that nobody, however experienced, could possibly ever remember, nor have any remote reason to. But the trainers held out the prospect of a working life surprisingly free of tedium. We were free to make whatever decision we saw fit, they repeatedly told us. Oh yes?! It was simply a matter of being able to justify what was neither the right nor the wrong outcome but the appropriate decision for that case as you understood the facts. I soon found out that this was quite untrue.

After two weeks of training days mercifully shorter than normal working days, we all moved on to the mentoring stage — loosely chaperoned individual work on 'live' cases: real cases currently in the system sent in by (so far as we knew) applicants who were indeed still alive, despite the length of time their files had been festering down at our parent office in Croydon. Not that we had much idea of what we were supposed to be doing. It was evident that we were to lead a mushroom existence — fed knowledge on the basis of a minimal need-to-know criterion sufficient to be able to carry out administration processes without having to follow how anything fitted together with anything else. The way I had always done things, of first understanding and then on that basis doing; was turned upside down and divided. Doing and more doing without bothering to understand appeared to be what was required. But without a framework to peg the processes to, it was more difficult to remember what the processes were.

Time and again the large white cardboard Home Office files — a system that was in the throes of being completely changed — containing passports, completed application forms and documents held together with green string, came back together with multiple choice assessment sheets covered in red ink. One or other of the two young women caseworkers who acted as mentors to a sub-group of us would explain repeatedly how to remedy our botched decisions; when they weren't completely rushed off their feet, that is, which was a lot of the time. Some of it stayed in my head, but then some procedure would be changed, or another e-mail would arrive telling us to take something else into account. And this was the simple stuff.

At the time (early September 2003), all of the work was being done under what was called BRACE conditions. We were told that this was a way of working to quickly get shot of a large backlog of cases that had been hanging around for months. The checks that we had to do were much reduced from what would normally be done. Nobody said what BRACE stood for. Perhaps it had something to do with the 'brace position' that air hostesses demonstrate as the best way to survive a crash landing? (in which case the Home Office knew more than it was letting on). After all, the essence of this crash posture is getting your head down and putting your hands over your eyes, which seemed to be more or less what the BRACE guidelines involved. As a word it conveyed strengthening, but what it entailed was loosening. We guessed it must be an acronym. No-one bothered asking when we were ushered to someone senior for a get-together in the middle of the office floor when yet another procedure change would be foisted on us. Or maybe I did ask and the convoluted answer I got more or less immediately slipped my mind? 'Backlog Reduction Accelerated Clearance Exercise', as I eventually discovered it stood for, does not trip off the tongue nor slide easily into your memory circuits.

I was clueless as to the management structure. Nobody bothered to tell us about this either. The need-to-know rationale again. There appeared to be people who were more like line managers, in charge of office processes and overseeing and appraising staff; and other people who were senior more through their experience of immigration law, of how applications were made and handling cases to make decisions. Who was the grey-haired slightly geeky man who sometimes gathered us together in the middle of the office? Was he a number-crunching cattle herder, or did he actually know about the work we were doing? Certain names would crop up regularly on e-mails, but we had no idea who they were. There were e-mail threads of discussions between senior caseworkers that were 'cascaded', as was the rather pretentious term used, down to the underlings. There was plenty of jargon but … nobody told us what it all meant.

The cascade of e-mails could become a deluge, though no advice was on hand as to how to store them in a meaningful way for later use and cross-reference. (Somebody eventually told us, about four months later.) Dozens and then hundreds started to stack up in my e-mail inbox, many of them fathomable only with great difficulty, some referring to highly obscure nooks of the many different kinds of applications Managed Migration received. As with any e-mail thread, they went backwards in time (the most recent reply first, followed by what it was a reply to, and so on), adding to their mystery. It was evident that nobody had thought that it would be much more efficient if reasonably regularly someone collated all the e-mails on, say, marriage cases, and produced a concise page or two that explained all of the changes so that you could be confident about being up-to-date on all aspects of handling marriage applications. Large parts of the day consumed by bottom-rung caseworkers scrolling down their screens playing hunt-the-ancient-email so-and-so vaguely remembered we were once sent, could so easily have been freed for more time for considering cases.

We were given a few hours computer training over a couple of days on how to use G-CID — the 'General Caseworking Information

Database' [I think] — the Home Office IND's system for recording case details of all applications. There were siblings of this, notably A-CID, which the asylum boys used; and into which we couldn't enter. (I thought this acronym had a real resonance: the sci-fi 'universal acid' eating through all it touches is a good asylum metaphor, given that asylum is one of the preferred routes to disappear through supposed controls to gain de facto settlement in Britain.) Apart from set fields to 'populate' (as this deadening task is humanely termed) there was a blank section for making notes. We were given some stock phrases but staff were at liberty to put what they liked in here, though nothing that was more opinion than fact. 'Seems like a right so-and-so, this geezer', or 'obviously dodgy fellah — minded to refuse when he doesn't bother to reply to my fishing letter' would have got one of our mentors to ask you to delete and to substitute some anodyne piece of meaninglessness. This was because applicants could, through the Freedom of Information Act, get to see what we had written about them. What soon became evident was that the bright sparks down at our parent office in Croydon had a penchant for making scanty and sometimes cryptic notes understandable only by their individual authors; if they bothered to make any notes at all — and full of typos into the bargain. Croydon seemed to us a black hole and, as with Stephen Hawking's revised view, this black hole wasn't just a one-way vortex but could vomit stuff: huge dollops of ancient forgotten applications.

After two or three weeks of mentoring, which meant five weeks in all if you include what passed for initial training, we were sent back to Aspect Court to be placed in our work teams and let loose on our own to decide on all of the various applications, most of which were either students or people attempting to settle under the marriage rules, and quite a few grannies and other dependent relatives. I say we were let loose, but all of our work was checked. Everything contained numerous mistakes as I, for one, was still not far short of bamboozled. I realised that most new entrants, unlike me, had backgrounds in administrative drudgery that had accustomed them to focus entirely on sequences of seemingly pointless actions without being fazed by not having the faintest notion of what any of it was really for. This was a twenty-first century satanic mill; producing not widgets but less tangible outcomes that had far more profound effects on people's lives — both the applicants' and all those around them. Instead of releasing great plumes of polluting smoke and foul effluent into the river, our impact on the environment was (in respect of a large proportion of the caseload, but obviously not all of it) to further divide cities, with the new influx of people tending to live in whole areas of inner cities where it seems only immigrants, and only immigrants of certain nationalities, concentrate. Not that this was in any way on my mind at the time. I did not have any particular reservations about the work, and even if I had I was keen to get settled and build a platform as soon as possible from which I could spring forward to a better, and better-paid, position.

In saying that I thought most of the others were unfazed by routine tedium and perhaps either did not know or did not care about the wider context or implications of their work, I do not mean that my fellow workers were dim. Quite the opposite. As regards this sort of work, I was the dimmo. Perhaps I was the awkward questioning type because I was such a scatterbrain as regards memory and was so slow off the mark that I used probity to blind people to my deficiencies. After all, the best questions look like the stupid ones, so perhaps you have to be a bit stupid to ask them. The new workers were a very varied bunch, and mostly conscientious, and of a calibre well above what the Home Office could reasonably have expected, given the low salaries on offer. More women than men but not by a large margin, with young and older in a good mix. Quite a few were middle-aged and, presumably, having to settle for jobs that paid less or no more than jobs they had previously held. Some people had just shifted sideways from council or other government work in the hope of a more varied (or cushier?) existence. For some perhaps it was just for want of a change. A number were young university graduates trapped by the small supply of employment that actually needed a degree and deemed over-qualified for most jobs that did not require one. Most of us were under the impression that the opportunity to move on was far better than elsewhere — and this is the reason many of us applied — making up for the very low starting salary (£12,300 for an administrative officer) making irrelevant the slow annual incremental rise over eight years to a heady sum between 15 and 16K.

Also on the plus side was the refreshing eschewal of clock-watching. The notion of time-keeping had been completely thrown out of the window. There was no clocking on, which surprised me because the flexi-time system allowed you to get into work any time between 7.00 and 10.00 am and to leave between 3.00 and 7.00 pm, with almost any slot and duration for lunch. Given the ease with which you could have put in on average a lot less than a full day's work, at first I suspected that the swipe card needed to enter the floor doubled up as a clock-in card, but it was generally thought that this was sophistication beyond the ability of the Home Office. I never got the impression that staff had much confidence in the Home Office doing anything well. I did not take any liberties, because cheating on the clock would be a slippery slope that eventually would lead to being found out. Then it dawned that they could look at the times you logged on and off your computer, so I always logged on even before I took my coat off. But some people never seemed to be around. Management might not be seen for days, or seem to regularly come in at ten and leave at three or four. With several different internal phone directories (most out-of-date), flexi-time, 'family emergency' leave, part-time and job-share, it was a red flag day if ever you actually got hold of the person you needed to speak to.

We were, over time, supposed to meet targets of the number of cases on average we decided daily, but this was months down the line, when we were more experienced. For now we were to concentrate on learning the job and on accuracy — irrespective, within reason, of how long we spent on each case. But even those who had been here for some time and so were having to meet targets, could take long tea breaks whenever and were free to wander to chat with friends. As long as targets were met then management was unconcerned how a caseworker apportioned his/her day. No way could you describe Managed Migration as an unpleasant work environment. Neither was there any sense at all of an oppressive hierarchy, though of course there was a rigid management structure in place just as there is in any workplace. Here it masqueraded as a flat structure of teams in keeping with all of the equal opportunities posters you had a hard time avoiding. The cynical went on to view the more than bearable sides of life in the Home Office as buying off our low intrinsic work satisfaction and as a substitute for low pay. Several ex-bank workers and insurance clerks spoke of how much better it was here than in the relentless target-driven grind of their previous jobs. 'There's more to a job than money.'

The job wasn't without interest. Every case was different, in some detail at least. Unfortunately, the tendency was that as you became more familiar with the nuances, these too became routine. It could then become a battle between the caseworker's attempts to feel that he/she was making a contribution through teasing out extra facets and special cases to keep the job interesting, and management's central task of throughput. The crux problem of production lines everywhere.

I was learning the ropes the quicker to get off 'probation', but I was already thinking that if I couldn't get advancement to something interesting, then I might be able to move on to other jobs where the salary was high enough for me to cut down my hours or job-share. Such were my horizons. But I had begun to settle to quite an ordinary working life, that at the time I expected to remain just that.

* * *

The mismatch between the immigration rules — the legislation, which I was starting to read neat (the Immigration Act being available in full on our computer 'knowledge base') — and the guidance notes (and how we laxly interpreted the guidance notes) was not making it easy to get a confident grasp of how we were supposed to be working. It might make sense in terms of getting shot of backlogs but not otherwise.

I had not long come off being mentored, and on the team in which I was newly placed I was asking a lot of questions of one of the two senior caseworkers — the one who had been set to oversee my progress — and other, more experienced folk; more so than other newcomers tended to. That you had to regularly ask for advice was an enjoyable part of the working day, especially as I was under the wing of someone it was a pleasure to have to regularly approach: a bubbly (in the nicest sense) warm and unembarrassingly almost over-friendly plump woman who shone through the whole team. You did not need an excuse to walk about the floor and interact: it was a requirement of the job. If you were anyway sociable you felt less inclined to work stuff out for yourself when instead you could get out of your chair and wander across for a chat.

The work naturally lent itself to team building. But you never really got the sense of a team. After all, nobody wanted to be there working every day, and nobody had opted to join this particular bunch of people. I was the only newie in ICS12 (that was the title of my team: 'Initial Consideration Section Number Twelve), so my prolific question-asking wasn't too much of a problem, but there was no other rookie I could compare with to judge if I was being a pest. All of those I had trained with had been spread across other sections. I had wondered if I had been placed here separately from others of the new intake so they could completely surround me with experience and stop me corrupting some of the other new blood before they were anaesthetized by a fast absorption of Home Office culture. But perhaps I flatter myself that management was much bothered.

After a very short while, my on-team mentor got shifted to a temporary promotion, though not before she pulled me up for work not up to standard. I had a progress meeting with her and my team leader and it was pointed out that in about one in five of the cases I had dealt with, I had not 'validated' them. It was agreed that this was simply down to eagerness to look to see if there was the evidence needed and then forgetting to go back and do the initial routine. I assured them that it wasn't that I was bored, though I was starting to wonder if soon boredom would start creeping up on me. One of the caseworkers had dryly warned me that although work here is fine for a while, after some months you think different. I was not intending to hang around to find out: the idea was to get a promotion as fast as I possibly could. Trouble is, I would have enough on my plate to counter any impression that I was a boat rocker; if they twigged I was bored as well, then they might think less of promoting me out of the way than getting rid of me altogether.

'Validation' was simply placing a red tick in a box on the last sheet of whichever application form and signing your name to confirm that at least a bare minimum of evidence had been supplied to allow consideration of the application. It was important for legal reasons, because it would louse up the Home Office's position if the decision on the case was a refusal but the applicant then appealed. 'Validation' was complicated in a supremely non-intuitive way. If by the time the case got to us it had already been in the system for more than eighteen days then it had to be validated come what may, yet in other circumstances it might be 'not yet valid' or actually 'invalid'. The procedure defied logic and was a series of inter-related knots that could only have been designed by a committee, though not a committee of people who would have to work with the result.

With the life-and-soul of the team now in another building, my deputy team-leader became the main recipient of my questioning and she rarely showed real impatience though I think she must have felt it. A petite early middle-aged meek woman, you might think she was impatient when really she was just being a little unconfident. She had been here for some time, so she was the one to go to about procedures especially, and how to interpret the guidance notes − it is a hallmark of guidance notes that you could do with a still bigger volume to explain them, notwithstanding that the guidance notes themselves are a whole lot fatter than the actual legislation, of course. Anyway, I got my head round everything after a few weeks sufficient to be 'signed off'. This meant that my decision-making would no longer be fully checked. It was assumed that I now had enough experience to make reasonably accurate decisions and management could run the risk of only randomly sampling work to pick up on any problems. Being 'signed off' also meant being able to put in for overtime.

I had heard about overtime and the generous pay (between two and three times normal rates) interested me, and showed how keenly management wanted staff to put more time in: to clear backlogs. It was available every weekend. Some staff did it routinely, as the only means of making a living wage. I asked about what work we would be doing: ECAA (European Community Association Agreement) cases. These were the applications from nationals of the eight states that were set to join the EU on May 1 (mainly East European countries, plus Cyprus and Malta) plus the two other states which were to accede a few years later (Romania and Bulgaria). I had had no training on this 'workstream', as the different sorts of applications were called, though I had come across it during mentoring. None of us had heard of the scheme until we encountered it here at work and few people in the country at large would have been aware of it. The infamous one-legged Romanian roof-tiler was as yet entirely unknown to all but his intimates and friends (and unknown presumably to anybody who actually needed roof repairs).

As it happened, some staff on our team had been given ECAA work and I copied a scribbled single sheet of notes one of them had, carrying instructions of how to handle these applications. A doddle really. Like all Managed Migration casework the cases arrived in blue plastic crates of separate clear plastic pouches containing passport and documents. For ECAA there was no need even for an application form, so we were spared all the rigmarole of 'validating'. Most of the applications were from people already in the UK who wished to 'switch' from some other immigration category. Most had arrived simply as visitors, though some had been seasonal agricultural workers, students, working holidaymakers, au pairs, etc.

The idea of the ECAA was to bring in those who wished to set up as self-employed, especially tradespeople. The scheme had been in operation for a number of years, allowing people to come in initially for twelve months but they could then renew for three years and settle after four. Applicants could apply for 'entry clearance' in their home countries rather than come here and then 'switch'; either way without having to fill in any kind of form and for no charge. This would be regardless of any adverse immigration history: I once had to grant the case of a man who had been 'removed' from the country and simply came back within days to claim under the ECAA. This seemed ridiculous. Cases like this were in effect an official endorsement of flouting the law.

The original guidelines based on immigration rules were torn up so that from the first day of last August (2003) the only requirement was a business plan. This could be a single sheet of paper containing no financial data of any kind, usually prepared by one of a plethora of 'representatives', many of whom simply produced identical plans for all their clients: for a builder in the case of almost all males and a cleaner in the case of almost all females. No evidence whatsoever of any ability, experience, training or qualifications was required — and not even the most rudimentary command of English, oral or written — and an applicant was free to arrive in the UK entirely penniless, without any necessary equipment for his/her supposed business and without any address, private or business. Supposedly any subsequent application would be subject to proper checks but again, from August last, requirements were similarly relaxed. All that was needed was proof of some payment of National Insurance contributions (just a few pounds would do), a photocopy of the most recent tax return (which may or may not actually have been submitted), some accounts (their own would do, uncertified by an accountant) and 'some bank statements' (the actual vague instruction we were given). Astonishingly, if none of these were submitted we were still required to grant a further year. The 'normal requirements' were supposed to include evidence of payment of tax, bank statements over the past twelve months, declarations that all work had been and would continue to be self-employed and that there had been and would not be recourse to public funds. This last, of all things, was specifically withdrawn in the 'current flexibility requirements'.

There was the comedy of warnings to caseworkers regarding certain representatives. Some were regarded as too unscrupulous to deal with, so we had to hand cases to ECAA team senior staff. It was hard to spot the difference between the activity of these singled-out representatives and most of the rest. In any case, the position of how to treat these changed and reversed and then changed again: one week we must not deal with a particular rep, the next they were about to be registered and were deemed OK, then later we were told to look closely at the applications before granting. But to look for what? You could play a little game to keep yourself awake: guess the name of the rep from simply viewing the business plan. Because reps usually produced identical business plans for all their clients this became quite easy and the game very quickly became too boring to play. It was clear that few of the business plans submitted had had anything to do with the individual on behalf of whom they were being submitted, if indeed the applicant could even subsequently read the application or understand the business culture of which the process was supposed to be a part.

Initially it was mentioned that we should be aware of 'disguised employment'; that is, when someone was purporting to be self-employed but was actually an ordinary PAYE employee. But when-ever I queried with senior staff a pattern of similar or identical sized BACS or BGC (or cash) weekly payments into bank accounts, I was told simply that this was not inconsistent with someone self-employed with a regular contract. Oh yes? Pull the other one. When we were set ECAA work to do during the normal working week, an ECAA team caseworker came to our team meeting — we all gath-ered round a conference table once a fortnight or more — and she admitted that it was: 'difficult to prove disguised employment, especially at present when the Inland Revenue seem to accept most of our applicants as self-employed'. She appeared to be admitting that ECAA team staff regarded many (if not most) applicants as bogus, but were at a loss to know what to do in the face of lack of interest by the tax authorities.

How little an ECAA 'businessperson' had to show he/she earned to still be accepted as not falling foul of immigration rules was start-ling. Several times (before I gave up) I took to senior staff cases of applicants who by their own admission earned paltry sums yet were living (sometimes with dependents) in London or the South-East where a rent alone was likely to swallow almost all income. Yet I was repeatedly told that we should be very reluctant to refuse on the grounds of insufficient funds: 'It's none of our business'. If people were happy to be dirt poor then it was not for us to pass judgment. Never once to my knowledge was a benefits check made on an appli-cant, regardless of it being obvious that on the levels of income declared survival was possible only by claiming public funds. Indeed they would be eligible for benefits on low-income grounds and could successfully apply if they fraudulently did not disclose that although they had a National Insurance number that did not entitle them to claim benefits. NI numbers are scandalously easy to obtain, obviating the bother of stealing one, or of inventing one. There are twenty million more NI numbers than there are people in Britain, so you could probably think one up that as long as it was in the correct format would stand a good chance of not belonging to anyone else and so available for yourself to use. The possibility of approaching the Inland Revenue to check if there was a record of the person working and paying PAYE was never even broached. Even on occasion when I drew attention to clear fraud I got the same 'it's none of our business' answer; such as when someone was declaring a low income offset by a reduced cost of maintenance by flat sharing, though at the same time claiming a single person occupancy discount on Council Tax.

* * *

The first overtime day I did was a little strange. The atmosphere was quite different to a normal workday. A quite junior staff member was in charge and someone had CD music on more or less the whole time that you could hear across the whole floor. Some of the dedicated ECAA team were there to answer the inevitable questions that cropped up — not that you necessarily got the same answer from different caseworkers. The work was straightforward — too straightforward. I then had e-mailed to me a full set of instructions as they had been set out for August and these pointed out the difference between how the rules said we were supposed to process ECAA cases and how, from August 1, we were actually going to deal with them. This filled in the gaps in the handwritten instructions I had been using and I found I had not been following the right procedure with some cases. It still meant that the task was a production line. I didn't mind, because I could earn in one seven-hour stint what it took me half a working week on normal pay rates. Still not exactly a fortune, but it is surprising how any qualms disappear when you feel you are not being taken advantage of.

On succeeding Saturdays or Sundays (we could work either but not both on the same weekend) we started to be given not just 'switching' cases but also 'leave to remain' applications — from those who had already completed a year as self-employed builders, cleaners or whatever. Procedures for these had also been heavily cut down. Some reps — not all were shysters — were sending fat sheaves of invoices, tax returns, etc, but we were supposed not even to bother looking at most of the documents: superfluous to consideration. Hang on a bit, I thought — and I said to fellow workers, including some of the ECAA team — we are virtually automatically granting these people three further years of residence, which will passport them to 'indefinite leave to remain' (permanent UK settlement). Can this be right?

The refrain I got in reply was that at least we know who they are. Uh? I don't get this. If we know who they are and if they don't comply with the rules, then they should be deported, right? Well, no they won't be, apparently. Apart from the likelihood that a lot would appeal, there aren't the staff to tramp round the country looking for these guys and then forcibly chuck them out of the country. And even if this were done, they would just hop on the next plane or ferry and re-enter. (If you recall from the Introduction this would be a 're-moval' as opposed to a deportation.) Better to have them in the administrative system than to have them in the country under no administrative control at all. This still stumped me. So what we do is just a charade then? At this point whoever I was asking would side-step to shift the ground of the argument. This new line was 'who cares?', because these people will mostly be within the EU in a few months time anyway. Er, yes, but they won't have the same rights of access to jobs and benefits as citizens of longstanding EU nations will they? Nobody seemed to know. Well, I knew that there was no way that Germany, France and most countries were going to let Latvians, Poles and all the rest have free access to their labour markets and benefits provisions; not for some time. None of this added up.

Overtime days now really were more of a chore. You could work through lunchtime (normally a mandatory break) and still get paid for it, so the overtime days I did were a straight-through seven hours starting at 7.30am. I was mindful of the 'stats' (number of outcomes — decisions, rather than 'extensions' — per day) that I reckoned would have to be fairly good if you wanted to keep regular overtime work. So I sort of shut my eyes and blasted through, doing maybe fifteen cases in the shift, starting fast and slowing as I knew I would hit an overall good rate of work. A true automaton for one day after the end of the weekday week. If I worked fast for the first couple or three hours then I could go and find someone to have a light-hearted moan-in with. There was a nice, friendly petite woman who seemed to know me (I sometimes meet people and forget that I have done — a male disease: ultra mild Asperger's Syndrome perhaps?) but she normally worked in the other building, so I only saw her on overtime days. She was always good for lively conversation. Usually nobody from my team came in for overtime, so I got to know a few other people a little. The absence of bosses gave the place the air of the kids running the school — the lunatics running the asylum was just a normal workday.

Endless weekend overtime on the ECAA BRACE exercise still did not prevent an ever-mounting backlog of ECAA cases, until we started receiving e-mails from management warning that a backlog of 11,000 'switch' and 'leave to remain' cases would shortly mean all teams stopping work on all other types of casework and taking part in a highly accelerated ECAA clearance exercise. 'Son of BRACE', known as 'ultra ultra BRACE' (what had happened to mere 'ultra BRACE' we had no inkling: the father appeared to have begotten his grandson) was not so much a method of working as no method at all. Lax checking became no checking whatsoever.

A friend — yes, there was one person I thought I could consider a friend — who was later to get the sack (see the appendix) told me what it was called. I thought he was pulling my leg, so I tossed the absurd phrase at the man I reckoned must be its author — the Sheffield Managed Migration deputy chief Neil Best — in a team meeting which he came to address before the exercise started. He didn't bat an eyelid: either at the term or at the fact that I knew it. He simply acknowledged with a 'yes'. 'Ultra ultra BRACE' for God's sake! This was getting to be like an episode of Thunderbirds. Big boys with their silly toys.

The ultra ultra BRACE exercise duly took place and was accomplished (if that is an appropriate description) in a week and included Bulgarian and Romanian nationals. We were told that: 'in the interests of fairness and consistency the exercise will extend to the applications made by nationals of the two countries that do not accede (Bulgaria and Romania)'. Apart from those who applied well after their leave-to-remain had expired, 'all other applications are to be granted 12 months/3 years leave to remain with no further consideration into the merits of the ECAA application, nor must any further requests be made for documentation.' In other words, we were to spend day after day in the archetypal administrative duty of literally glancing at a case and accepting it. Apart from recording details on computer this was literally rubber stamping, in that the only process performed was the despatch department stamping the passport. That's right: we never ourselves put immigration stamps in passports; not for any type of case. That was done in a secure area, presumably so that nobody could set up a lucrative business on the side. Some loopholes they had thought about.

The justification for such an easy way out of the mess of an un-expected deluge of applications, we were told, was that 'the refusal rate across all categories of application is 2.1 percent. This low rate and the nationalities involved point to a low risk of applicant in terms of immigration and security'. What this amounts to is the department compounding its own incompetence; using the results of its own amazing lack of scrutiny to in turn justify no scrutiny at all.

This still left an accelerating build-up of cases that would require other 'ultra ultra' clearance exercises in the near future, but on top of that are all the entry clearance cases, which we were told 'will not come under the remit of this exercise as a high proportion of the backlog of these applications involve applicants not achieving free-dom of movement on 1 May.' In other words, Bulgarian and Roma-nian nationals, who do not get free movement until 2007. The size of this backlog can be judged by the comments of Neil Best at one of our January team meetings. He told us that in just one week there had been 2,000 entry clearance applications from Bulgaria alone. For this reason, from February four entire teams in addition to the dedicated ECAA team were used just to process these entry clearance cases.

The numbers we were dealing with completely blew apart the Government's repeatedly stated upper estimate of the total expected influx of workers from all of the acceding nations after May 1, of between 5,000 and 13,000 (which became 13,000, before David Blunkett dropped making any estimate). Apart from the fact that these figures show this to be a wild under-estimate, the suspicion must be that the whole ECAA exercise was a deliberate ploy by the Government to siphon off as many individuals as possible to be here before May 1, ostensibly as bona fide business persons, so that they do not appear in the figures for those post May 1. Of this the Govern-ment has remained silent.

There was a written response by Beverley Hughes to a parliament-ary question by Simon Hughes MP, that as of July 2, 2003, the Shef-field Casework Unit (alone) had already handled 20,128 ECAA applications, of which 17,027 had been decided. On the figure we were provided of a refusal rate of just 2.1 percent, then the Govern-ment's supposed overall figure of 13,000 after 1/5/04 had been well exceeded by the previous July just on the figures from Sheffield. If you add the ECAA work (now stopped) at Croydon, then this must have been well exceeded by the first of May 2003 — an entire year before day one of accession. Since July 2004 the rate of ECAA deci-sion making has rocketed. Not only has BRACE been in continuous operation since August 1, but staffing levels in the Sheffield Case-work Unit of Managed Migration have climbed steeply, with large intakes for initial training in July, August and September 2004. Then there were (and continue) the massive clearance exercises. The num-ber of people from EU accession states already here officially must run into many tens of thousands, and that does not count those who have simply arrived as visitors and overstayed without declaring themselves. Even discounting these, the Government's upper esti-mate may be out by a factor approaching an order of magnitude even before the starting pistol, as it were, was fired.

What should have caused alarm and the reaction of properly applying immigration rules (followed by tightened legislation) instead propelled the Government into exactly the reverse. Rather than managing migration the Government has simply tried to hide the actual figures, and in so doing has actually compounded the mess. The state of the processing of ECAA applications was well summed up by a senior caseworker on the ECAA team when I asked her incredulously if what we were being asked to do was correct. 'Look, we all know it's pants; so don't ask me about it because I'll just get annoyed.'

The Government itself still does not like being asked about it, because after promising that there would be a register of EU acces-sion state migrants after May 1, when Mayday came to pass and journalists enquired about the rate of arrival of these people, the Government said that it was not keeping any figures. How conve-niently lax of them. This register turned out to be a *voluntary* signing up of those under ECAA, and so necessarily a small subset of the actual numbers.

* * *

What we did not know as we beavered away at the relentless stacks of ECAA cases was that at the other end of the fax machine (which we used for 'entry clearance' cases) James Cameron, the manager of the 25-strong visa section of the Romanian embassy in Bucharest, had over a period of two years persistently complained about open systematic abuse. He had sent between thirty and forty e-mails to his bosses at progressively higher levels. Neither did we know that he had many times contacted Sheffield expressly to try to prevent the granting of UK entry to certain individuals, but that this had had no effect whatsoever. The Home Office had always ignored and over-ruled him. One day Cameron, manager of UK Visas, Romania (a joint body between the Home Office and the Foreign Office) interviewed yet another obviously ineligible applicant: a member of the family of someone who was already in Britain — in business as a roof-tiler, supposedly. Cameron looked through the paperwork and asked the piggy-back applicant before him a rather awkward question about the man she was hoping to join: how does he manage in his occupation if he has only the one leg?

What was particularly amiss here is that it was only when their dependents applied that the obvious unsuitability of people who had been granted ECAA status came to light. Cameron himself interviewed other dependents, or applicants themselves, who were just as incapable of doing the work they claimed to be their trade; such as an electrician with several missing fingers. But it was the one-legged roof-tiler who caught the public's imagination and became the shorthand for the whole immigration mess for many a newspaper cartoonist.

* * *

Just how lax had been the whole ECAA fiasco was exposed in a bombshell report published in June 2004. Nine out of every ten applications that the Home Office insisted should be accepted would not have been granted by British embassy visa section staff ('entry clearance officers' in UK Visas) if they had been allowed to make decisions and not been over-ruled. That was the headline-grabber from the National Audit Office's fiercely damning report into ECAA applications from Romania and Bulgaria. The irony was not lost on the media that earlier in the same week this report was published, James Cameron, the 'whistle-blower' in the Romanian embassy who managed the entry clearance officers there, was barred from returning to his posting, issued with a 'final warning', and now faced the sack through the Foreign Office's trumped-up charge of being 'on-the-take'.

Everything that both Cameron and myself had said at the outset was repeated by the National Audit Office. Applicants had no skills, no English and no knowledge of what was in the so-called business plans dodgy reps submitted by the case-full on their behalf. They didn't even know what a business plan was, and all the business plans from any one rep were all the same: pro formas for builders (men) and for cleaners (women); they were not credible, and where they did contain figures these were not realistic. As if that wasn't enough, applicants had often previously entered the UK illegally or had claimed asylum.

For once the Government had to contend with a report from a body independent of the Home Office, and it was so damning I might almost have started to feel sorry for them if they hadn't done a spot of their usual inept news management. Seemingly caught on the hop, the embargo date/time on reporting was suddenly put back a day: so it would coincide with another whitewash Sutton report on the same subject. But, as before, Sutton couldn't put on a thick enough coat of the white stuff to stop the real story showing through. Rather than what the Government intended, his report was drowned by that of the National Audit Office.

The NAO's David Clarke spoke out: 'The suspicion there is clear. They weren't really coming across to set up a business. They were coming across to take up jobs and therefore displace potential jobs here.' The chair of the Public Accounts Committee, Edward Leigh MP, pulled even fewer punches: 'It is simply outrageous that there were no consistent standards in dealing with these applications, with entry clearance staff and Home Office staff having widely different interpretations of eligibility. Instead of being of one mind, they're like the two heads of Dr Doolittle's pushmi-pullyu. Indeed, UK Visa staff reported that they would have rejected nine out of every ten applications approved by the Home Office. This lack of common purpose is intolerable and jeopardizes the credibility of the UK's immigration system.'

In the most transparently and pathetically feeble attempt by their Government masters to bury unwelcome information, the NAO's main findings are published in text of a minuscule font size in the last page of the last appendix to the report:

> There were many examples of Bulgarians and Romanians obtaining a tourist or student visa and then applying to 'switch' once in the United Kingdom under the ECAA regulations. Some applicants applied to switch very shortly after entering the United Kingdom. This raised doubts over the initial intention for the visit had been as stated [sic], or whether in effect, a visa had been obtained by deception.

Blunkett was interviewed on TV and came back with the lame retort that these people were self-employed and so not exploiting the system; but that is of course exactly what they were doing, as the report stated. Not only at best would they be taking jobs from others, but as Blunkett is only too well aware, nobody knows if they went on to work in the black economy or even if they eschewed work altogether and claimed benefits instead. In his ministerial statement on the Sutton report he again contradicts the NAO: 'Neither does the report find that Home Office officials knowingly processed applications based on forged passports, or that they were complacent about organised criminality in Romania and Bulgaria'. We could be thankful for this small mercy, except embassy staff had been telling the Home Office of these problems for years and the Home Office simply ignored them. The NAO's report finds that: 'The use of forged documents is endemic in some of the countries covered by the visa regime.' Yet everything was approved.

The hopelessness of inter-departmental communication was dealt with at one point in the main body of the report, and through this some of the crucial issues identified in the appendix were touched on:

> Entry clearance officers in Bulgaria and Romania did not generally receive explanations from Home Office staff when their recommendations not to approve the application were not acted on. Instead they received a standard letter instructing them to issue the visa. In addition they did not receive feedback when they had issued visas to Bulgarians and Romanians as tourists, students or seasonal workers but these visa holders 'switched' to the European Community Association Agreements when they were in the United Kingdom. They found out about 'switching' when dependents of those that had switched applied for a visa to join their relatives. The issue was important as there was a suspicion that applicants were obtaining a tourist or other visa by deception and really wanted to enter the United Kingdom to apply under the ECAA. In addition, entry clearance staff did not receive any feedback on what had actually happened when the visa ran out after one year; ie, whether that applicant had successfully established a business.'

Perhaps the most telling phrase was in the tiny writing of Appendix Seven: 'Home Office staff believed that they were not able to make it any more onerous for Bulgarian and Romanian nationals to set up business in the United Kingdom than for British nationals.' This, even more than the revelation that nine out of ten applications should have been refused, is the killer statement within the report. It gets to the core of the problem within Home Office, Government and the Labour Party ... within the culture of the intelligentsia. Astonishing though it is, it would seem that any and every person in the world is more worthy than one of the British subjects our self-appointed betters have (what they seem to feel is) the onerous task of serving; or, rather, presiding over. As citizens of the UK we have responsibilities — not least the payment of taxes, either direct or indirect — and rights accruing through our obvious stake in residing here. Our foreign friends are rendered more worthy than the mere British citizen in being given the same rights without having to show any stake; while imposed on the rest of us is the obligation of support for the system of immigration through taxation.

In fact it's even worse than this — while the Home Office is happy to welcome disabled Romanian roofers to the ranks of the self-employed, the Inland Revenue has ruled that the typical British building subcontractor is a 'disguised employee'. And the notorious Inland Revenue IR35 ruling had the consequence of forcing many freelance IT and engineering contractors to become PAYE employees and contributed to the collapse of the software consultancy industry in the UK. This has led to widespread emigration by skilled professionals.

Migrant Enclaves

I previously asked if anyone had ever counted the cumulative costs of our divided Northern towns and cities, having raised the issue of immigrant enclaves at the outset and then returned to the problem when I went into economic questions regarding immigration. I explained that the enclaves — mainly of Pakistanis and Bangladeshis — are a result of an obviously foolish policy of settling people who were prepared to accept even lower wages than those starting to be shunned by local workers in industries that were clearly overmanned and crying out for investment in technology. Unskilled migrant workers were the very last thing that was required and they now add to the unemployment queues headed by the workers they displaced. I now want to look in some more detail at the problems enclaves pose and what the Government has proposed to deal with them.

British Pakistani and Bangladeshi enclaves (and those of Indian Muslims — about thirty percent of Indians are Muslim) have become more homogenous two generations on, with the divide from the wider society in some respects actually getting worse. Mohibur Rahman of the Muslim Council of Britain, commenting on a depressing Cabinet Office report wrote that: 'Younger generations of disadvantaged groups are not showing signs of breakthrough'. Forty percent of young Pakistani and Bangladeshi men are unemployed and some are being recruited into gangs. At the same time many older people in these communities have re-created a life as lived 'back home' that is more traditional than that of those they left behind who have now moved on. Muslim enclaves are growing rapidly not because of large family size — though that is a factor — but through the massive rise of immigration for the purpose of family reunion (or family creation in the case of marriage). If you combine marriage with dependent-relatives cases then collectively family reunion is by far the biggest caseload in Managed Migration and far and away the most prominent route to full settlement. This is why, as Ann Cryer, Labour MP for Keighley, alerted, half of the Asians in West Yorkshire don't speak a word of English. Anyone can bring in new marriage partners, parents, grandparents, children and brothers/sisters (or people so masquerading). This is reflected in Home Office figures released in May 2004, showing a 21 percent increase in applications for full UK settlement in 2003, and that 40 percent of all of the grants for full settlement had been for Asian applicants. (Another 32 percent were in respect of Africans, notably Somalis, with certain nationalities also tending to form enclaves. Ditto Turks in North London. Few people may know that there are well over a million people from Zimbabwe here in Britain. But I have here in mind Asian Muslim enclaves as they are probably the most intractable and certainly the most numerous.)

The people gaining entry in this way are mostly non-English speakers with no connection to Western culture and hailing from backward rural areas. Having passed a 'critical mass' the enclaves have become more rather than less impervious to integration with the wider host community. Both the increasing size of enclaves and the sort of people who are being added to them combine in negative effect in this regard. On top of this are mytho-political developments. Attitudes become entrenched in history and folklore and this can be a potent base for what may eventually deteriorate into inter-communal strife. Quite apart from the economic consequences, the impact of immigration here is described by the Institute of Community Studies as 'a social disaster'. To claim that migrants in the North (and in the Midlands and London) have made a net economic contribution and are the source of social enrichment is an obvious dishonesty plain to everyone on the ground and is a major reason why people in large numbers do not vote. Some now are openly prepared to cast their votes for the British National Party, after decades of incredulity that politicians (including the Conservatives) have not only done nothing but said nothing apart from insulting and libelling the mass of ordinary decent people as racists. Few would dispute that small numbers of people from a radically different culture can bring about some sort of social enrichment, but this would most likely be nominal and inconsequential. With increasing numbers, diminishing returns must set in regarding this effect very quickly and then it is likely to go sharply into reverse as forces of internal cohesion pull the newcomers away from the proximity with the host culture necessary for mutual enrichment.

On a worst-case scenario, if numbers continue to explode it can be envisaged — it is not inconceivable — that there could be escalation to near civil war as occurred in Northern Ireland between much more similar traditions. This possibility may have seemed remote if not improbable until recently, but in the first few years of the new century we have witnessed Muslim riots in UK cities — notably in Bradford — and the development of a worldwide violent antipathy by Muslims of various shades not just to the West but to the USA and Britain in particular. As correspondents from abroad have noted, in Britain more than anywhere else there is widely available and openly on sale on the high streets of Muslim areas books advocating violence against non-Muslims.

Now I might hesitate to make the Northern Ireland parallel for fear of attracting the charge of being alarmist, but I do so advisedly: it was cited by the Government:

> The idea now is to take a more co-ordinated approach to the problem. We did the same in Northern Ireland in the 1980s when as well as deploying police and troops on the streets we had a massive programme of investment in the local community, raising living standards.

This is written by Home Office Permanent Secretary John Gieve in a confidential report leaked (as all controversial Home Office material is these days) to the Sunday Times at the end of May 2004. The report is on a project codenamed 'Contest', appropriately named to contest the terrorist threat posed directly and indirectly by UK-domiciled Muslims. Gieve estimates that between 10,000 and 15,000 Muslims in Britain 'actively support' Al-Qaeda or related terrorist groups. These figures are based on government intelligence, opinion polls (showing that 13 percent of UK Muslims thought terror attacks against the USA were justified and 26 percent felt no loyalty to Britain) and the fact that 10,000 UK Muslims attended a conference in 2003 of the extremist organisation Hizb ut-Tahrir, which thrives in the UK but is actually banned in Germany. This is clearly a very serious problem in itself, and looks far worse when you consider that the 10-15,000 is just a subset of what is likely to be a far larger number of those who offer passive support.

On the morning of May 19, 2004 the Cabinet Secretary, Sir Andrew Turnbull, chaired a meeting of civil service mandarins, following a letter he had sent to John Gieve. In this letter, Turnbull had outlined 'the problem', as he called it:

> There is a feeling that parts of the Muslim community, particularly younger men, are disaffected ... This includes some that are well-

educated with good economic prospects. Al-Qaeda and its offshoots provide a dramatic pole of attraction for the most disaffected.

Winning 'hearts and minds' is what is called for, Turnbull declared. At the meeting, Gieve presented a paper titled 'Young Muslims and Extremism', which is the report quoted from above in the cited parallel of Northern Ireland. Gieve looked more closely at Muslim disaffection:

> Muslims who are most at risk of being drawn into extremism and terrorism fall into two groups: a) well-educated with degrees or technical/ professional qualifications, typically targeted by extremist recruiters and organisations circulating on campuses; b) underachievers with few or no qualifications and often a non-terrorist criminal background — sometimes drawn to mosques where they may be targeted by extremist preachers and in other cases radicalised or converted whilst in prison.'

> Extremists are known to target schools and colleges where young people may be very inquisitive but less challenging and more susceptible to extremist reasoning/arguments. There is evidence of the presence of extremist organisations on campuses and colleges. The 1924 Society, Muslim Media Forum and Muslim Cultural Society all have extremist tendencies.

Even when such groups are banned, it is pointed out, they simply re-emerge under a different name. To combat this, Gieve focuses on imams (prayer leaders in mosques who are also leaders of their community), proposing to identify and support imams who are not antipathetic to Britain and the West, and to ensure that imams coming here from abroad are sufficiently well-educated and knowledgeable about Britain and the English language.

Ultimately the internal terrorist threat the Government has identified is an intractable problem. The hatred by Muslims across the world is not just against the foreign policy of the USA and Britain. Whatever happens in Palestine, Iraq, Saudi Arabia, Sudan, Afghanistan, etc., Muslim feeling will not be diminished, as some commentators have proffered the analysis that the hatred, or extreme ambivalence, is against modernity itself. But at another level below an abstract kicking against the brick wall of the future is the bare group-against-group status competition — our 'in-group' versus 'out-group' again. It is as simple as that. Such root social aggression will find any peg to hang itself on, but clearly it will manifest as Islam against the world, for the obvious reason that Islam is what dominates and structures peoples' lives in the Muslim world and sets them clearly apart from the rest of us. The USA is the leading nation and so, despite its reluctant- if not anti-imperial nature, is the most detested;

just as its being the principal economic powerhouse makes it the most envied. As the parent of the Anglophone world, Britain is second only to America as the target for Muslim wrath.

Young Muslim men in traditional societies and enclaves suffer considerable sexual frustration, hidebound as they are by cultural restriction of sexual activity to marriage, when marriage is less and less realizable because of failing economic conditions. This is set to be strongly exacerbated by the fact that it is Muslim countries that are experiencing the biggest population explosion; set to expand from about a fifth of the world's people today to a total of a full third by 2025. Under this set of conditions it is hard to see what will assuage the Muslim collective sense of humiliation at the thwarting of their conception of the worldwide state of all Muslim people: the *umma* as a political union. The demographic and economic pressures do, of course, further drive migration to the first world, notably Britain.

I hear in local communities people with wise heads not given to rash statement predict that Britain will rue the day it ever allowed settlement of large numbers of Muslims. It is not enough that the majority of the 1.6 million UK-domiciled Muslims do not support the idea of a violent route to universal political *umma*. Of course it is the case that the majority of UK Muslims do not. But it is not enough even that there may never be such a majority. A majority is not required. A sizeable minority of sympathizers and a core of diehards would be enough to make a Northern Ireland. This is not at all to say anything like this will come to pass in Britain, or that it is particularly likely. My gut feeling is that it isn't, but visceral sense works only on a short timescale. We are all optimists: that is the human condition. We can be optimists while we are at the same time cautious, and recognize that some graffiti is indeed on the wall. It may be by confronting it that we can clean it off.

The Government is not entirely oblivious and is contemplating pulling the wool over our eyes and over our mouths. In July 2004 David Blunkett announced a proposal to introduce a new criminal offence of incitement to religious hatred, specifically to protect Muslims. Not hatred, but vehement opposition is the only rational response to Muslim extremism, such as and notably Wahhabism. No doubt, voices of firm but reasonable hostility to Muslim extremism will be vulnerable to the workings of such an Act and it will serve to curtail freedom of speech in the very area where we will most need it.

Even without such an illiberal Act there are plenty of forces of suppression already. One example is the ruling of the Association of Chief Police Officers that it is the duty of policemen at all times to actively promote race equality. On that basis the Association announced in July 2004 that any officer found to be a member of the British National Party would be dismissed. This raises several serious questions of a conflict of interest between police duties and politics. Does actively promoting race equality at all times mean not arresting street robbers? What about democracy: the BNP is not a banned organisation, their stated policies are not 'beyond the pale', and most members presumably are quite ordinary non-criminals.

The problem with legislation to deal with 'hate' is that the difference between hatred, dislike and ridicule is a fine one. The present Government, let alone any foreseeable government, cannot be relied upon to apply such a law either sensibly or impartially.

The main thrust of Home Office supremo John Gieve's 'Contest' agenda has to be economic, hence his illustration of Northern Ireland. But apart from this making more concrete the depth of Government alarm, throwing money at the problem would be to make systematic and much more pronounced precisely the complaint made by people who live near to ethnic minority enclaves: that recent immigrants are given special favour over indigenous whites. Gieve's mistake is to take a simplistic, pre-judged analysis of the problem:

> ... the broader task is to address the roots of the problem, which include discrimination, disadvantage and exclusion suffered by many Muslim communities.

The analysis is that the problems experienced by these communities are caused from without and not from within. (I will explain below Gieve's mistake in terms of a bogus 'top-down' as opposed to a 'bottom-up' view of discrimination.) The very fact that male Muslims are three or four times more likely to be unemployed than is the average across the whole population is seen as self-evident incontrovertible evidence of discrimination and exclusion. But this does not follow at all. A correlation does not demonstrate a causal link, as any social scientist knows. The report cites the very low rates of economic activity amongst women as if this too is entirely a result of discrimination and exclusion, when clearly it is a cultural property of Pakistani and Bangladeshi enclaves, where the wife usually stays at home in a standard pattern of single-earner households.

In any case, as Heidi Safia Mirza from the Centre for Racial Equality at Middlesex University points out: 'these figures don't record home working, time spent on family-run businesses, and unpaid work, so the idea that they don't participate isn't very helpful'. Of course, far from female economic inactivity being imposed from without, this is a pattern in defiance of a very new norm in wider society. It cannot be considered any form of disadvantage because a majority of Muslim women as well as men see single-earner households as desirable. Furthermore, this is no 'false consciousness': the leading researcher into women and work, Catherine Hakim at the LSE, has shown that the full-time working woman is the aberration even in Western culture, and stay-at-homes together with 'adaptive' types (who try to balance work and life) make up between 70 and 90 percent of women and thereby constitute the norm; not full-timers. Furthermore, this is freely chosen (as Hakim and authors of recent major studies on part-time work have conclusively shown). We are most certainly not in a position to tell Muslim enclaves how to apportion work amongst men and women, because the pattern is not down to discrimination, it is not down to exclusion, and it is also not down to disadvantage. It is a policy chosen by the community. If this is a trade-off between social and economic considerations then it cannot be considered a mark of disadvantage in need of rectification. Those people who would maintain otherwise, when wearing another hat, are the same people who might level charges of 'cultural imperialism' against this sort of thinking if it was voiced by white advisers in a third-world country. Yet this is common stuff in the columns of the Guardian, and if it is not racism then it is feminist-inspired.

In many ways, exclusion is working in the opposite direction: it is actively pursued from within against the wider community; not in the direction we would assume. Not only female inactivity, but the Muslim male unemployment rate could also be easily explained by various factors related to the properties of Muslim enclaves, needing no recourse to any residual explanation of discrimination. For example, if you have a large family and no economic contribution from your wife, then there may be little benefit to working for a low income, given that total benefits will probably almost match an income from working, even if you include tax credits. Various considerations may intervene, such as that the need to support a large family precludes being able to afford to run a car and this restricts the range of feasible work. Against a number of family-related factors that may be working against you getting work, it is not improbable that any discrimination is likely to be in the other direction: actually in your favour. While some men may find the benefits system dissuades them from working, others may take the decision that in-work benefits make working for low hourly wages just as profitable as a much better-paid job. For this reason, at the low level of wages typically on offer, an employer may well consider Asian workers as more willing to accept both pay and conditions and more compliant than someone from the white labour pool. Without specific research all of this is speculative of course, but it rings far truer than the standard cant.

Throwing money and special schemes at Muslim enclaves is likely not only to be unjustifiable and perceived as reverse racism by the white majority, but may even be counter-productive. Yes, it would seem to make good sense to provide assistance if it can be shown to be seed money to help people to help themselves; but is it not more likely that assistance will just facilitate a continuation of an enclave mentality? This is more than likely given the inexorable increase in the size of Pakistani and Bangladeshi communities through rampant chain migration and large family size. At least, if there are economic stresses on a community, then there is increased pressure at the margins towards integration with the host community, as some feel more motivated to gain a better education and then find better jobs.

Inherent problems, no matter what approach is taken, are well illustrated by social housing. There are Muslim housing associations that obviously exacerbate community segregation, but if housing associations make efforts to attract Pakistanis and Bangladeshis and whites, then there is likely to be less uptake of accommodation from all quarters. With even small percentages (as low as 5 percent) of non-whites in a housing area 'white flight' tends to occur, but equally Muslim non-whites tend not to want to stay among whites. This is why Muslim housing associations came into being. Exactly the same dynamic applies to education and the debate about faith schools. The problem of integration in West Yorkshire schools is worse than it was twenty years ago. There is no answer except not to make the problem even worse than it is by continuing to allow mass net immigration.

It seems that perhaps Trevor Phillips, the chair of the Commission for Racial Equality, knew about the forthcoming Government tack, his volte face on multiculturalism being a prelude. The CRE announced recently that it is no longer to fund projects that encourage separatism, but not everyone will see this as an advance on the previous position of active encouragement of the promotion of separate identity. For all that the CRE will argue that future targeted assistance is to promote inclusion in the wider society, money that is given to Muslims to help them simply to do the same things as the rest of the population may well be seen in many quarters as just as unfair as funding multicultural projects. It is still special treatment. It will be objected that an unemployed person is an unemployed person regardless of their skin colour, and that the help available should likewise be colour blind. With a much higher proportion of Muslims unemployed than in the wider community, then the Muslim community would in any case thereby receive far more Government assistance than the size of this community would seem to entitle on a pro rata basis.

What is often lost sight of is that an enclave within society is not a negative feature for those within it, regardless of how much of a burden it may be to the host society. Its purpose is direct contest with the outside; those within perceiving their membership of an in-group opposed to the external out-group. The extended family structure of Pakistani and Bangladeshi communities provides social capital that has profound economic as well as obvious social and health benefits. It radically reduces the need for income (through reciprocal services not requiring money payment, sharing and subsidy of accommodation, altruistic financial support, efficient channelling of money from older people who have a surplus to younger people with children, etc) and facilitates employment through sharing of labour market information and nepotism.

Of course, there can be envisaged a benign situation where the perception is of membership of a narrower in-group together with a weaker but nonetheless salient membership of the wider community. For instance, I could say that I feel more of a Yorkshireman than I do a British citizen, but that I am both; despite the in-group of a native of 'God's own country' being antithetical to the out-group of Britain as a whole. In fact, the dual identification tends to mutual reinforcement, so that the more strongly I perceive myself as a Yorkshire-phile the more I am conscious of being British. This is the positive side of multiculturalism, you could say, but it is nothing like how multiculturalism is usually envisaged; which is that the more exotic and irreconcilable with its host is the 'sub-community' then the more worthy it is considered to be.

A dual identification tends to work when the narrower in-group is not overwhelmingly the stronger identification and this appears very much not to be the case generally regarding certain ethnic minorities. Indeed, it is claimed that the sense of being an in-group of an ethnic minority enclave is if anything getting still stronger in the case of Pakistani and Bangladeshi areas. The more genuinely excluded — those with the weakest overall perception of member-ship of in-group(s) — tend to be poor whites; and those poor whites living close to ethnic minority enclaves also tend to feel that this real-ity is rather rubbed in their faces.

It might be said that many poor whites live in enclaves and why should we not consider these at least as problematic as those of eth-nic minorities? The answer is that there is little if any parallel and for a number of reasons, not least that their members always consider themselves as belonging to the wider society, and primarily so. The inexorable growth through uncontrolled chain immigration is a fun-damental difference between ethnic minority enclaves and what have been pejoratively dubbed 'white trash' estates. The latter are not subject to unnatural expansion. They are also less apart from the mainstream culture — existing largely because of the lack of oppor-tunities compared to the ease of a life on benefits. They are far less homogenous (containing people who are in many ways part of wider society), less geographically demarcated, and very fluid at the margins — with many people able to be brought into the wider com-munity and offspring much more likely to react against their upbringing. The white underclass is, in short, not an intractable problem (at least not in theory, if the political will can be mobilized); albeit that there may be recalcitrance, criminality and endemic seri-ous drug abuse. The importation of ethnic minority enclaves is in effect an attempt to replace the working class areas that have descended into dysfunction; but this strategy is one of the prime causes of the social disintegration that produced 'white trash' enclaves in the first place. In turn, the ethnic minority enclaves are now producing their own underclass of disaffected youths turning to drug abuse and crime, and with a vengeance. The collapse into dysfunction of certain sections of the white working class is being reproduced within the replacement ethnic minority enclaves. Any bets on the Government not only refusing to stem the flow of new recruits to the ethnic minority underclass, but opting for immigra-tion of other nationalities to repeat the same sort of social collapse? You guessed it: they are already doing this.

* * *

The approach of the Government shows that there is a basic problem with its concept of what constitutes discrimination — which has wide import: to sex as well as to race — and I am here going to pin it down and so push home the points I have made above. In a nutshell there are two very different ways of defining discrimination, but only one of the two is a correct definition and the other is bogus, yet most people are unaware that they are conflating and so confusing the two. One view is that discrimination is something actively done by someone (either intentionally or inadvertently) to someone else, not excluding neglecting to include someone for consideration. The classic situation here would be an employer choosing between white and ethnic minority job candidates on the basis of their skin colour. Discrimination in this scenario can often be fixed by tackling the behaviour of the person doing the discrimination. This is what could be called a 'bottom-up' understanding, and is what most people readily understand by discrimination.

The opposite view is a 'top-down' position, which is to look for any skew in distribution (of, for example, jobs between whites and ethnic minority groups) and simply to deem any skew that is found to be down to discrimination. This is the way that public policy makers tend to think about discrimination — and is the view that John Gieve, the Home Office supremo, takes — but it is fallacious, because all kinds of factors could correlate with being a member of a particular ethnic minority group and it is this that actually explains the skew and not discrimination.

To use an example from above: Bangladeshi women tend to raise larger families and for cultural reasons are homemakers rather than workers, and where they do work it is likely to be home-working or work within family businesses (both of which are not picked up in official figures) and this explains the low work participation rates of Bangladeshi women. Discrimination against them by employers is not the main factor and may not be a factor at all — and may indeed work in a positive direction.

A correlation is a co-variation between two separate factors that may be down to a third common variable that has nothing to do with the other two. In this case, the third common variable is family lifestyle, and this mediates between ethnic minority and employment rate. This cannot be considered to be discrimination; neither 'direct' nor 'indirect' (it is not 'indirect' discrimination, because family size and lifestyle is a question of choice: it is not something you could do nothing about). Furthermore, if measures are taken to address the skew and, as in this case, there is a zero-sum scenario (selection for jobs entails one person's gain and correspondingly another person's loss) then this is practicing discrimination against those who are not afforded special assistance.

In the example here cited, people in Bangladeshi communities have made the choice (albeit that it is a traditional cultural practice that conditions individual decisions) to provide themselves with the social benefit of a lifestyle of large families and single-earner households, and have thereby opted to undergo the opportunity cost of foregoing work for (many) women. As in the case of anyone in Britain who does the same, there are extra in-work benefits for the sole earner to offset to some degree the economic trade-off. It is not appropriate to do more than this, either for people generally or for any sub-group where this is the norm, because this would be a case of 'having your cake and eating it' and therefore unfair to the majority. If the authorities intervene to provide targeted help for Bangladeshi women to encourage them into work, then this is discrimination against non-Bangladeshis: against white men and women, and men and women of other ethnic minorities. It is also discrimination against these communities in attempting to impose social engineering to produce what is a very dubious supposed advantage and against the community's norms.

There are further problems with targeting help at sub-groups of the general population. One of the reasons why we find discrimination objectionable is that it is treating people not as individuals with their particular differences from the sub-group norm, but treating them as if they were typical of their group and conforming to the group norm. Notwithstanding that there may be some justification in this − we do this all the time and seem sensitive to the downside only when sex or race discrimination appears salient − many sometimes or often feel that this is in contempt of personal individuality. But this is precisely what is done when help is targeted at a sub-group to try to combat discrimination, or supposed discrimination. It is hypocritical to argue against one of these and then to support the other.

There is also a wider question of the appropriateness of state intervention to compel employers to make great efforts to try to eliminate discrimination, because getting any particular job or being able to get any job at all is not an entitlement. If an employer does not give someone a job then he is not taking anything away from the applicant that he/she has any right to; but merely not conferring on them the benefit of a means of acquiring an income in a particular way. Although there is a reasonable consensus that, unlike present-giving between friends and acquaintances, giving out jobs is in the public domain should be regulated; employers (excluding the public sector) are paying out their own money in wages/salary, so there has to be a good reason for intervention. A 'top-down' concept of discrimination — which is likely not discrimination at all in the 'bottom-up' sense — does not come close.

The problem of conflating notions of apparent disadvantage with discrimination is a significant one, because it artificially inflates people's sense of social injustice and will fuel the sense of 'in-group' versus 'out-group', especially in the situation of a profound divide as with the ethnic minority enclave. The classic example of disadvantage masquerading as discrimination is the situation of disabled people. We routinely say that disabled people are discriminated against when they can't get autonomous access to somewhere. But a moment's thought confirms that we are not talking about anything actively or even passively done to disabled people by the rest of us. Almost without exception we all feel consideration for disabled people, and the built environment more and more is designed with disabled people in mind, despite the often considerable extra costs. Inevitably, sometimes disabled people require assistance to gain entry or to move within a building and, as this entails requesting help instead of being able to do something for themselves, it may cause them to have unwelcome feelings of dependency. The simple fact that life for disabled people is bound to be harder than it is for the rest of us — and no technological fixes will ever change this fundamentally — in no way means that they are discriminated against. Yet this is a usual way to talk about their problems. In this case, 'top-down' discrimination is always misleading. (For a full discussion of discrimination issues: see Matt Cavanagh's seminal book, *Against Equality of Opportunity*.)

Now, the case of ethnic minority groups is different and there is even less reason to talk loosely about discrimination. The disadvantages (or supposed disadvantages) they suffer from — difficulties with the English language, a sense of cultural disengagement with what is perceived to be a foreign culture, a profound unfamiliarity with how our labour markets work, economic support problems through opportunity costs sustained in characteristic lifestyle choices, etc — are not fixed problems ethnic minority groups and individuals within them can do nothing about. They can be rectified by personal initiative without the necessity of any co-operation by anyone else. These are problems which any immigrant should fully expect to face and any immigrant should expect the host society to demand that he/she addresses through his/her own efforts. There is no onus on the host society to divert substantial resources in this regard and there is no justification in members of ethnic minority groups feeling aggrieved about what they may perceive to be their disadvantage. Immigration is a special opportunity and if immigrants (and their dependents and offspring) are not prepared to grasp it, then they have to question why they came here and why they remain. The host society's obligation at most is that it should treat them the same as any other citizen; neither any worse nor any better. Indeed, as many nations do, it would be reasonable, after a 'good Samaritan' welcome, not to treat recent immigrants as equals of the rest of the population until there is some indication of having or seriously desiring a stake in the host society.

* * *

That Asian enclaves are becoming an increasing social problem could not be better demonstrated by the warning from the Met that the only way to stop these communities turning into 'crime-ridden ghettos' run by gangs dealing drugs and using guns, is to set up an Operation Trident style task force, the first phase of which is set to be up and running in summer 2004.

Community leaders have been taken by surprise, as have police, because South Asian communities have been assumed to be relatively law abiding. What seems to have happened is a mushrooming of 'white collar' crime — at one time the only crime that Asians practiced at similar or greater rates than across the wider population — to include violence. Now figures show that Asians in Britain are four times more likely to be involved in organized crime — including international drug smuggling and passport scams (these are immigrant enclaves with global connections after all). Drug and especially gun crime — notably the use of sub-machine guns — has increased disproportionately over the past few years; ditto kidnappings for ransom.

Tarique Ghaffur, Britain's top Asian police officer, explains: 'There is often a denial in the community that things are actually happening in relation to serious crime. What that allows are criminal role models within communities to flourish. The last thing you want is those communities themselves to create their own crime-ridden ghettos.'

'Asian parents have lost control', says Britain's first Pakistani Peer, Lord Ahmed of Rotherham; 'community leaders need to get behind this new police campaign.' He criticizes mosques for not doing enough.

The devil seems indeed to have found work after a fashion for the very growing number of idle Asian hands, for all that the communities to which they belong are closer knit than the wider society that surrounds them. That much of the crime stays within the enclave as Asian-on-Asian violence is no consolation to the rest of us on the outside.

* * *

The power of the enclave is well illustrated by a recent Guardian newspaper account of the very area in which I lived for many years until I left in 2000 to return to Sheffield. This is Highfields, a Victorian quarter in central Leicester. Almost half the population of the city is non-white and the great bulk of those are Indian Asian. Of these a minority are Muslims, but they still stick together.

> It is possible to walk the streets of Highfields for hours and never see a white face. The shops, from confectioners to drapers and butchers, are all Asian, and predominantly Muslim. It is possible to live a Muslim life barely touched by secular culture. But even enthusiasts for this way of life admit that, unchecked, such self-sufficiency can push a community dangerously far down the path towards becoming a ghetto. ... Today it is almost a self-contained administration. You can get practically anything you want — from housing and sports to schooling and medicine — delivered with an Islamic perspective. And the community is determined that it stays that way.

> 'We had a problem with young people who experienced mainstream culture and found something was missing,' (according to Yaqub Khan, a local community leader), 'but they did not have enough knowledge of Islam so they found themselves stuck in the middle of two cultures and directionless.' ... Those who were without direction a few years ago have grown up and, largely, turned to Islam — not just as a religion but as a full cultural identity.

The account describes strict Muslim schooling, centres for Islamic instruction, a social work day centre for elderly Muslim women, community centres that organize circumcision, Muslim sports and social facilities, loan funds that do not involve payment of interest, and so on:

All this, an almost separate society, has been fashioned through negotiation by community leaders. There are Muslim councillors in Leicester, but mainstream politics seems set apart from the Highfields community. 'The councillors are reasonably effective, but because they are not much involved in the community they tend to toe the party line more often than the community line,' says Manzoor Moghal, chairman of the Federation of Muslim Organisations in Leicester. 'They are more part of the political system than the Muslim community and ordinary Muslims tend to turn to the mosque or community leaders.

Moghal then twists the problem round when he says: 'We need to reach out to mainstream culture to educate them about our community'. Does he not think that the bigger problem is of Muslims not being sufficiently educated about the culture of the wider society in which they must function? This could not better illustrate the extent of enclave separateness.

* * *

The problem of the enclave was very well told in the BBC2 strand, This World, broadcast on July 8, 2004, as I was finishing writing this chapter. It neatly illustrates the intractable dynamic between an ethnic minority enclave and the wider society. The scene is Australia: Redfern, aka 'the block', a Sydney suburb set aside for Aborigines, who were of course the indigenous population but are now just one of Australia's minorities. The original hope was for an autonomous Aboriginal area with control of its own housing stock; a decent and close-knit community. After high hopes, the Aboriginal Housing Trust left all the houses in appalling disrepair through (it is strongly intimated) nepotistic corruption. As the physical fabric decayed, so did the social: broken families became the norm and the streets filled with rootless young males. Drug use, dealing and associated crime became ubiquitous, and the area is now visually and spiritually a run-down ghetto.

Money was thrown at the place by the Australian Government, including a new community centre, and when that became dilapidated a second new community centre; which was opened with full multicultural fanfare without bothering to remove the ugly graffiti on adjacent walls. Police patrol more or less constantly but rarely make arrests for drug offences, despite heroin dealing being fully open. Some commentators regarded the police inaction on drugs as a means of containing the dealing and attendant crime within the enclave so that it did not spread to white communities. Despite the leniency of the police they were hated, and resentment towards the wider society brewed even in the elders of the community, but nobody could explain in interview why they felt this way. It was as if white Australia was just a scapegoat for what they felt inside.

One day, a seventeen-year-old Aborigine, Thomas James Hickey, nicknamed TJ, was cycling in the area when he heard a police car travelling fast behind him. The officers were chasing a mugger. It is presumed that TJ mistakenly thought the police were chasing him. He had an outstanding warrant against him and some cannabis on him so he did not want to be stopped. He quickly pedalled round a corner but hit something and was thrown over the handlebars on to some spiky railings which impaled him. He was taken to hospital but died. It was Valentine's Day 2004. Everyone, not least his mother, refused to believe the police and regarded TJ's death as murder. He was 'chased to his death'. The next night, catching the police entirely unawares, there was a full-scale riot, with the police and property the target. The scenes of police cowering behind shields and helmets in the face of about 100 fearless youths lobbing chunks of concrete and petrol bombs, could have been Bradford or (less recently) Toxteth.

Elders said that they did not agree with how Redfern's youngsters behaved but could understand it. They had learnt how to contain their rage but youth found it more difficult. The Aborigines felt like second-class citizens and victims of discrimination. The reaction by the majority white Australian population was disgust that the endless money in the form of social security benefits and communal infrastructure had been violently thrown back in their faces by a subgroup it regarded as drunken layabouts. It set back race relations by several years. The reaction by the authorities was to clear up and put yet more money into the area, which still further antagonized the taxpaying majority. The one thing that everybody agreed on was that money would do little if anything to solve the problems of Redfern, but that nothing else could either. Ideas on what would be the right political approach were ventured by few. A number of factors needed to be taken into account; there was no obvious solution. That slow incremental progress was the best that could be hoped for was the most optimistic outlook.

In George Orwell's Dreams

The name 'Managed Migration' is unintentionally comic and could be straight out of *1984*, being a classic 'Newspeak' term George Orwell might have dreamed up. Overwhelming levels of migration and the inadequate management thrown at it, clearly required a name to try to contradict the reality. My experience of working for six months as a frontline caseworker was a long and deepening experience of a progressive institutional failure to apply the immigration rules. Even apart from the substantial amount of time the rule book was effectively torn up completely, we were always at two removes from the legislation, with the guidance notes and then what was euphemistically called 'pragmatism' that management directly, or indirectly through senior caseworkers, ensured everyone applied in practice. The law I was supposedly working to implement had been lost sight of.

The overriding principle, often mentioned as justification for a seemingly unfathomable reason for granting an unworthy application, was that if it arrives on your desk then you should grant it if at all possible, because if you don't then he/she/they will simply disappear and stay in the country illegally anyway. At least this way, it was reasoned, we could keep some sort of tabs on people. With so few resources allocated by the Immigration Service to 'removals'/ deportation work it was recognized that there was slim prospect of anyone who was refused actually being found and 'removed'/ deported — nil chance in the case of a family that had been here for any length of time or anyone elderly.

The whole Managed Migration exercise provided a semblance of administrative control over temporary and permanent migrants, but in effect we were an arm of the Government's effort to supply spurious information to the Office of National Statistics. The process involved allocating to ourselves a proportion of incomers to reduce the massive numbers of those gaining illegal entry or (much more commonly) overstaying, the extent of which David Blunkett admits he has not the slightest idea. This is because embarkation controls were removed in the mid-1990s, with the result that nobody has any notion of how many of those admitted to the country actually subsequently leave. (Embarkation controls were removed in two stages: first by the Conservatives, when they were last in power, in respect of EU citizens – this was seen as being in keeping with the free movement of all EU nationals across the borders of member states. But then, quite inexplicably, in 1999 the Labour Government removed the controls for all other nationals, heedless of the obvious dire consequences for immigration and security.)

Exacerbating matters further, from last August most types of application were charged for, so stress was placed on our being a customer service organization with tight deadlines for decision making. 'We are in the business of granting people' was an expression often heard, according to one of my colleagues. Even so, there were always backlogs and sudden arrivals of huge volumes of cases that had been held up or put somewhere and forgotten down in the main Casework Unit at Croydon. Any decision which looked remotely like attracting an appeal with any chance of success was turned around to a grant. How many people this charging (at £155 a time) put off even bothering to make us aware of their continued presence in the country nobody knows, but it placed still further emphasis on routinely granting applications instead of examining them. On the face of it we were making some money for the Treasury – at least paying our own way – but of course the long-term costs of failing to apply immigration rules properly render this immediate gain in comparison insignificant. Charging completed the destruction of the gate-keeping function. Under the ethos of the political Left's international open door, the accent was all on the applicant's rights and our responsibility to uphold them, instead of whether or not the applicant should be allowed in.

Fostering a lack of proper consideration was at the core of management strategy, with targets set for the number of daily decisions a caseworker should make. If a case was too complicated to easily decide either to grant or to refuse, then a caseworker had an option to 'extend' (as was the term) to a team of more experienced caseworkers; but out of fifteen cases we were supposed to handle daily only three should remain without an outcome in this way. Crucially, you earned no credit whatsoever for an extension, no matter how well considered; only for a grant (or, much more rarely, a refusal) did you earn a 'stat', as management referred to them; yet 'extensions' often entailed more work. 'Why give the 'stat' to the guy in CLS?', it was often said (the CLS being the corresponding team of more experienced caseworkers that dealt with our ICS team's extensions. To this day I don't know what 'CLS' stands for.). Neil Best, the chief numbers man, attended our team meeting and I asked him whether this proportion had been arrived at by research. He admitted it was simply a target handed down from senior management. In other words, management had a budget for staff and made estimates of likely caseload and divided the one by the other to come up with the rate of decision-making required.

It was understood that these targets were unrealistic, especially for new caseworkers (who would take between three and six months to be regarded as experienced) and, as I have said, it was a relaxed civil service work environment with a refreshing eschewal of clock watching. Even so, it was made clear that meeting 'stats' was the only route to advancement away from the production-line style of work of a first rung caseworker. The temptation to which you were fully expected to succumb was to cut corners. Unstated as of course this was, it was a difficult task to assimilate the deluge of e-mail updates of procedure and guidance into the already massive body of knowledge you were expected to have at your fingertips and apply them to make accurate decisions. Caseworkers who had initially made good notes detailing what evidence had been submitted and why they made the decision they had, progressively cut down the information they recorded. As I have said, our counterparts at Croydon frequently made virtually no notes at all and so spared us any useful information about a previous application that could help in deciding the current one. In this way ill-considered granting was compounded because, in the absence of a warning note about missing evidence or breach of conditions, a previous grant was often taken to be reason itself to grant an extension of leave to remain if there was doubt about the current application.

On top of the routine failure to implement immigration rules, whenever there was a significant backlog then all cases were assessed under what was termed 'BRACE conditions', as described in Chapter 7. This was the jargon for a rubber-stamping exercise of varying severity. Latterly we were under 'ultra ultra BRACE', which literally meant that you opened the plastic pouch in which the application was held and, without any consideration whatsoever, granted the case. I have explained what the BRACE acronym stands for — 'Backlog Reduction Accelerated Clearance Exercise' — though this appears to be a forced re-naming after the manager who devised it, Bill Brandon, left his post. It seems that originally it was 'Brandon's Accelerated Clearance Exercise'.

With these general concerns about how casework was done, together with the more specific concerns that I had — the obviously inadequate processing of ECAA, marriage and student applications — I decided it was no exaggeration to put it to Home Office minister Beverley Hughes that our function was a smokescreen for the fact that immigration, both legal and illegal, was out of control. I likened us to those civil servants who compile figures showing that NHS waiting lists have shortened (when everyone knows the real problems lie elsewhere).

The minister was to pay us a visit on December 4: that is what put into my head the idea of going straight to the top. There was a supposed 'open forum' for the very purpose of asking questions of her, but only a handful of picked individuals were invited. Not being amongst them, I put my questions in the form of an approved e-mail that I sent to those few who could have asked on my behalf.

Knowing that I would never be allowed to ask such explosive questions in person, I had a plan to get them put to the minister. A few days before the visit, by chance I found myself talking to someone who had a typed list of all those who had been invited to the 'open forum' with Beverley Hughes. 'DON'T tell anyone I gave you this', she emphatically implored. Armed with these names I decided I would go into work the very first thing the next day — 7am — and quickly write my questions and then e-mail them to Internal Communications. I rang them up and, as I expected, a young-sounding presumably junior staff member answered. I had reckoned that senior staff would not yet have come into work, so she would make a decision off her own bat. Obviously she would not let me do what's called a 'global' e-mail — one sent to everybody across all of Managed Migration — but she might be willing to agree to a fallback position that would actually give me what I needed. I said that what I wanted to e-mail was a set of important questions a lot of people were looking for answers to, but that if she really thought it inappropriate to circulate them generally, then they could be sent only to those who would be in a position to ask the questions on my behalf:

the dozen or so actually invited to attend the forum. The Internal Communications officer would be unlikely to deny me this because 'Int Comms' is the body you must go through to get a global e-mail okayed, although it was not clear about what their role was in a more restricted circulation. What mattered was that I could then claim that I had gone through normal channels to get approval. She readily said she couldn't see why I couldn't send it to just those on the list. I did so straight away, before any manager got wind of it and stuck his oar in.

Next I went to see one of the top four managers, a woman who was very approachable and who I got on with in the brief time I had ever spoken with her, and originally my line manager (actually I thought she still was: so much for Home Office information). I showed her the questions and said that I had got approval and sent them as an e-mail. The idea was that I was presenting her with a fait accompli. She could hardly query the legitimacy of the questions if they were already in the hands of all those in a position to put them directly. Worse, to query and then prevent their being asked would serve merely to highlight management worries and so give the force of my questions credence. It would be a 'shutting the stable door …' job without even the consolation of cutting losses. I asked her if I could go to the forum myself and put my questions in person, because I could not rely on others. A rhetorical question if ever I asked one. She said she would take them to the head man, the kindly and respected George McIntosh. Shortly afterwards she came to see me, having secured agreement that my questions could be put to the minister by some means or other, though not in person. This was fair enough. They would have been foolish to allow me to attend. I am sufficiently articulate and knowledgeable as to the procedures to severely embarrass the minister, given that she probably would not have command of her brief to the extent of fully knowing what was going on. What manager would set themselves up for a flea in the ear from a minister as she ends her one and only visit to his part of the department? There was no time, with the minister on her way as we spoke, for managers to give her advance warning to enable a considered response. I left it in my manager's hands, allowing that the minister would be spared embarrassment on the day but that they would have to send it through internal channels. You never know, I thought, eventually it might reach her.

Then my manager's immediate boss, Neil Best — the number two in Managed Migration at Sheffield — saw the e-mail. I had e-mailed him as one of those invited, not knowing his position. He flashed me a one-liner asking who on earth had given approval to send it and why. I replied to say how I had gone about getting approval and that his boss — the chief — was happy with what I had done. I discovered that without informing me he had then e-mailed all of the recipients to tell them, ever so not so subtly, that they need not bother humouring my request to be my proxy. This was a 'business' meeting, he wrote; not for raising 'personal' matters. 'Personal' matters?! If you're going to brush something under the carpet then get a big fat brush, you could say.

As I expected, the questions never left Sheffield. To her credit, my (original) line manager I had first spoken to, alerted me to this fact a few weeks later. She told me that they were being held up by Human Resources, which in Sheffield is a somewhat aloof bunch of officers on an equal opps kick, kept well away from us; their building being the best part of a mile away. The Business Support Unit, ironically it is called. No surprise that they were obstructing my complaint. I had two betes noir in that department: one specifically on the equal opps side and another on the general HR and training side with whom I had had a feisty meeting. It was this last who was responsible. She gave me the excuse that my new line manager had discussed with her that I should send an e-mail of the questions. This was the first I had heard of this. Then she objected that the last question was not appropriate, and that it was insulting to refer to Hughes as a junior minister because she was a Secretary of State. She was wrong in this: Beverley Hughes was indeed a junior minister, but it was a trivial point and I concurred. So the questions were sent by e-mail from HR Sheffield to Beverley Hughes' private office and when the e-mail bounced back it was sent to another recipient in the same office. But right up until the day of my disclosure, Sunday March 7, I was still waiting even for so much as an acknowledgement. This was by then more than three calendar months since I had first tabled my questions.

Hughes' excuse was that someone new to her office had failed to alert her to the e-mail, but I had another e-mail exchange with the HR senior who had sent the e-mail on my behalf, pointing out that I had had no reply of any kind and asking her to chase it up. This she agreed to do and this she did, speaking to people in the minister's private office. This was followed up with a message containing the details of the e-mail together with a message to contact Sheffield HR. Then another staffer in Sheffield HR also followed up.

The minister's private office repeatedly rebuffed efforts to process my questions: no less than four times. Was this chain of events really all down to staff incompetence, or had staff consulted with the minister and agreed to feign communication breakdown so as not to have to deal with my awkward questions? It's yet another reason that Hughes' account of her conduct is hard to believe.

I later found out that the chief, George McIntosh, thought I should have been disciplined simply for raising these questions! But did he think that at the time, or was this for the benefit of the investigation? Anyway, here are the questions in full, including the last question which was withheld, in the form that they were sent by e-mail to the minister:

> It is welcome that a politician from the government with a ministerial position overseeing part of the Home Office has made herself available to answer questions from Aspect Court staff that Civil Service management may not feel able to answer or that are in fact outside their ambit. Answers to the following questions could be important in helping to raise staff morale here at Aspect Court.

> As Civil Servants we see our work as public service, but there is the widespread view that the emphasis at every turn on decision-making over full consideration of cases — and granting rather than refusing — and not properly applying immigration rules, means that in fact we are concerned not with the proper management of cases but with the creation of statistics not in the public interest but in the interest of the Labour Government. In the same way that NHS waiting lists are widely viewed by NHS staff and experts as not reflecting reality in the health service, so it is widely held that migration statistics hide illegal economic migration. Could the minister dispel this impression?

> The workstream we deal with where there is perhaps the very least adherence to immigration rules is that of ECAA applications. Again, the widespread view is that we are dealing with the aftermath of an ill considered political decision; rubber stamping the arrival of large numbers of economic migrants who in fact have made a very weak if any case that they are likely to be successful by any criteria as self-employed businesspeople. In this way, some of the anticipated flood of economic migrants after the accession of new states to the EU are displaced to the figures for earlier arrivals of ostensible additions to the business community. Could the minister explain why this may not be the case?

> We were recruited on the understanding that we were entering the fastest growing area of Civil Service employment, with excellent prospects of rapid advancement. This appears not at all to be the case, and this lowers staff morale, even to the point where some staff are resigning. Rumour has it that Treasury caps have put a brake on expansion, but the feeling of many is that we were simply misled. In view of the much supe-

rior performance on all criteria by Sheffield staff over their Croydon counterparts, and the ongoing problems of retention, recruitment and costs at Croydon, can the minister assure us that the opportunities we were promised will indeed be forthcoming?

During the junior minister's previous brief she complained in the media about a Channel 4 programme which, she claimed, excused or supported paedophilia, when commentators agreed that the 'Brass Eye' slot was lampooning the very media generated hysteria about paedophilia which it could be said the minister played a part in creating. The minister then admitted she had never seen the broadcast. This begged the legitimate question of her grasp of her brief and sense of proportion; qualities essential for any ministerial appointment, not least her present one. Could the minister tell us what she learnt from this experience?'

The last paragraph — that, as I say, was never sent — was rather cheeky and you could say disingenuous, but the point is a valid one, and I thought it would have given Hughes the opportunity to laugh it off and show some humility. Or do I mean that it would have demonstrated that she had none? I was thinking of it in the context of a meeting, you see, not as correspondence. My (original) line manager thought it was way too cheeky and suggested that I cut it. I said that I was quite happy to carry the can for it. She said I could send it via my MP, but I pointed out that he is not part of the Government (a member of the Lib Dem opposition, in fact) and that would be a case of putting it in the public domain, which — prior to 'whistle-blowing' as I know too well — is supposed to be against the rules.

Anti-Racism Hysteria

It is to be supposed that it is the fear of social unrest, or at least of widespread discontent gaining more coherent expression, that is the reason for the longstanding obsession with anti-racism that has reached levels that can only sensibly be described as hysterical. This in turn has had a dire impact on freedom of speech, as well as convulsing organizations with wasteful and divisive overhauls in a vain effort to combat supposed 'institutional' racism. In addition targets (quotas in all but name) for ethnic minority recruitment and advancement have been imposed that if anybody had the courage to challenge would likely be found to be illegal. It seems, however, that anti-racist hysteria is more to do with the mindset of the political Left — as I explained in Chapter 6 — and is really all about suppressing debate on the subject of immigration. It is inherently hypocritical, with an obvious double standard. The concerns are those the intelligentsia fears about itself; not what it fears about the behaviour of ordinary people.

As the most recent (at the time of writing) high-profile example, the boorish Ron Atkinson — for whom it is hard to have sympathy — was sacked from his TV and newspaper jobs for using (albeit when he thought he was off-air and so in private) the word 'nigger' to describe a black person. Commentators rounded on Atkinson en masse in a spectacle of denouncement so emphatic it was nauseating to see their fear of not being seen to conform perfectly. This fear was quite tangible in the over-earnestness of every member of the panel on the following Thursday night's BBC1 Question Time. But the question that many people would like answered is: when has any non-white ever been censured for using words like 'honky' ('honkie'), which is a US import that black people sometimes use to derogate white persons; or 'gora', which Indian Asians use for the same purpose? According to the *Encarta* dictionary, 'honky' is indeed an offensive term. Certainly I have never heard it used as a term of endearment, even if often it is more joke than jibe. 'Nigger' is actually used by some black people to describe each other in a brotherly or endearing way, demonstrating that it has lost its offensive connotations, at least to the extent that it can be used ironically. It is rather a nonsense then, to discipline a white person for using a term because it is supposed only to be used between black people and is deemed offensive only when white people use it to describe blacks, but then the opposite is true when blacks use it in respect of each other. As for 'gora' (a Hindi word) I have yet to find it in a dictionary, though internet searches confirm that it is meant as a derogation (specifically referring to 'white male'; white female' would be 'gori'); ditto 'Angrez', meaning an English person.

Atkinson has a record second to none for bringing black football players to the fore; indeed he was a pioneer in this respect. Black players he has had dealings with queued up in his defence. In the context of his bad temper and foul mouth, it seems clear that he was not being racist but — as he himself described — 'an idiot'. At worst he was 'unconsciously' racist, but what does that mean? 'Discrimination' is an active term, so to discriminate against someone really you have to act intentionally, although acting unwittingly is often also regarded as discrimination, if less culpable (this is the correct 'bottom up' view; I deal with the bogus 'top down' view in Chapter 8.) It seems Atkinson was using 'nigger' in the way some people, and probably he himself, might have casually used it in the past; having unguardedly drifted back to his younger self in his mood of annoyance. He could have been dropped for his foul mouth generally and the idiocy that was indeed revealed by his 'nigger' jibe, more than for his supposed racism. You could even argue that if Atkinson was actually a racist by sentiment but despite that did so much for black footballers by his actions, then he should receive commendation for so demonstrably overcoming his prejudices. For all that the entire world of worthy commentators lined up to condemn him, in the minds of most ordinary people Atkinson is not really a racist at all, and people will not take kindly to those who would insist otherwise; in defining racism so loosely that any slip or fleeting moment of non-malicious abuse is seen as an indelible mark of inflexible xenophobic hatred. The irony is that the cowardly conformists who were so keen to gang up are more guilty of irrational intolerance than Atkinson.

Terms for 'black person' rapidly go in and out of vogue for reasons of fashion. The more politically correct and defensively euphemistic the term, the more likely it is to be seen as risible by the general population, who may then turn it around to be used, often in a shortened form, as abuse, necessitating a replacement word. Since none of these terms are intrinsically abusive, then ones that have dropped out of favour are available for resurrection as pet forms by which those whom the term had previously abused refer to each other. Hence the dual use of 'nigger'.

'Paki' is widely used, for the obvious reason that it is short for 'Pakistani', in the same way that 'Aussie' is short for 'Australian'. 'Paki' is often not derogatory in use. (You might often hear 'I'm going down the Paki shop', and not the slightest slur is intended.) In some places the ethnic minority enclaves are almost exclusively populated by Pakistanis, and 'Paki' is also often used in ignorance to describe anyone (descended) from the Indian subcontinent, Pakistani, Bangladeshi or Indian, simply because many white people are unable to distinguish between them. Unfortunately this is unlikely to go down well in places like Leicester where the overwhelming majority of the ethnic minority is Indian.

But none of these uses makes the term offensive per se, although it is of course used pejoratively, and so much so that it has come to be thought of as offensive. So it is that the word 'Paki' too has been appropriated by the politically correct to be deemed offensive irrespective of how it is used. It can be useful in distinguishing between those people of Indian subcontinent origin and those of African or Afro-Caribbean descent, for whom 'black' tends to be reserved. 'Paki' is therefore sometimes used to mean 'brown' — which is itself not used, fortunately, given its obvious connotation. There is no term that can easily replace it in areas where Pakistanis are the exclusive ethnic minority or where they are preponderant or the ones to have first established themselves, so 'Paki' remains current for general use as well as for use pejoratively in places like Bradford and Burnley.

'Indian' might be preferred, because as yet it does not have the negative connotations, but this can only be a matter of time; I have often heard it used as a generic term of disdain. The biggest problem with it is that it is taken as an insult by Pakistanis. It also has a distinct and quite antithetical meaning of primitive North American tribesmen. People think of wigwams, braves in headdresses whooping in a war dance round the fire, firing bows and arrows, and taking scalps. An Indian is also a lowly worker, as in: 'too many chiefs and not enough Indians'. The scope for derogation is far and wide. In Bradford and Burnley it would be far better to stick to 'Pakistani', though as in Leicester, the generic 'Asian' would be fine even at an anti-racism organization posh dinner party.

'Asian' is the 'preferred' tag, because it is so anodyne and general that it minimizes the possibility of insult. Though apparently I must be corrected by the judges' bible, the *Equal Treatment Bench Book*, that states that the term 'Asian' should not be used by judges because it is a 'term of convenience'. The mind boggles as to what inconvenient word should be used instead, and why on earth we should put ourselves to the trouble. 'Asian' gives a clue about origin without implying that the person is not a British national. The only problem with it is that Asians are a diverse collection of peoples. Japanese and Chinese are Asian and they are easily distinguishable from Indian subcontinent peoples by everybody. It may be laudable to signal that you are not implying that someone is not a UK citizen, but multiculturalism is (or was: should we talk about it in the past tense now?) about allowing — celebrating even — cultural roots; so from that perspective we should not be subsuming distinct ethnic minorities under a wider and more meaningless category. Instead we should be highlighting the specific ethnic difference: shouldn't we? This appears to be what the judge's *Bench Book* is suggesting. That takes us back to 'Pakistani' which inevitably will be shortened to 'Paki', so we have come full circle. Perhaps this is the idea: that any and every term for an ethnic minority group should be deemed offensive, to persuade us of the ridiculous notion that the treatment of such groups by the wider community is always discriminatory.

The reality is that no decree from on high will ever force ordinary people to desist from making simple shortened versions of everyday words, and given the myriad and fast-changing sensitivities it would appear to be a fruitless exercise even if everyone took notice. Whole communities are not any day soon going to talk only of 'Pakistanis' and not 'Pakis'. Nor should they. The idea is as absurd as if we were told never to speak of 'Aussies'. Even if terms could be forced underground, other cryptic slang would quickly emerge. The famous case comes to mind of British soldiers in the Falklands who were chastised for calling the locals 'Bennys' (after the cerebrally compromised Crossroads soap character), so the squaddies simply substituted 'stills': they were 'still Bennys'. Doubtless if they had stayed for a long tour, 'stills' too would have been proscribed and yet another term would be substituted, and so on. Of course, the troops did not seriously hold the locals in contempt; it was more a case that the Falklanders would have to have been near saints to have been worth the trouble and sacrifice of dislodging the Argentinians.

It is not that ordinary people are insensitive and careless with these sort of words, because both 'coon' and 'wog' have pretty well fallen out of use, despite neither of these having pejorative origins. Both words date from early last century, and everyone accepts that they are offensive and there is no mistake in understanding that it is abuse when anyone uses them. 'Coon' is a word from the Portuguese 'barracoos' for a type of shed that came to be used to house people waiting to be sold into slavery; and 'wog' is derived, or so I thought, from 'golliwog', a cloth doll featured by a nineteenth- century American writer who never intended a racist slur. (There are alternative suggestions for where 'wog' came from: meaning 'warden on guard' in Indian imperial times; Greek 'workers of the government' in Australia; even 'worthy/white/westernized oriental gentleman'. None of them at all derogatory in origin.) Even in retrospect the golliwog could be seen, in the context of the time, as innocuous if not enlightened, with white children taking their little black friend to bed with them. With the lack of civil rights, condescension to blacks was not on the radar screen, so inasmuch as golliwogs were in any way representative of black people they could not have been a negative force undermining relations between the races; if anything they would have contributed to cross-race amicability. I actually had one as a young child and I also recall the golliwog as the emblem on Robertson's jam and, as has often been pointed out, there were definitely no overtones of racism. The figure had no association of any kind with the idea of a black person. It was sensitivity to the possibility of such a misconception that made the company drop the logo, not that any rational case could be made that it was inherently derogating. A case could be made that there is derogation to a degree by a caricature in the appropriation of 'golliwog' shortened to 'wog' to actually describe a black person, but even this presupposes an originally pejorative intent. It would seem instead to have been an obvious folk process that the familiar 'golliwog' would be borrowed colloquially to refer to the unfamiliar black person.

There is a core problem in trying to engineer the cultural outlawing of terms people use to describe others of different race/culture.

Even when such words are being used pejoratively it is usually still a fairly gentle use. Rather than an expression of virulent racism, it is often an almost humorous or wry observation of difference. Far from causing friction, this is the way that people belonging to separate groups accommodate and assimilate to each other. A blanket ban on gentle ribbing followed by some less subtle winding up, prevents communication even getting off the ground. This harks back to the 'in-group' versus the 'out-group' and how members of one group can become members of another, providing the numbers of would-be entrants are small. We call it 'winding up', Americans call it 'hazing', and it is associated with initiation ceremonies that face new workers, new students, army recruits, etc. It is a way that the group has of testing potential loyalty of a would-be member; and whether it is pronounced to the extent of 'hazing' or much more subtle, it is universally the natural way humans join groups and as such it is indispensable as a tool of racial integration.

This is what the Yorkshire comedian Charlie Williams was about. At one time a national TV star, now highly unfashionable, nonetheless he made a contribution in working men's clubs to break the ice and build communication between races. His act was saying: 'look at me, I'm a 'darkie', and like you I can take the mickey out of myself and make you white guys laugh your socks off'. He may seem anachronistic today, but not within mass culture at the time. He was in no way unique. The Irish comedian Dave Allen remorselessly took the St Michael out of the Irish, focusing on their Roman Catholic religion, yet Allen was both Irish and Catholic himself. Humour requires that anybody and everybody is potential fair game, and this is how Bernard Manning persistently defies his various and vociferous misguided critics. He claims sincerely that his comic performances are not racist. And he's right. No comedian would retain mainstream popularity if his humour was actually malicious. Comedy works by attacking all and sundry, on the understanding that the selected targets are at worst held in sneaking regard. A comedian who was in fact racist would never use race as a topic, especially in today's climate.

The silly word game that the authorities are foisting on us is an attempt to use semantics to simultaneously deny the existence of a problem and to highlight its seriousness in a circular argument that collapses in on itself. It is a classic way to duck a challenge. It is to blame ordinary people while proclaiming that they themselves, our self-certified leaders, are spotlessly above the fray but somehow doing their best.

If we insist that the use of terms that are acceptable in local communities is not acceptable in polite company because they are, or are tantamount to, racism; then we end up pushing the majority of the population into the category of 'racist'. This is an arrogant lie, and everybody knows it. It impoverishes the label when it comes to be used where it is needed: to describe those who really are in a nasty way provoking gratuitous dislike, with no intention and no reasonable prospect of working towards any accommodation between people. Applying this to white people and not to anyone else really is racism and seriously compounds the offence felt by the majority. Inevitably this is a route to an eventual major backlash.

* * *

A classic instance of double-standard racism applied against whites and not against blacks is the history of the eventual censorship of the Black & White Minstrel Show. The B&WMs were a dozen white male singers masquerading as black (plus a dozen white chorus girls), and their shows were obviously an acknowledgment of, and deference to, the power of the black voice; a fact that is widely recognized today as ever in the surprise people express at a convincing soul music vocal sung by a non-black. It was a straight impersonation begun in the US almost 200 years ago, and was never a caricature. Indeed, in the 1960s it was criticized as breaking a taboo of depicting inter-racial sexual relationship. As with comedy not working if it is actually malicious, light entertainment cannot work if it is actually derogatory, and the B&WMS was the most successful light entertainment show in entertainment history, running for over twenty years and achieving Saturday night BBC TV audiences of sixteen million. I remember these even as a child, as a teenager even, and they stood out to me as an affront to musical taste, not as an affront to 'coloured people' as they would have been referred to at the time. The social anachronism was a harking back to 'variety' and Al Jolson (a Jewish man who wore 'blackface'), and nobody has ever convincingly explained the basis of racial offence. If the B&WMS deprived blacks of jobs, that presupposes that plenty of talented black people were interested in the particular work of performing a hackneyed style that was in any case within mainstream and not black culture. Even so, some black actors were auditioned — though turned down — before finally, in the mid-1970s, one black person did indeed join

the B&WMS: none other than a seventeen-year-old Lenny Henry —
perhaps the only contemporary comedian to consistently lampoon
blacks. This was several years after Diana Ross blew a fuse when she
saw the Minstrels troupe sat in the stalls for a Royal Variety Performance rehearsal of her and the Supremes in 1968. The troupe members were perplexed and mortified, unaware that in America
'blackface' minstrelry was seen as unacceptable by the time of the
heyday of the civil rights movement. The BBC defended the show
against charges of both racism and sexism and did not axe it until a
decade later, in 1978, since when the B&WMS has been deemed
taboo — the BBC refused to show footage for its fiftieth birthday
celebration.

To look at a parallel, Othello has traditionally been played by
someone blacked up, but today this is also often considered offensive and the character is usually played by a black actor. But what is
the offence in an actor attempting to display his versatility by playing someone of a different race? Alec Guinness played an Indian
character in the 1980s film of *A Passage To India* and no-one found this
odd. Countless white actors have blacked up on both TV and cinema
screens.

Why should offence taken by someone, or by some group of people, be enough that whatever it is that offence has been taken to is
thereby deemed offensive per se? Apart from humouring those who
claim offence: no reason at all. On the contrary, it is a denial of freedom of expression in the service of pandering to paranoia, on top of
an erroneous assumption, in the cases that arise in the context of
race, that enmity between people of different races can only flow one
way. When, in 1968, Diana Ross got her way and the Black & White
Minstrel troupe were ushered out of the stalls and denied a viewing
of a Supremes rehearsal for a Royal Variety Performance, Ross gave
a 'black power' salute. An appropriate gesture, as Ross was indeed
abusing her own power. This was the offence, not the male Minstrels' blacked-up faces; as arrogant as other of Ross's tantrums. It is
ironic that Ross's close friend Michael Jackson has adopted 'white-
face'; permanently. Nobody has thrown a tantrum about that, of
course. The only critics are some black people crying 'sell out!'

There is plenty of evidence of racism from ethnic minority groups
to whites and between ethnic minority groups. Hidden in the report,
Statistics on Race and the Criminal Justice System, published in 1999 by
the Home Office, it is revealed that ethnic minorities per capita were
responsible in 1995 for something like twenty-five times the number

of racial assaults as were whites. This is based on the 1998 *British Crime Survey* that estimates 382,000 offences were racially motivated in 1995, and this figure breaks down into 143,000 where the victims were members of ethnic minorities, but the much larger figure of 238,000 for white victims. Of course, the report does not discuss this. In particular it does not discuss that this discrepancy is even greater than it appears, for the obvious reason that the percentage of ethnic minorities in Britain in 1995 was roughly 6 percent (as against, of course, 94 percent for whites). From this you can calculate the difference in propensity to carry out racial assault as a factor of 25. Even this would seem to considerably underestimate the extent of Afro-Caribbean perpetration, since some — presumably most — of the ethnic minority victims will have been Asian (by far the larger category of ethnic minority people in the UK, several times more numerous than those of African or Afro-Caribbean descent) and their assailants not white but Afro-Caribbean. This is a more than reasonable suspicion given the fact that Asian males are arrested and imprisoned at rates of about half that of white males: Asians are more than anyone not perpetrators but victims of assaults. To confirm that the Home Office stats are not aberrational: in the USA, Department of Justice figures for 1997 show the rate for inter-racial violent crime differs by the even greater factor of 50. (And this too is a gross under-estimate, since bizarrely Hispanics are counted as black when a victim but white when a perpetrator!) The idea that American whites are seen to have money and the relatively dispossessed blacks target them for this reason, is not supported by the fact that 85 percent of black-on-white violent acts are assaults of varying severity and rapes, none of which have profit as the motive. And, as in the UK, 'institutional racism' flies out of the window with the figures for arrest and imprisonment of Asians being considerably below the per capita figures for whites.

Although such overwhelming evidence comes from the Government, prominent politicians insist on denial, even when the issue is raised by their own fellow party MPs. So it was that the Labour NEC member, Shahid Malik tried to deny free speech both to Phil Woolas, the Labour MP for Oldham & Saddleworth, and to no less than the former director of the Joint Council for the Welfare of Immigrants and Labour MEP Claude Moraes, who backed up Woolas; when Woolas raised the issue of black-on-white racist violence during street disturbances in 2001 on his home patch. In an interview on Radio 4's Today programme, Woolas said:

We had a series of very, very nasty and sinister attacks in my area against white people where it is very clear that the motivation is racial. What I am trying to do in Oldham is build a consent for a multi-cultural society, and to do that, we have to be seen to be even-handed. At the moment, unfortunately, we are not.

If we can show that there is an even-handed approach, recognising that of course, the bulk of discrimination and attacks are against the ethnic minorities, then I think that everybody will benefit and the BNP will be the losers.

Following this up with a letter to the CRE chair, Trevor Phillips, Woolas wrote:

Politicians across the party divide have failed to be seen to condemn racist violent attacks against white people as strongly or forcibly as such attacks against Asian and black people. My view, and I believe that of my constituents of all ethnic backgrounds, is that this fact has diminished confidence in the communities and damaged race relations.

Despite Woolas' testament — and he is the local MP for where the trouble occurred, remember — despite backing from the former JCWI director and an MEP, and despite concrete and comprehensive evidence from Government figures, this is the response from Shahid Malik:

These comments are very disturbing. They are irresponsible remarks and absolute nonsense. The comments feed far-right organisations like the BNP who hijack the remarks. All right-minded people condemn racism, be it black on white, Asian on black or white on Asian. Mr Woolas has no basis for his view and is clearly out of line with Labour party thinking.

Living in a predominantly (overwhelmingly) ethnic minority area for much of my life — and this was a free choice, I should add — I can attest to the problem first hand. More racism was evident between different ethnic minorities and from ethnic minorities towards white people than in the direction it is usually expected of white to ethnic minorities. The Leicester Bengali community is much maligned by many Indians, some Afro-Caribbeans are openly racist towards Asians in general, and there is an argument voiced by some of their white student victims that mugging by Afro-Caribbeans is, or is tantamount to, a racist crime.

This last is a great unspoken of the 'not in front of the children' lobby. In many inner-city areas in Britain, mugging is committed disproportionately by young Afro-Caribbean males, and whereas this same sub-group is liable to victimization by fellow blacks in 'dissing' incidents (disputes over mutual respect), and turf war

between gangs or over drugs; whites, being not of the black community, appear to be regarded as fair game for street robbery. Denial of
this particular reality is widely regarded by ordinary people as a
most risible position held by the 'not in front ...' brigade. Media
silence on the fact that the typical mugger is black was finally broken
in 2002 by the editor of the black newspaper, Voice, when the Met
calculated that 63 percent of muggings in London were perpetrated
by blacks — a massive incidence given the small proportion of the
population that people of African descent constitute — and the
Home Office found, in a study it commissioned itself, blacks to be
the principal culprits for most mobile phone theft. Silence was broken, but only in respect of blacks perpetrating crime; the idea that the
crime they commit could be construed as black-on-white racism is
still a no-go area. But since this interlude of candour, discussion even
about the fact of black perpetration has, to say the least, been muted.

Blacks are many many times over-represented in prison across all
categories of crime, accounting for over 22 percent (on 1998 figures)
of all those detained for robbery. It is absurd to ascribe this to any
large degree to 'institutional racism' as the Macpherson Report
fudges. If a mugging victim reports the crime, then one thing he will
know for certain is whether his assailant was white or black; and if he
was white then the police can hardly make a case against a black supposed perpetrator get past the CPS and make it to court. Financial
deprivation does not stand up because 8 percent of prison inmates
convicted of sex offences are black: another over-representation. The
real issue, of course, is that people are personally responsible for
committing crime. Not only that, but it places society in moral jeopardy if it does not continue to act according to that principle. It is a
pernicious moral totalitarianism that dictates that such a stark problem as this cannot be legitimately aired and contributes to the sense
that black assailants have of being able to get away with their crimes.
Meanwhile anyone with 'street sense' knows to play by the sensible
'rule of thumb' that predominantly Afro-Caribbean areas or where
blacks deal drugs or pimp girls, are places where extra caution
should be exercised; irrespective of their own politics, however
virulently anti-racist.

* * *

There is a racism industry, about which a conspiracy of silence still
prevails. Some black and Asian people, for personal gain, use the
assumption that all white people are racist towards all ethnic minori-

ties. The only occasional voice to speak out must, of course, be an ethnic minority spokesman. The rest of us are not allowed to talk about it and are not reported by the media if we do — unless a white scalp is in the offing. Thus it was that the newspaper columnist Yasmin Alibhai-Brown talked about the use of racism as 'a poison to destabilise and terrorise organisations' already used by too many in the wake of the Lawrence enquiry and the debacle at the Law Society. It is all too easy to make a spurious allegation and to receive a pay-off to head off the embarrassment of an agency or company; paradoxically the more so if the organization has a reputation that makes it less likely to be thought guilty of such a charge.

Nobody explains why there are blanket ethnic minority quotas masquerading as targets when large sections of the British ethnic minority population actually fare better than whites. This is true of the Hindu Indian populations, that easily outdo native whites in school/college qualifications. This is in stark contrast to Pakistanis, Bangladeshis, and Afro-Caribbean males (Afro-Caribbean females actually also outperform their white counterparts). However this startling difference in average performance is explained, it completely undermines the case for special favourable treatment in any way for ethnic minorities taken as a whole. If institutional racism existed, or if there were large numbers of people with racist attitudes, then how is it that Indian Hindus are so successful? And how is it that Asian Britons in general are substantially less likely to be arrested or imprisoned than are white Britons? Where is the institutional racism that the police have been officially accused of?

David Coleman puts his finger on a profound general problem and nails it succinctly:

> This transformation of the United Kingdom into an ethnically corporate state providing group rights for some over and above individual rights for all is of dubious constitutional propriety and has never received democratic sanction. Such practices and 'group rights' are explicitly rejected as divisive and counter to the principle of the equality of citizenship in some other European countries, notably France.

This is precisely the outcome expected by the moral totalitarianism of the political Left that places any and every minority over and above the mass of ordinary people — the mindset of our current intelligentsia I explained in Chapter 6. As I discuss below, the foundation of our sense of outrage over discrimination is the unwarranted contempt implied in treating someone not as an individual but as merely a typical member of the sub-group to which he/she belongs. It is the height of hypocrisy therefore to somehow attempt redress by dealing with the individual via assistance given to the sub-group, thereby succouring the very root of the offence complained about.

* * *

Political censorship is rife, and lurking in the wings to destroy the careers of people simply if they can be wilfully misconstrued as lumping together all members of an ethnic minority, even when it is clear that they are referring to a proportion of them only. As the latest instance of this, for omitting the qualifying word 'some', Robert Kilroy-Silk was sacked by the BBC when he described Arabs as 'women oppressors', 'limb amputators' and 'suicide bombers'. Not the wisest remark, to be sure, but fully in keeping with the style of how the one-time Labour MP (and now UKIP MEP) succinctly introduced the many hundreds of feisty daily half-hour morning TV discussions he presided over. It is a tabloid style that befitted the slot as commissioned by the BBC. Such pithy shorthand is the very stuff of newspapers and it is indisputable that much of the practise of all three categories of offence Kilroy pointed to is not just by certain individual Arabs but at the behest of prominent or majority sections of entire Arab communities, and this goes even for suicide bombing. It was perfectly clear to everyone that Kilroy did not mean that all or most Arabs carry out such acts (though feminists would side with Kilroy here on 'woman oppressors'), as we all know they do not. Was the problem thought to be that some people might, merely through hearing Kilroy, start to think that every Arab you could meet would try to blow you up?! Contrast the reaction if a woman had said things about men that clearly all or most men do not do. This is done so regularly on the BBC that you would be hard pushed to write complaints to keep up with the never-ending series of instances. It is never censured.

It is beyond any excuse that what is supposed to be our public service broadcaster, and for which we each (are supposed to) pay a poll tax, systematically perpetrates the political abuse of suppressing discussion of anything related to immigration, through obviously unfair character assassination. But the cracks are showing in the elite's façade.

Another key part of anti-racist rhetoric — and another one that the BBC and the media generally propagate unchallenged — is the notion that Britain is a nation of immigrants. This has now been widely and comprehensively debunked. As David Coleman — an Oxford University demographer — wrote in the Spectator in 2001:

> English population history is known better than almost any other in the world; it has been reconstructed carefully from the 16th century. ... Immigration forms no part of the story. ... Surnames and genes confirm a British population little affected by immigration for a millennium, with many traces of ancient local settlement.

You have to go back a millennium, Coleman argues, to the Anglo-Saxons and Danes to find the last colonists, and even then they comprised only 10 percent of the population. The Normans came in tiny numbers and were 'demographically trivial'. Later waves of immigration were few and far between. The biggest influx was of Huguenots, but these numbered only 100,000, which was about one in sixty of the population; the earlier arrival of Flemings totalled even less at one in a hundred, while the Jews who came in the nineteenth century constituted about 0.3 percent. All of these peoples were quickly assimilated, not least because they were culturally little different from the host population as well as being relatively small in number.

The first generally noticeable immigration was the post-war arrival of blacks from Commonwealth countries, but this was halted before the totals reached even 1 percent. Immigration was such a novel prospect as recently as the 1970s that there was a furore over 20,000 displaced Ugandan Asians. Immigration has grown since then but suddenly exploded from what it had been by multiples through the late 1990s and into the 'noughties'. Even so, still well over nine out of ten of the population are native white. The New Labour mantra that Britain is a nation of immigrants is a myth.

In parts of the country, such as Pennine South Yorkshire where I live, even the Anglo-Saxons had little impact, and genetically the local population today is a mix principally of 'Celtic' and Norse. Perhaps this is why we are so troublesome up here and resent an out-of-touch central Government and so-called intelligentsia telling us that we must think and believe utter nonsense.

* * *

If it isn't the 'we're a nation of immigrants' rhetoric then along comes the one about Britain once colonizing the world. We were very much 'over there', this argument runs, so we should not complain if people now want to be 'over here'. This falls down because Britain's wealth today has nothing to do with 'plundering' an empire, which is long dead. The empire benefitted a small elite only, while the great bulk of British people were exploited in conditions worse than those endured by third-world sweatshop workers today. Britain was the cradle of the industrial revolution and that is what made it wealthy. In some ways the inertia of painful change from old heavy industry set us back compared to some nations that were late arrivals on the industrial stage, so that per capita wealth is higher than it is in the UK in many places abroad, most of which never had an empire. We gave the world the means to escape drudgery and for many nations this meant a much less painful and much speedier transition from an agricultural-based economy than British people endured, because more recently developing nations were unchecked by having to pioneer a sequence of new technologies and could short-circuit social problems by implementing the fruits of painful lessons learnt in Britain. On top of all this, economic analyses show that British rule almost invariably created much more wealth per head of the colonial population than would have been managed otherwise, and much more than the ex-colonies managed to create after independence. (See Niall Ferguson's books, *Empire* and *Colossus*.) We do not owe a living to large numbers of people in those parts of the world that for whatever reason were particularly slow to follow our lead. In any case, it does not help those under-developed countries and the vast bulk of their people for us to take in what for them would be a very small proportion of their collectively vast populations. It is a nonstarter as a development programme, and if anything it is actually the reverse (for reasons I outlined in Chapter 4).

There is a case that the under-developed world suffers from unbalanced trade agreements with the US and EU, the latter of which, of course, we are a part. Well, if that is the locus of the problem then that is where action should be taken. In the case of African states, which are the real economic basket cases of the world, it is endemic political failure above all that is the problem. Bottomlessly corrupt leaders, individuals, civil services, armies and entire regimes, together with tribalism and nepotism have laid waste a continent, where people starve because even food aid is appropriated by the corrupt and withheld from the people, if not used as a weapon of war. In Africa too and across the world Britain is blamed for the slave trade, but historians have shown that slave trading had been voluminous across Africa for millennia before the British empire, run both by Africans and by Arabs. It took British philanthropists to stop it's perpetration by Britain, but in Africa it has continued, as it still does today, run by Africans themselves.

There is no justification that anyone from anywhere can be 'over here' today on the basis that many years ago a few of the British elite were 'over there' or reaping the rewards from empire back at home.

* * *

Anti-racism hysteria dictates that we do not criticize either groups or individuals who choose to come here. 'Managed Migration' functions as a service to self-selected immigrants who can usually circumvent the unusual outcome of a refusal by recourse to human rights legislation the Labour Government so thoughtlessly allowed to be hooked up to immigration law. The result is that London has a reputation bar none as a haven for the world's terrorists at the very time when there is much Government rhetoric about combatting the terrorist threat. David Blunkett regularly curses the judiciary but the blame for the absurd legal knots in which the hapless Home Secretary is tied lies with the very Government of which he is a key part; indeed, with departments that he oversees.

We welcome people who openly despise us. Some telling quotes have been gathered by Anthony Browne. He cites 'one of Britain's most celebrated race commentators' as describing as 'the empire strikes back!' when endorsing the sentiments of a Ghanaian immigrant who wrote:

> It is only the naïve who believed they could celebrate the achievements of empire and not pay for some of its consequences … surely it is all right for their descendants to enjoy the fruits of those struggles and sacrifices.

And a Bradford City Council forum attracted the following posting:

> Well I tell u what get my goat u English were not complaining when u wonderfully took over the Indian subcontinent, got what u needed. And white flight? I think u are more than accustomed to it u have been doing that for centuries in and around the world once u had pillaged, gorged and sent back what u needed. Guess what? What goes around comes around.

Responses to Browne's articles included this invective:

> It is indicative of the 'chickens come home to roost' phenomenon, spread out over decades. You screw over enough parts of the world, their children will eventually settle in your own backyard. After all, Britain must be the best place on earth, considering that your ancestors beat that notion into mine, right?'

And Browne found this posted to a BBC website:

> A strong thirst for wealth once took the British all over the world. Ironically now it's payback time.

The great majority of UK citizens would, if they were asked, want a government that will ensure that people who feel this way are not allowed to settle here. Of course, there is no question that those who are fully settled here are allowed full rights in freedom of speech: as I have been arguing above, free speech has been a major casualty of the refusal by those in powerful positions to allow discussion about immigration. The point is that although we give all citizens the right to free speech, that does not mean that we automatically grant every-one who requests citizenship the right to settle; and if we know or if we can find out that someone is likely to disparage the very nation he wishes to welcome him, then should we not veto his application?

It is one thing to hear a native Briton express such sentiments as those quoted above from a politically Left perspective in some sort of *faux* atonement for their association with the past through their own descent. Such people are inextricably part of the wider British com-munity and all bar the most extreme are unlikely in any way to try to do serious harm to individuals simply to express their political views. But this is not the case with respect to a foreign national newly arrived who has such an attitude. It is not just that he holds deroga-tory opinions of Britain and British people in general, but that he has no stake in our society. This is a combination that would seem to be a much greater risk that he is a real danger to people. It could become a justification for all kinds of anti-social and criminal behaviour; and is in extremis the mindset of someone who may aid and abet terrorism, and even go on to carry out such acts directly. At the most innocuous level, you would almost expect deceit from such a person, and with enough people like him there is a deleterious effect on social capital: the basic trust people can expect to safely place in each other.

It is hard to see how you could screen applicants, particularly if many if not most go through the intermediary of a legal representa-tive. A minority of immigrants only may have undesirable or even hateful prejudice, but it cannot but add to the argument against net mass immigration. Of course it would not be at all right for us to feel prejudice against immigrants in general because of what may only be a minority, but equally if we have made such efforts to eliminate prejudice within ourselves against foreigners, then we should demand at least as much from them. And who is to say that 'payback time' notions are not in the majority? A substantial minority would fully justify a 'rule of thumb' judgment to be wary.

The reality, I suspect, is that the practical, ethical and political con-straints will serve to scupper any suggestions of vetting applicants for UK settlement. In any case, experience of vetting procedures shows that they have limited usefulness. Ask social housing tenants. The impression of the problems caused by a failure of vetting is the reason most people would feel some horror at the prospect of falling off the housing ladder and having to consider being housed by the local council, or even by a housing association.

The lack of action against opinions such as those increasingly heard from various sorts of Islamic extremists, as well as the 'pay-back time' sentiments, will indeed undermine the case for mass net immigration in the minds of the general public. For want of discrimination (to use the word in its positive sense) it is unfortunate but understandable that all immigrants will indeed to some extent be tarred with the same brush.

Anti-racism hysteria dictates that there is to be no dissent not only regarding the specific groups and individuals that come to Britain but over the very idea of immigration in general. Beverley Hughes, in one of her replies to Bob Ainsworth, the Labour whip, about abuses in Romania and Bulgaria, talked about the 'entitlements' of applicants. 'Entitlement' is the language of rights without responsibilities. It is astounding to ordinary people that someone who is not a British citizen is simply 'entitled' to become one and woe betide anyone who suggests anything should be put in their way; especially when as everyone knows there are usually severe hoops to pass through for any British citizen to secure citizenship elsewhere.

Political sensitivities preclude discussion, but at some remove from voters, in the European Parliament, there is a better chance of someone airing their views, albeit fruitlessly. So it was on July 2, 2002, when Bruno Gollnisch MEP commented on the Ceyhun Report:

> Europeans are racist if they reject the immigration policy. This approach involves forced guilt, moral inquisition and permanent psychological conditioning. The Ceyhun report is a further step towards moral totalitarianism. It contains such a broad definition of the racist offence that it is becoming difficult to say what is not racist. Therefore, a simple reference to national origin may be considered as a racist act or as racial discrimination. Ultimately, the mere fact of setting aside public sector jobs or the right to vote for nationals falls foul of this aberrant legislation. The report also has a repressive edge, making it a crime to express one's thoughts. Freedom of expression is giving way to the principle of compulsory cosmopolitanism. This 'anti-racism' hysteria is the psychological level of the process whose aim is the general colonisation of Europe. One right is finally recognised implicitly in the report: that of keeping quiet and supporting those who are destroying our freedoms and our identities. This document is the manifesto of collaborators of future foreign occupations.

Bogus Students, Sham Marriages

Problems of how Managed Migration applications are dealt with apply in common to all the various types of applications we deal with (such as dependent relatives, au pairs, working holidaymakers, domestic workers in a private household … a long list), but there are additional major procedural inadequacies that bedevil particular types of applications other than ECAA: those for students and marriage. The trouble is that these are by far the two largest types of applications. Out of several dozen kinds, students make up the best part of a half of all cases, and those intending to settle as married partners of someone already settled make up a very large portion of the remainder. Yet these are the case types which are dealt with by the most cavalier adherence to immigration legislation, despite clear knowledge by the Home Office that very widespread abuse is taking place.

In common with other caseworkers, I soon got the impression that quite a lot of the student applications were, shall we say, dodgy, if not almost cheekily fraudulent. The high proportion of applications which did not contain the required information, or the absolute minimum that might just enable us to give the benefit of the doubt was striking.

As I did at the start of doing this job, when most people think of students they think of university undergraduates and these are what I assumed I would mostly be dealing with. But this was not the bulk of the people who applied. Most were coming here (ostensibly, that is) for part-time courses, especially English. In these cases the answer on the application form to the question about the hours per week of tuition was almost invariable: 15 hours. This just happened to be the absolute minimum hours per week that under the rules a course could be considered as full-time; and under the rules you can't come to Britain as a student if your course is not full-time. What seems to be happening, then, is that there is a wholesale working of the system — a collusion between 'students' and the colleges (or should that be 'colleges'?) to get people into the country posing as students when in reality they are here just to work, or mainly to work. This may be on the black market or it could be 'legitimate'. If you are granted leave to enter/remain a student then you get what is known as a Code2 stamp in your passport that states you are not allowed to have recourse to public funds but that you are allowed to work — part-time, supposedly. The stamp can get you above-board employment, and if you can get your foot in the door then of course many employers turn a blind eye to the distinction between full- and part-time. In any case, a lot of work extra to basic agreed hours can mean in effect that the worker is full-time rather than part-time. What's more, a student can bring his partner or even full family with him, and anyone other than the lead applicant (the student himself) is free to work full-time.

This must be the easiest way to enter the UK as an economic migrant, given that all of the checks that are supposed to be in place regarding students are generally very laxly applied. For example, an applicant is supposed to show proof of funds or sponsorship, to show that he/she will have money for support while doing the course, but any kind of letter from anyone appears to suffice, especially if there is the offer of accommodation. Untranslated Spanish or Chinese is fine, as is a brief handwritten note from (literally) anyone. The point of checking on funds and/or sponsorship is to ensure that the applicant will not need to work in order to support themselves and to pay their college fees. Effectively waiving these checks is an open encouragement to come to the UK to work.

There is a loophole at every turn. That the return address for the passport is usually given as a different address from the one stated as where resident is seen as normal and is never questioned. Shouldn't this sound a loud alarm bell that fraud may be being perpetrated? An enrolment letter for the course is required, but proof of payment of fees is not; so anyone can apply and be accepted on a course and then simply fail to turn up and not even be out of pocket. In fact a letter merely offering a place will do (as we were only recently reminded). Yet it is known that considerable numbers of economic migrants are prepared to pay college fees as a cover for their real intentions. It must be expected that many more will try the route whereby they incur no cost at all.

Many economic migrants just register at one of the large number of bogus colleges set up to hoodwink the Immigration Service and Managed Migration is fully aware of this problem. I remember getting an e-mail between senior caseworkers that was circulated to one and all, complaining that:

> unfortunately, the common factor I have found in all of my investigations on the LEE (a confidential list of all known educational establishments) and bogus colleges is that although Ministers recognise that student abuse is on the increase, there is little or no commitment from anyone to investigating potentially bogus colleges/students unless a particular case or college has hit the headlines — IS visits are very very rare, and the message coming from IS at quite a high level is that this kind of thing is currently low on their list of priorities. The only thing I can suggest is that any suspicions you have should be sent to ICC* who currently have responsibility for LEE but have little time to devote to it so the chances are that little or nothing will be done with the information … there are no systems in place to adequately provide meaningful stats and there is little commitment from IS.

Yet it was recognized that not only was there a problem but that it was a problem requiring investigative skills. My own practice was to check to see if the college had a website if I felt it was dubious. But another cascaded e-mail pointed out that: '… the 'scams' are very complex and the fact that a college has a website is not an indication that it's bona fide,' Nevertheless, I used to do my own simple checking that a website exists and a simple phone call to check that the contact number was in operation. For my trouble I was given a formal reprimand (by written notice and in a special meeting) from my team management for the deemed sin of: 'making extensive enquiries on the internet and by telephone into the legitimacy of colleges and educational establishments (making in depth inquiries is not the responsibility of caseworkers).'

'In depth'?! Hardly. Well, since there was either nobody or almost nobody centrally checking up on colleges, in however shallow a fashion, then whose responsibility was it other than ourselves, the caseworkers? In any case, given that I was not falling short of set targets for decision making, then not only was there no reason why management should have been concerned, but they should have recognized my effort to make more fully-informed decisions.

Belatedly, two Croydon staff were allocated to update LEE, but when I rang them, and they took some tracking down — the Home

Office is notorious for the difficulty of locating staff internally — one of them replied that colleges unknown to the Home Office would still not be visited, so the large number of establishments not on LEE or listed but given the residual code 'H', should be treated normally in the absence of any information. So what changed?

The laxity of checks goes further. When a student (or an economic migrant purporting to be a student) applies for an extension of leave to remain in Britain, he/she is supposed to supply bank statements, but when these show unsourced deposits we were encouraged to simply assume that they back up what is stated on the application form. Round figures deposited in cash or by any other route are taken to be from a sponsor (and never assumed to be earnings from working). Why? Why not demand to see evidence?

Students are not supposed to work for more than 20 hours per week and are not supposed to support themselves wholly or mainly from earned income, but few caseworkers refuse on these grounds. Applicants are supposed to send in evidence to support their claim that they are working part-time only, but very few do, and seldom do caseworkers request such evidence. We were told not to refuse on hours worked unless it was substantially above 20 hours per week, and even then that refusal should not be on these grounds alone — despite the fact that the legislation clearly allows and requires this. I was myself again formally reprimanded by management for: 'going out for information on how many hours a student is working (when all other aspects of the case are clear cut).' But again, why should management have been concerned? Rather they should have been appreciative.

Applicants should submit bank statements that cover the whole of the previous three months, but many do not, and in any case an applicant may choose to send statements covering a period out of term-time when the 20-hour restriction does not apply. They need not bother. A senior caseworker circular stated:

> Whilst it is preferable for an application to contain the last three months original itemised bank statements, caseworkers should look at the merits of the case and decide whether on the basis of the information already received, this is necessary.

In other words: there is no need to bother. But in practice, even if the application enclosed no bank statements at all, a handwritten letter by a friend, or from someone living in a bedsit in the same house, purporting to be a sponsor would usually or often secure a stamp in a passport. In any case, it is frequently obvious that the account for which statements are submitted is not the account used for usual transactions, and when I raised this, yet again I was told: 'it's none of our business'. This seemed to be particularly crazy. Don't most people have more than one bank account? Is it not the easiest fraud in the book simply to show details of the account you don't actually use and to hide details of the one you do use? Again, it is so easy it is a wonder why anyone goes to the bother of forging documents. Apart, that is, from those who have no money to put into any bank account. Occasionally someone spots forged bank statements, but detection is rare, not least because there is no training.

It is hard not to be demoralized when time and time again you raise your suspicions with someone more senior on the team only to be told that it need not concern you and to grant on the basis of the paltry information supplied. I lost count of the number of occasions I raised doubts and I was told to grant the application anyway or only to request a particular kind of information and not the full set I thought I needed. During training I remember the advice that if you had to send for further information then it was best to ask for everything conceivable rather than find that there was something else you required which meant having to contact the applicant for a second time. More and more, it seemed, this practice was frowned on. I got away with it to some extent because for a time there was an experiment to fuse what had been separate ways of working of two types of teams. I was in an initial consideration team, and we had a corresponding team that dealt with all of the cases that for one reason or another we could not decide on straight away. When we changed to taking on this function ourselves, a caseworker could follow through with enquiries. But this way of working was abandoned as being inefficient. Job satisfaction went down and inevitably unworthy applications were more likely to be granted through a diffusion of responsibility. Caseworkers had to meet their 'stats', and if a case had been ducked by the ICS caseworker then the person it next came to (in what was known as the CLS team) starts off with the idea that he can maybe get a 'quick win', as it were, simply by not agreeing with the ICS worker's assessment and not bothering to send for further information.

Clear evidence that the situation had got so out of hand that even senior caseworkers had simply forgotten what they are supposed to be doing came with an e-mail between senior staff cascaded to ordinary caseworkers: 'Are we still OK to refuse students solely on the fact that they cannot support themselves/fund their study without working?' The legislation clearly stating this is then actually quoted. The reply: 'I can see no reason why we cannot refuse on this point alone'. This alarmingly points up that even when the legislation is there in print before their eyes, senior caseworkers are so bound up in guidance and the dilution of this in 'pragmatic' practice that it has come to take precedence over the law. (This is not to censure senior caseworking staff, because my experience was that the quality of staff, both junior and senior, was higher than the Home Office should have expected given the low rates of pay. It is an indictment of top management and in particular their political masters who have pressured staff to behave in this way.)

Even the tabloids could not have been prepared for the ultimate student scam, this time perpetrated by the National Health Service. In July 2004, Unison complained that foreign student nurses, who should not be working more than 20 hours under the regulations for immigrant students, were actually been made to work full-time — for 60 hours per week — in NHS hospitals.

* * *

Apart from student applications, the other major proportion of Managed Migration casework consists of marriage applications. (In fact, if you subsume marriage applications and dependent relatives under 'family reunion' then this is a much larger category than students.) There was controversy when the 'primary purpose' rule was axed in 1997 — fulfilling a promise by New Labour to its ethnic minority voters — and it was presumed that the obvious invitation to abuse this opened would be met with proper scrutiny of applications, but this is anything but the case. That abuse is rife is shown by another senior caseworker e-mail circular sent in December:

> Marriage abuse within the immigration system is an increasing problem. INDIS estimates that there could be in the region of 15,000 sham marriages each year. Reports of suspicious marriages from registrars have been rising from year to year.

It is estimated by research done by registrars themselves than at least one in five marriages in London are contracted primarily to circumvent immigration law. Of course, this must be merely the tip of the iceberg. Apart from the contrived marriages entered into in the UK, most marriage applications are in respect of those contracted abroad. There are no estimates of the proportion of these that are bogus, but the French do have an estimate with respect to their own caseload. At a seminar of the Franco-British Council in 2004, M Barry

Delongchamps said: 'There is widespread fraud over marriage certificates issued abroad: up to 90% of them were fraudulent'.

Applicants can enter the UK either as a fiancé(e) or as a spouse of someone present and settled, or they can simply switch from whatever temporary immigration category they are under into marriage. An initial two-years is granted as a 'probationary' period, after which full settlement follows. To be granted the first period all that is required is a marriage certificate — there is not even a requirement that the couple should be residing together — so you might imagine that there would be very extensive checking when it came to a settlement application, but scrutiny is as lax as that afforded student applications. The two questions supposedly to be answered are: can they support themselves without recourse to public funds and, is the relationship subsisting? Regarding the latter, the rules state that official documents addressed to one or other of the couple at the shared address should cover the range of the probation period, but such are rarely supplied. Usually the minimum is all that is received: a total of five documents (such as gas bills, medical cards) addressed not to both parties at the shared address but to one or other party, and often in the ratio of 4:1. So a single document addressed to the applicant, and on any date within the two years of the probation period, would suffice — even though self-evidently this proves nothing. This was exactly the situation in the very last case I handled, as I described in Chapter 3.

When it comes to funds, the familiar relativism surfaces: who are we to say what minimum income is sufficient? This is the same line as before: 'it's none of our business'. These are customers after all. I have had just one instance agreed by a senior caseworker to run a benefits check — this was one of only two benefits checks that I have done in the whole six months I worked at Managed Migration. In this case the couple, with a child, actually stated that they were both unemployed and claiming benefits. I still had to go through the rigmarole of consulting with two levels of senior caseworking staff for approval, making up a pro forma to fax off to a central checking agency to then await a reply hours (or days) later. Again, just as with ascertaining subsistence of relationship, the full probation period is ignored and the last (or recent period of) three months is usually all that is looked at; wageslips for a short period are all that is required. When I queried the possibility of the applicant being workless and/or receiving benefits for the rest of the period, again I was assured it was nothing to be concerned about. It is possible, therefore, to gain settlement simply by signing up for a temporary job for three months and having no further engagement with work thereafter.

A very large proportion (I would very roughly estimate 80 percent) of marriage applications are from individuals from the Indian subcontinent (Pakistan, India, Bangladesh). I would estimate that a large proportion of the remainder are from Africa and a good number from East Europe. Few — very few — are from people who share cultural ties with the majority indigenous UK population. Marriage is used as a major gateway for secondary economic immigration and is only in a small minority of cases what it is supposed to be: the result of a genuine emotional entanglement with a foreigner.

The consequence of challenging the short-cut practices that were particularly evident regarding the processing of student and marriage applications, was a written reprimand delivered at a meeting. I responded in writing, countering by explaining that I was simply implementing the immigration rules. So another meeting was held, I thought to discuss my reply, but discussion was ruled an irrelevance and I was told that I had answered by my improved performance all of the points and it was therefore not necessary to address my corrections to the points management had previously made. Instead, all of the points made against me were subsumed under 'requesting further information when it isn't required', and the assessment was that 'checking indicated that in all cases the inquiries were appropriate'. A convenient dodge, it would appear, to avoid discussion of the failure by Managed Migration to properly implement immigration rules.

The vast scale of abuse of immigration becomes apparent when you draw out the lens to look at the overall picture. I have detailed the across-the-board systematic problems with all applications and the multiple failures that apply specifically to the processing of student and marriage cases as well as to the ECAA caseload. Managed Migration deals with well over 500,000 applications annually (the figure provided by Ken Sutton in his report into the processing of ECAA cases). This workrate dwarfs the 200,000 or so Work Permit grants, and is in addition to asylum, clandestine entry and illegal overstay. The Sheffield Casework Unit of Managed Migration is the recently formed junior partner of the main office at Croydon; even so a director e-mailed staff in February to say that Sheffield was 'on track to achieve around 130,000 decisions by the end of March', but that this was despite 'the delayed introduction of Aspect Court' (one of the two premises) 'from May to July 03 and the very gradual build-up of staffing and knowledge through the Autumn and Winter months.' The rate of decision making will therefore now be greatly in excess of that suggested by a 130,000 annual figure with the greatly increased capacity phased in. While Sheffield may still not yet be making as many decisions as Croydon it can't be far off, but the problems uncovered at Sheffield must be replicated at Croydon. It would seem that if anything the situation at the parent office is likely to be worse, since it was generally apparent to Sheffield caseworkers and admitted by management that Croydon caseworkers had a cavalier attitude to casenotes and were by all accounts resentful and jaded, so were making still less well-considered decisions than were Sheffield staff. The low pay meant that staff facing London and South-East costs could neither be recruited nor retained, so the quality of the staff who remained must be suspect. As for Ken Sutton's whitewash report: nobody believes that practices at Sheffield were isolated and not paralleled at Croydon. Indeed Croydon is where all of the problems in procedures must have originated.

Clearly there was a major problem and as there was no political will by the Government to tackle it, then for me it became impossible to continue working at Managed Migration without speaking out in such a way that the Government was compelled to take notice. And so it was. The question now, several months on, is what if anything has the Government actually done?

As if Home Office leaks were not enough for the Government to contend with, a new outlet for the truth about immigration emerged with the trial of a Chinese restaurant owner and one of his waiters on charges of people smuggling. Robert Owen, a Home Office expert with thirty years experience and on secondment to the National Criminal Intelligence Service to advise about Chinese Snakehead gangs, was in Swansea Crown Court on June 9, 2004, giving evidence on oath. Owen divulged some amazing information he described as 'highly classified'; that between 40,000 and 50,000 is the actual number of Chinese nationals living in Manchester, despite the official census figure for the numbers in the city being just 8,000. The 40–50,000 figure is actually from the Chinese immigrants' own local association: hardly a body likely to exaggerate the numbers of its own members over those here officially, because the difference would be the number here illegally and therefore potentially subject to deportation. Presumably, the association knew of the extreme unliklihood that the Home Office would take any action.

Now well under half a million people in total live in Manchester, so with 40-50,000 Chinese, that makes an incidence of about one in ten — comprising more than the nationwide entire percentage of *all* ethnic minorities who are legally here added together!

This is truly amazing. Chinese nationals are just one ethnic minority and way below the most numerous in Britain. What if there is a similar reality regarding other ethnic minorities? It must be assumed that this is at least possible. Then the scale of illegal migration appears to be even more staggering than anyone had suspected. Owen admitted that as to the total across the country of illegal migrants he could not 'guesstimate' even to the nearest hundred thousand (or should that be 'million'?)

Owen said in court that the current controls both on immigration and asylum could not cope, and that: 'it was accepted by [the Government] that the true figure of immigration was considerably higher than the official figure', and that the variety of routes into Britain were 'unbelievable'. Many simply arrive without documents:

> we have no serious removal arrangements whereby we can remove a person back to China without documentation. They have to be interviewed by the Chinese consul to establish they are Chinese, and nine times out of ten the embassy does not have the staff.

However, instead of simply turning up (and claiming asylum), most Chinese are brought here clandestinely by the Snakehead gangs. But rather than being smuggled through customs hidden in lorries, a much cheaper method tends now to be used: the gangs supply fake education documents so that the illegals can simply pose as students.

Now I seem to remember raising this. It definitely rings a bell. In fact I reckon I must have processed some of them.

Chapter 12 — Analysis

Scrapping Asylum

Asylum and immigration often get confused, and not only by the media. The Government has often complained that commentators mix them up, but it has on occasion confounded the confusion by undermining immigration procedures in order to try to meet Tony Blair's promise to halve asylum figures. Immigration Service staff were instructed not to carry out operations against illegal migrants (few such operations that there are) unless certain that they were failed asylum seekers. This was because failed asylum seekers could be 'removed'/ deported whereas those who had not already claimed asylum could then do so to prevent such action against them. Clearly, this would push asylum figures in the opposite direction away from the magic figure Blair was committed to achieving. This seems to be what went on with the illegal migrant cockle-pickers in Morecambe Bay. The local Labour MP, Geraldine Smith, complained that when she first alerted the Immigration Service nobody was sent; it was up to the police. Only when the deaths of several of the migrants made headline news did the Home Office finally act, but even then lamely — a few migrants were simply told to turn up at Immigration Service offices in Liverpool and then failed to do so. But it seems that inaction was the rule long before Blair's target. Harriet Sergeant noted (in *Welcome to the Asylum*, 2001): 'The Immigration Service discourages requests to come out and collect asylum seekers.' In any case: 'Charges of racism make the 'speculative raid' out of the question.' Meanwhile, the Sunday Telegraph claimed, Blair made deals with the Romanian Prime Minister that he would relax immigration procedures if in return Romania helped to curb their nationals' asylum applications to Britain. Whether this story about a deal is true and if it is whether it had any import, is debatable; but the story of the pulling of operations has been verified and is one of the most despicable aspects of the Government's appalling behaviour in the great immigration cover-up.

Rarely has government been caught fiddling the figures so brazenly and at such disregard for the costs to the country. The National Audit Office can verify the asylum figures (as it did, though only partly, in May 2004: see below) but cannot get round how the Government behaved in achieving them. However, even if you accept that the annual asylum figures really have halved and that those who would previously have claimed asylum have not come in by other immigration routes; that still leaves several tens of thousands of new entrants even in the very year that Blair focused his efforts. And that does not include those who have entered illegally or overstayed and not declared themselves, who may subsequently claim asylum if there are ever the staff and the political will to go out and try to find and 'remove'/deport them.

Of course, it would be a political problem both domestically and internationally if the UK made a decision to stop accepting people who have genuine claims to have been persecuted, but when asylum cases are processed through the courts it is found that well under 10 percent are genuine, with well over 90 percent being in reality cases of economic migration. It has been routine for some time that very many asylum claimants destroy their passports in-flight; either to then pretend to be from a different nation (where widespread human rights abuses are acknowledged in Britain) or because their government is known not to accept back anyone without documentation. Sergeant quotes a Pakistani lawyer's description of the documents supplied by many of those who come to him for help as 'blatant and endless fraud'. The IND's idea of proof of persecution, which they ask of refugees, is a newspaper article where they are personally cited. 'If you pay money to a Pakistani newspaper', the lawyer explained, 'you can get anything made up … I don't accept it as evidence so why does the Home Office?'

The 1951 Geneva Convention on Refugees (the international agreement on asylum), as implemented in Britain, is far more abused than it is used. This is compounded by a failure to 'remove'/deport those who do not succeed in their claims, an endless appeals process and the application of human rights legislation that the Government has imposed courtesy of the EU. Then there is the bizarre situation that we still accord people asylum status when the situation in their home countries has entirely changed and there is no reason why they cannot return. Not least important are the serious health conditions, such as HIV/AIDS, that also give entitlement to asylum (see Chapter 14). This makes asylum a promising route for anyone to try to gain settlement, so serving to attract still more applications. As in other countries, every so often an amnesty is declared for those who have had their asylum applications refused but then do not leave. This too feeds back to encourage a still higher rate of people willing to take the chance of arriving, claiming asylum and simply lying low for a while.

Even with just the genuine applicants there are serious questions as to whether the asylum agreement makes any sense. The 1951 Convention was entered into because of concern for those fleeing the Soviet Eastern block over the Berlin Wall. The numbers concerned were a tiny trickle and receiving them into the West had propaganda value to boot. Those that were dissidents had little chance of being able to make any sort of political impact in their home countries because of the heavy and all-pervading suppression of freedom of thought. These people had intelligence value for the MoD in a time of dangerous nuclear stand-off. With so very few asylum seekers and of such value, not many taxpayers would have objected to giving each one a mansion and expense account.

A more different world situation it would be hard to envisage than the one we face in the early twenty-first century. Now there are all kinds of places that are major sources of asylum seekers, all or most of them very poor — indicating that economic rather than oppressive factors are likely to be the key — and with African states topping the list. Most of these countries are amenable to change if only their dissident elements and middle classes remain. But many despots are wise to this, having seen examples such as Castro's Cuba. Instead of having to deal with dissidents, Castro allowed them to move to Florida from where they could do nothing apart from helping to keep pressure on the USA not to drop its Cuba boycott. They were powerless to try to effect change from within Cuba itself.

If a tyrant in, say, a sub-Saharan African state has what he sees as the problem of a recalcitrant area or tribal element within his country, then he has an option other than initiating costly civil war. Civil war would risk trade sanctions if not a blockade or even invasion from those with interests in the area or with a duty to act as international or regional policeman; not to mention the severe wrath of neighbouring countries flooded with refugees. Instead, our tyrant can now crack down in a very limited way, either economically or militarily, or with secret police, to make life so uncomfortable, or so unsafe, that a large portion of the supposedly troublesome population will of its own accord take advantage of the international treaty on asylum and leave the country. If people take this decision then all that can afford to do otherwise are not likely to move somewhere that is poor, where they will be an unwelcome burden and unable easily to make a life for themselves. They will eschew nearby countries (ignoring the widely-flouted rule that you should seek asylum in the first country you arrive in) and move to the West; and more than likely to Britain, because this is the one place that is easy to enter and remain in and has relatively large populations of similar nationality as enclaves in which new entrants can be swallowed; as well as the attraction of the international language of English.

But quite apart from the undesirability of the numbers involved, the 1951 Convention puts us in moral jeopardy, because without the agreement there would be less incentive for despots to so mistreat their countrymen. If the option of relatively minor provocation to provoke an exodus is not available, then our tyrant would have to contemplate the risk of civil war, and this would probably dissuade him from making any move. It may convince him that he has to reach some compromise, a political solution.

Admittedly it's hard to point to instances of conflicts where this rationale can be seen to have been a definite factor. We cannot easily get inside the mind of a dictator or to see the workings of the top echelon of a corrupt and secretive regime, so it would be hard to find what influenced the decision to oppress minorities rather than to accommodate them. Even so, the point would still be that the moral jeopardy is there and may play a part in precipitating man-made political famine, or localized genocide, or the jailing and torturing of many people.

The resulting wave of asylum seekers would be a humanitarian disaster, in that large numbers of people would be displaced from what they know as home, where live the people they know and grew up with, to come to a place they perceive as alien that they may have extreme difficulty in coming to terms with. There would be the strain of splitting relationships with all those left behind and obviously this would have a profound impact both on these entrants to Britain and on those left in the home country. Furthermore, if the wave of those seeking asylum are the leading people in the country or area from whence they came, then this may act to encourage the tyrannical author of the mess so far, to go the whole hog for a 'final solution', as it were.

Asylum is not the simple humanitarian policy that it first appears to be. It produces its own leverage on situations that can be envisaged as leading to anything but humanitarian outcomes. Added to the massive scale of abuse by those who avail themselves of it, then there are undeniable reasons why the treaty on asylum as we know it should be torn up and everyone sent back to start thinking again from scratch about what to do. The answer may be a much enhanced United Nations with teeth — though that is unlikely ever to emerge. We need some form of effective fluid global army that can threaten to intervene in the affairs of those states posing a serious threat to stability through warfare and displaced people. Assuming the UN would never agree to put up an offensive army, then given also that the USA has got colder feet, an international policeman would have to be a consortium of those within the UN who wished to go further than the minimal agreements that are all that the UN can muster. A two-tier UN, if you like. Unfortunately this too appears a long way off. What may eventually emerge is an acceptance of intervention by states in the same region, neighbours especially, with an interest in stemming the flow of refugees across their own borders. Since such countries are likely to be the more powerful economically in the region — attractive to refugees — they are likely to have commensurate military muscle with which to successfully intervene and dissuade escalation of internal conflict.

Asylum, as with migration, is a problem that has to be tackled at source. Helping people to feel safe and economically at least subsistent, if not with real prospects, in their own home countries is the way to a happier world for us all. This is the logic we should apply and it demands a radical reappraisal of asylum policy.

The resentment the public feels towards asylum seekers is, of course, a major political problem in itself, albeit that public concerns may be exaggerated. The exaggerations though are only in respect of the supposed pervasive criminal behaviour of asylum seekers — though there are no figures to disprove public perception — not in respect of their numbers or their cost to the taxpayer. Asylum seekers are not officially allowed to work, for the good reason that this would further encourage this route for economic migration. But asylum seekers, by being paid benefits instead — and as of right with no conditions — cannot other than lead to resentment from the public, who are obliged to work and can receive benefits only by showing that they are unable to work and then only if they pass means tests. It is usually made out that the public's attitude to asylum seekers is a xenophobia that gets it wrong on all counts, but this is not true.

* * *

Even if Blair's figures were correct, that the number of asylum claims had fallen to 40,000 a year; the annual figure is a small part of the problem because of the vast numbers in total through year-on- year compounding. Over the last decade, of the many hundreds of thousands of asylum seekers, 88 percent were either granted residence or were refused and are now unaccounted for and presumed to be still here. Less than 10 percent were granted asylum, another 17 percent the authorities were not so sure about were given Exceptional Leave to Remain — another category which is tantamount to a gateway to settlement — and a mere 12 percent were 'removed'. But note: 'removal' is not the same as deportation (see Introduction, above). So many of even this small proportion could easily have returned. The rest just disappeared: presumably into inner-city anonymity, or enclaves of fellow nationals, or to far-flung places to take up unregulated employment. So for the great majority whose applications fail, no 'removal' action is taken against them, let alone deportation. Targets in this regard are meaningless: Peter Tomkins, a former chief of the Immigration Service, no less, described them as 'picking figures out of the air'. This is a telegram to everybody in the Third World that Britain is the place to come to claim asylum, either 'legitimately' or as a cover for economic migration.

The total number of those who have come in claiming asylum currently living in Britain must be colossal, because before the almost certainly doctored figure of a halving of asylum applications for this last financial year, the numbers simply disappearing amounted to 50–60,000 annually. Well over 25,000 in addition to this figure were granted either asylum or ELR. That makes roughly 80,000 a year, each year, which is pushing a million in a decade — and may well be more given that 125,000 arrived in the year 2000 alone. The impact such a figure has on housing alone is massive, especially considering that most are in London and the South-East where the housing problem is much more serious than elsewhere. There is no way of knowing how many of these who are not receiving payments as asylum seekers or successful asylum/ ELR claimants are illegally in receipt of benefits. There is no way of knowing how many of these are working legally with a national insurance number, or working in the black economy and so not contributing taxes. Either way this puts others out of work and forces down their wages, in just the same way that the work activities of legals and fraudsters in the normal immigration categories do. It is hard to exaggerate the problem. Eventually, as with the immigration fiasco, government will have no choice but to sort it out. On present indications, as with immigration, the current Government shows every intention of leaving the asylum fiasco up to the next one.

* * *

In the wake of the immigration furore, in April 2004 the Government asked the National Audit Office to look into the question of whether the asylum statistics were reliable and if the fall in asylum claimants had been offset by a rise in other forms of migration. Tucked away on page ten of the report's summary, it is stated that:

> There are neither data sources nor estimates of the number of people living illegally in the UK. It was therefore not possible to assess whether some people have decided not to claim asylum but have entered, or stayed in the country, illegally.

Of course, this should have been the very first paragraph of the report — the 'key conclusion' — because it sets the parameters and completely undermines what the report otherwise appears to be claiming. Instead, the 'key conclusion' we are given is that:

> There is no clear statistical evidence that the reduction in the number of asylum applications has had any significant impact on other forms of migration.

But this is not at all to say that people have not indeed switched from claiming asylum to some other immigration routes. The report's 'key conclusion' section ends:

> Further research might usefully be carried out to compare asylum flows with the combined statistics for all routes of entry and by nationality. This would allow a broader picture to be obtained of any relationships that might exist between asylum and other forms of migration, rather than one based only on individual routes.

There are elementary mistakes in methodology that any statistical dunce would spot. This so-called research merely takes specific migration routes in turn — for instance, student or ECAA applications — to see if numbers in any single category had shot up suspiciously, in line with falls in asylum claimant numbers. When this is not spotted, the report makes the illogical inference that the two figures cannot be related! But what if numbers in categories had previously crested and the trend was downward, but this fall had been braked by the addition of numbers of otherwise would-be asylum claimants? This is especially likely for ECAA claimants, because the figures would be expected to fall with Mayday only a few months away. And what if would-be asylum seekers had distributed themselves across a number of different avenues? The report is facile and quite obviously a Government fiction designed to hoodwink gullible and lazy journalists and those friendly to the Government line.

Things get much worse for the Government in the report's 'key findings'. The very first is that:

> Where illegal immigrants are arrested and then not detained in police cells or immigration removal centres, they may be referred by the police or some enforcement offices to the nearest Home Office unit where they may make their application for asylum. There is a risk that some of these illegal immigrants do not present themselves at any of the Home Office units, do not make an application and disappear once more from view. The Home Office did not have procedures to check that all people so referred subsequently made an asylum application.

In other words, the Government would rather have these people disappear into the country as illegal immigrants than to become part of the asylum statistics. Well of course they would, just as they would rather have illegal workers unmolested by police and the Immigration Service, because when arrested they are likely to claim asylum and push the asylum figures up in that way. Both of these ruses constitute systematically applied negligence in the Government's political self-interest and are seriously against the national interest.

There are a list of problems with the Home Office data. 'The Home Office's presentation of the statistics is, in our view, materially misleading.' Only those asylum seekers eligible for National Asylum Support Service subsistence payments are counted; those ineligible number some 24,000 and these are recorded separately. These, including 7,000 unaccompanied children, are supported by local councils, bar a thousand who get help from the DWP (Department of Work & Pensions). To get the true figure you have to add this second figure to the Home Office's total of 76,245. This adds up to over 100,000. A large figure and a large cost to the taxpayer to be sure. Even so, it is but a fraction of the total of those who have failed in their asylum claims but remain here anyway, so the real question that needs answering concerns removals: of the many hundreds of thousands of failed asylum seekers, is the Government making any headway at all in deporting or even 'removing' them? This question was not looked into by the National Audit Office, but on the same day that the NAO's report came out, the Home Office released figures for the first quarter of 2004 showing a 27 percent increase in removals over the same period in the previous year to 3,320. This is, of course, from a very low base. So current removal rates are just over a thousand a month — assuming the figures are reliable, which the NAO casts some doubt on, given a percentage where 'removal'/ deportation could not be verified and the small and possibly highly unrepresentative sample used.

Now, even with Blair's much trumpeted reduction, the current inflow of those seeking asylum is still several times higher than the removal rate, albeit that the figures for the first quarter showed a fall from the previous quarter (10,585, down from 13,150). So the many hundreds of thousands of people who have come in over the past decade as asylum seekers and who are, we presume, still here are in fact still swelling by thousands every month. What's more, any increase in the rate of 'removal'/deportation is slowing to almost nothing: there was just a 1 percent increase over January, February and March 2004. In the most favourable light — not looking into illegal entrants or overstayers, nor expanded substitute legal migration helped by lax or non-existent procedures — the problem is not only not going away, it is still getting worse. The only consolation is that the speed at which it is getting worse is not accelerating.

* * *

Unfortunately for the Government, impossibly bad stories just keep coming. How about this one, in June 2004, for a gem? A Zimbabwean named Stalin Mau Mau was, along with hundreds or thousands of prominent members of Robert Mugabe's racist Zanu-PF party, actually granted UK asylum. The story gets even better: Mr Mau Mau and the rest allegedly did it by posing as members of the Zimbabwean opposition, the Movement for Democratic Change (MDC), whose members are the chief victims of Mugabe's thugs; and the organization that got them fake Home Office asylum grant letters and National Insurance numbers was formed in 2003 with £5,000 of lottery money! Members of the Mugabe government and senior members of Zanu-PF are supposed to be banned from entering the whole of the EU, let alone from the UK.

What is also surprising is that the scam was uncovered by the BBC: journalists from Radio 5 Live. They posed as would-be bogus asylum seekers and went to Birmingham to see Albert Matapo, the chairman of the group, Zimbabwean Community UK, and took along a tape recorder. Matapo's wife Grace demanded over £1,000 up front and her husband boasted about getting into Britain the adult children of several members of Mugabe's Cabinet simply by coaching them to say they were MDC members. Matapo had more than a thousand clients according to the ZCUK's ledger book. On the tape (several hours of it), Matapo is obligingly frank:

> For the purpose of winning, we advise you to tell the white man that you are a member of the MDC. How can you tell the white man that you are Zanu-PF when you want to stay in this country? We will teach you the one, two, threes of the MDC so that when you are asked who the president is you can immediately say Morgan Tsvangirai. But we are not teaching you to be an MDC supporter. Do you get what I am saying? So when we start talking about politics, don't assume that we want you to be in politics. All we are telling you is what the white man will ask you; what he wants to hear.

Rather miffed by this is Washington Ali, the top man in the MDC here in Britain, who is astounded that the UK is allowing the corruption, fraud and racism of Zanu-PF to become established here, while some of his own members he claims are genuine asylum seekers are being refused. Perhaps the Government might reflect that it is not very useful for anybody's community relations to have many members of both of two violently opposed factions all together in London. Mr Ali will have much stronger words to say than that in private. The idea of asylum is just what the word says: a refuge. The idea is not to create the same conditions ripe for oppression and murder in the very place that is supposed to be a safe haven.

There is much other evidence that large numbers of prominent Zanu-PF members — including, early in 2004, the bankers behind Zanu-PF's finances — have fled to Britain in the wake of the famine and ruined economy of Zimbabwe caused by the anti-white racist land reform policies of the very organization of which they are key members. They have plenty of their fellow countrymen to hide amongst: there is the staggering figure of well over one million Zimbabwean nationals living in Britain today. Such a colossal number from just one African country must reflect economic migration and bogus applications — certainly I processed considerable numbers of suspect student applications when I was at Managed Migration.

Stalin Mau Mau runs a supermarket in Leigh-on-Sea, but Harare residents will recall his election slogan 'down with the whites!' and his leadership of a gang that forced white farmers from their lands. His party leader brands Britain 'a vicious, racist and vengeful country', and has driven a quarter of Zimbabwe's population abroad.

The story was in the news but not at the very top of the news, which is a measure of how we have all got so used to appalling stories coming out of the asylum system. It is just that nothing any more, no matter how lurid and farcical, is astonishing.

Minding My PMQs

'Black Wednesday' would be too strong a description; 'Hash Wednesday' you could call it: a tag to describe what happened after perhaps unwisely (as I thought at the time) I took part in a Conservative Party set-piece at the House of Commons. David Leppard had called me to say that Michael Howard was trying to get in touch. Did I want him to give the Tories my number? 'Fine', I said. I have never been a Tory supporter, mind you. I remember Howard in Thatcher days. An oleaginous figure. Dracula, I believe he is now referred to. The man with 'something of the night about him', as he was once famously described by a Cabinet colleague and who holds the record for not answering the question: Paxman's memorable Newsnight interview when he repeated the same question a dozen times and Howard still failed to answer (though actually he comes second to Harriet 'speaking clock' Harman). I never felt that he was genuine (though I'm sure there is a nice man there under the façade). On the other hand, I have never been virulently anti-Conservative.

Sure enough, I was phoned by one of Howard's staff to offer me a VIP chaperoned visit to Prime Minister's Question Time; the first one after the story broke. Leppard later said that he advised me against taking part, but my recollection is that he saw no obvious problem at the time. My thinking was that I would not get support from the Liberal Democrats — too 'head-in-the-sand' and politically correct (it pains me very much to say, as a one-time Lib Dem activist) on immigration — and given that the Government, obviously, would try to attack me, then the Conservatives were the only game in town. Go for it, I decided. 'Go for it' I went, but with a simple ploy to try to defuse any charge of political bias.

I rang my MP, the Liberal Democrat Richard Allan (Sheffield Hallam), to tout the idea that I would see Lib Dem spokesmen and cross the road from Portcullis House to the Commons (which I wrongly thought was all the public exposure outside the confines of Parliament I would be subjected to) with a Lib Dem in tow as well as the Tory Leader and/or the shadow Home Secretary, David Davis. I had been a principal helper in getting Richard elected and I knew him well enough to know he would help me, aside from repaying a favour. So it was that I met Mark Oaten, the Lib Dem Home Affairs guy, in the Portcullis House lobby. He asked me to brief him on events as he had been away in New York for several days. After twenty minutes or so he waltzed off to consult and then came back to say that although he himself would be happy to accompany me, it would be against Parliamentary protocol to pitch a tent on the Tory's lawn, as it were (or words to that effect). No mention of any policy disagreement, albeit that Richard Allan and myself agreed to dis-agree on Europe and on immigration policy when we met in his Portcullis House office shortly afterwards. I must admit that I have never researched what Lib Dem policy on immigration is, exactly, but I can't imagine it is less than liberal (obviously) and most likely oblivious to reality. With now no heavyweight Lib Dem (if there is such a thing) in tow, I started to get an uneasy feeling that I was about to tread too firmly on political turf for my own good health.

Meeting David Davis' aide, Tracey, she led me through the corri-dors to Howard and Davis. I had been reasonably impressed with Davis' performance on the immigration issue and told him so. I exchanged pleasantries with Howard, though meeting him in the flesh did not dispel my impression of him. This deteriorated when we walked on a pre-arranged circuitous route to the chamber, which took us on to the pavement in front of the Commons and he engaged me in a slow conversation on the issues with gestures to suit that were obviously intended for the cameras. It was a piece of acting, on which his attention was fixed to the detriment of the ostensible dis-cussion, that rather embarrassed me. Various press and TV cameras were lying in wait and I made a point of saying that I had never voted Conservative and was not about to start — I currently vote for no party, large or small, and I've only ever voted Liberal Democrat. That's safe ground for someone on the immigration issue, I thought. There are not many racist liberals, 'woolly' or otherwise.

We had agreed that I would not pose for any photos, but on the doorstep of the Commons I instinctively turned in sync with Howard and Davis and realised straightaway but too late. You can see me raising my hand and showing an 'I'm not a part of this!' expression in the photos that appeared in the papers. What the heck: this was a media event of mutual benefit, and it's not every day you get to be guest of honour at PMQs. Tracey took me up to the gallery. Various well-known people (well, at least one who I could name: Cecil Parkinson) graced the seating across the end of the chamber, from which you would have had a good side-on view of the despatch box exchanges. We were sat at right angles to this, overlooking Blair from well above and behind him, with a great view of his bald patch and not much else; from just about the same place as a few weeks later the Fathers4Justice 'bomber' scored a bulls-eye with a condom full of purple-dyed self-raising flour. Now that's what I call a publicity stunt. I would love to have done something similar but although this was certainly the place, for many reasons of course it was not the time. I can't say that the atmosphere caught me. I have seen PMQs so many times on TV and with speeches conveyed through microphones the occasion sound-wise was not markedly different from being perched in front of the TV at home; from where you had a view from a perfect angle in close-up. I suppose I felt a bit of distance from it. Embarrassment at being in some ways the lead player in a charade was one thing, but the cameras and press outside made it hard to reassure myself that I could hide my awkwardness.

Immigration was to be the focus of Howard's questioning. 'The one person who has behaved impeccably throughout this is the one person who is suspended', Howard slowly boomed. 'It so happens that Mr Moxon is here today', he went on. 'A Liberal Democrat', some of the Labour bank-benchers loudly muttered to remind him. 'Will the Prime Minister meet with us?' Of course he wouldn't, as we all knew he wouldn't, and the PM wasted no time in saying so. It was a rhetorical exchange that made me slightly uncomfortable again, though there was no sign of a cringe from anyone on the floor of the House. The Lib Dems looked fed up, as well they might. It was a set-piece all right, and rather than being any sort of protagonist I was like an ornamental gift on the sideboard that had to be on display so as not to offend whoever had given it.

More interesting was what followed. I was escorted by David Davis to a tea room where we had an illuminating chat about the ins and outs of strategy, what might happen to me, and what might happen to Beverley Hughes short of the unlikely outcome of her resigning. We met Jack Straw en route. I have witnessed before how politicians can be very friendly cross-party. The two clearly get on well. Then it was off to a private room to meet the Tory leader. I had decided to make the best of it and speak up for a few important things. I emphasized the breadth and depth of the failure of immi-

gration procedures and I went into some detail about specific problems at Managed Migration, but that it was not the fault of staff at
Sheffield; rather the politicians at the top who declined to face up to
the constraints of reality while saddling civil servants with the consequent problems. I pitched that jobs should be moved out of London wholesale to Sheffield, where the quality of recruits was far
higher despite lower pay, and overheads overall were a fraction; the
upshot being that even with a staff expansion, costs would fall and
performance would be much improved and a much needed major
contribution to the Sheffield economy would lead to additional sav-
ings by reducing unemployment.

A bit cheeky my next tack: I said that they (the Conservative Party)
should quit being scared of political correctness. 'Stop doing a
Portillo!', I admonished; fight the damn thing head-on. There was a
widening gap between ordinary people and those in control and the
parties were insufficiently distinct. You're not meant to be the Liberal Party, for God's sake. Labour are motivated at root by disdain
for people and the Lib Dems on the immigration issue as on other
areas of policy are nowhere. So Tories need not be frightened of
being seen as anything other than dead centre. Left–right is an out-
dated way of looking at politics anyhow.

I can't think that this could have been entirely novel thinking to
them, but I hope I put it across well.

Howard sat without much changing his expression. Slight amuse-
ment perhaps — or is that his more or less permanent supercilious
pulled face? Possibly the same kind of disdain for an ordinary chap
like me as I had just lambasted his opponents for. We all shook hands
and Tracey, with another sidekick, ushered me out on to College
Green, the favourite place for TV crews to collar hapless politicians,
or for spinning politicians to bamboozle hapless journalists. On this
day the hapless one happened to be me. I hadn't thought about the
media stuff that was lined up. First off was a BBC News24 crew. If I
recall correctly the interviewer was on a feed to my earpiece. First
question was about my ideas on fundamentalist Islam. On what? I
don't know much about Islamic fundamentalism, and — lacking any
media training — I said so. The thing was going out live. I was read a
few words that were an extract from a Panorama website posting I
had made, apparently. What on earth were they talking about? I was
still thinking aloud instead of dismissing an irrelevance in favour of
a substantive question. Do you advocate the use of nuclear weapons
against Muslims? Do I WHAT?! Time was moving at two different

speeds in my head as I was racking my brains to know what was going on while at the same time trying to take part in an interview. There must be a context to explain it, I said, but I was at a loss to know what it was and nobody was showing me the text. All I needed to say was that I had no such views and ask for a question on the issue at hand. But I didn't. The damage was done. Sound clips went out on the Radio 4 PM programme, and video on TV channels. Cheap journalism. The other TV crews picked up on this new twist of the clearly mad whistle-blower, including Libby Wiener from ITN. 'You're very good at it', she said, referring to my appearances. I pondered: what is she going to try to trap me with? I told her I had seen her once: at a Lib Dem conference in Glasgow. She was chewing gum vigorously the whole time, looking pretty bored. (Subtext: I know you're not all sweetness and light.) I almost declined the interview because of sheer tiredness (through getting up very early for the train) but reluctantly gave in and then perked up and actually enjoyed it. Was any of it used? I never got to see the evening bulletins to check. That's one trouble of being in the thick of the news. You don't get to see the news yourself, so you have no idea how you came across or what angle the media are taking on the story.

I knew it was not a positive one, judging from the constant calls I was getting on my mobile phone back at the Sunday Times building in Wapping where I had gone to work with David Leppard on the second Sunday's story. I kept repeating that I was very tired, that I had not seen the website posting to know what the context was and I couldn't recall writing it. Leppard was somewhat irritated by me. I was being more of a distraction than a help. The mixture of tiredness and confused shock was not a little upsetting. The Lib Dems, I heard, were now saying that they had never met me, that they had refused to meet me because of my extreme views! Is this the party I had campaigned for all those years and had stood for as a candidate alongside a Muslim running mate in a heavily Muslim ward? I was no longer even a member, but I was tribally Lib Dem; I wouldn't vote for anybody else even though I no longer felt able to vote for them. This made me fully realize that the three-day media scrum since the story first broke had graduated from honeymoon to serious row. I felt physically unwell; gut wrenched, literally. It felt strangely not too unlike when there's a girl you really really like, and you know you've not much hope, but simple hope makes your chances feel even; and then she tells you nicely but straight. Leppard kept telling me to ignore it all. He was teasing out of me a few clarifications of detail in my original submission for the following Sunday's pieces on abuse of procedures in marriage and student cases. I was still composed enough to see how a journalist worked to make something as clear as possible, rather than artfully well-written. Ideas and actual phrases were repeated and progressively expanded to always ensure a reader could follow the thread with little effort and that the precise meaning and nothing else was being conveyed. Not like creative writing at all.

Later we went on-line to find this dread web posting. It was fairly lengthy. I still couldn't recall writing it, yet it seemed obvious that it must have been from me. 'It's bollocks': Leppard's summary dismissal of the piece as having no merit worth discussing was almost reassurance. He began to laugh. 'It stuffed Michael Howard's little set-piece, didn't it!' Given that the Tories were the only party on my side I couldn't quite see how this could be a consolation. I imagined how they might well be a bit miffed. He could see I was shook up, so he invited me for drinks with some friends, including the paper's news supremo, Mark Skipworth. These people, at least, did not see me as a weirdo with a 'towel-head' phobia — and please note the inverted commas indicating my distancing from the colloquialism. It snapped me out of it for a while. Then I had to go to the hotel the BBC had provided so as to be in London for the Daily Politics show in the morning. I phoned a friend for a long chat. The calming effect was short-lived, and I relied on sleep to dispel despondency.

I walked to Millbank well ahead of when I needed to be at the BBC studio there and strolled on the riverfront. I took a call from someone on the Daily Politics show staff. A long quiz about the infamous web posting. What could this possibly have to do with 'whistle-blowing'? That was the item on the programme for which I was to guest. I had had time to think and I was now able to defend myself. The quote is taken out of context. It is absurd to say that I have a view of advocating nuclear weapons against Muslims. The text makes it clear that I was writing about a possible future scenario, decades hence, a future involving a far from improbable Wahhabi sect take-over of oil- and nuclear weapons-rich Middle-East states, leading to a similar situation to the Cold War nuclear stand-off. Moreover I was referring to a specific sect and not to Muslim fundamentalists generically. I was *describing*, not advocating.

McCarthy-era trials came to my mind of novelists who were interrogated for supposedly holding the views expressed by characters in their books! On that basis, Agatha Christie must have been a serial murderess. Beverley Hughes had already owned up to the truth of my disclosure, so anything about me was irrelevant to the story. Having a go at me at all, let alone a smear, was just bad journalism. How does the media expect 'whistle-blowers' to come forward if they are treated like this? After a conversation that went in a circle, the woman from The Daily Politics told me that I would not now be required as the show had been re-organized. 'You mean you don't want me because of this e-mail!', I caustically replied. No, she insisted, that was not the reason. Oh yes it bloody well was. Talk about 'pull the other one'. Sometimes women especially don't give up on the most obvious of lies, as if sheer persistence could bluff.

I was angry now, more than I was upset. I had arranged to meet Leppard again to work some more on the second instalment of my tale-telling about the Home Office. I arrived and although I managed not to irritate Leppard as much as the night before, he was concerned. I'm sure he was not so bothered about me as about the security of the next Sunday's story. He suggested I stay in a nearby hotel for a night or two. He didn't really say why. While I recovered from the ordeal and where I could easily meet with him to work on the story? Or where he could keep tabs on me to make sure I did not go off the rails in some way and spill the beans and torpedo his upcoming front page? In the hotel I was away from my home landline, contactable only through my mobile phone. Even more importantly, I could not be doorstepped.

Either way I was happy to follow his advice. My room at the Tower Thistle was right by Tower Bridge and just about the nearest hotel room in all London to Traitor's Gate! How marvellously apt. The hotel was out of my price range but paid for by the newspaper — I was allowed under the 'whistle-blower's Act' to receive expenses, after all. I woke up not feeling too bad but much more isolated, with all of the fun aspect of what was going on completely lost. I consoled myself with a very large breakfast and ploughed through the papers. When I found out that a glass of wine from the hotel bar cost a fiver, I ventured out in search of a bottle. I was not going to abuse the Sunday Times' hospitality. I walked around the Wapping marinas a little but mostly read newspapers. Coverage was not a disaster, save for a page three story in the Independent. The Mirror, I learned later, had done a tabloid version of the Independent's line, but who believed anything Piers Morgan's boys' publish? Not after the obviously faked Iraqi prisoner abuse photos he stupidly published a few weeks later and that led to his eventual sacking. It is a red top after all: the one New Labour paper (except on Iraq). I rang Tracey. Yes, the Conservatives were miffed. Well they shouldn't have set up TV interviews then, should they?

I whiled away three days, occasionally meeting David, taking phone calls from him to clarify this or that detail; ringing people back home, getting back on an even keel. This was helped enormously by that week's BBC1 Question Time show. The hapless Beverley Hughes had been booked on to the famous panel on the Thursday after the story broke. She could hardly cry off such a highly public prior engagement, when the questions to be asked inevitably would be about her. She was announced by Dimbleby as 'the minister for immigration, asylum and counter-terrorism'. I had never heard her full title before. A dustbin of the three areas of government any sensible career-minded politician would run a very fast mile from.

She did very well in answering the first two questions thrown at the panel. The third question was the one that everyone had to expect: 'Has the Government lost control of immigration?' Theresa May said that it had, as obviously she was bound to say, being a principal opposition spokesman. She was scathing about Hughes, who she thought should resign. The one person who had stood up to tell the truth — she emphatically intoned and bore into Hughes — was the one person who was suspended. Very loud audience applause.

Dimbleby brought a couple of the audience members in. One man admonished: 'there was no problem bringing talented people into the country', but 'the Government has completely lost control of immigration into this country'. Then a woman, who declared herself an immigrant who had lived here for 15 years, contributed: 'I really do think there is a need for planned immigration in this country … to be absolutely up front' about it.

The two 'liberally minded' panelists aired their prejudices next. Alain de Botton, a philosopher and son of immigrants, called the furore 'overdone and unnecessary'; while the splendidly named Lord Razzle (a Lib Dem) got the prize for the biggest yawn as he complained of a story whipped up by the popular, right-wing press. So far so very predictable. Then came the Independent's trenchant columnist, Bruce Anderson, to really 'tell it like it is':

> Let's remind ourselves what we're being asked to believe. We're being asked to believe that civil servants decided off their own bat to change policy in a very basic way to let through thousands of people; that had they got away with that, it would have saved ministers from embarrassment. So we have to assume that civil servants decided to introduce a

new policy bending all the rules, possibly even breaking the law, in order to save the Government from embarrassment; and ministers knew nothing about this.

Anderson went on to cite the Government's highly contrasting 'insistence on chains of responsibility' re corporate management:

> If the ministers did know, it's scandalous; if the ministers didn't know, it's scandalous: because they are not running their department even in the most basic way. If you were a private sector manager, Beverley, you would go. I'm afraid, I think, if you've got any political self-respect you would resign.

Our Beverley was neither crying nor indignant with rage. A cool customer. 'I have had better weeks in politics, I have to say … I have never ducked an issue of responsibility in my life', she said, and proceeded straightway to break what she would have us believe is her habit of a lifetime. 'A team in Sheffield had changed procedure without telling their managers'. Now this was illuminating. Here she was placing the blame at the level of a team — the ECCA team at Sheffield — which is the most basic admin unit. This is below any line manager. She may even mean that it is down to the senior caseworker on that team: the team leader being on the operations side of things. Anybody at Sheffield knows this cannot be right. All of the managers at Sheffield were fully aware of the clearance exercises. She was going to have to retreat a long way from this position.

'Steve Moxon has been suspended', Dimbleby interjected. 'Why haven't the civil servants for whom you're responsible beneath you, who he said did this — why haven't they been suspended too?' 'I can't intervene in any way whatsoever with personnel matters', Hughes replied, 'That is how it has to be. People are shaking their heads [she was referring to the audience.] It is not right for ministers to take on personnel issues. If we were to be accused of interfering with the independence of the civil service on these matters we would rightly be accused of behaving wrongly. We are not allowed as elected representatives to make those personnel decisions. I must not have anything to do with that. It would be quite wrong.'

This was something else she was to completely contradict, in her answer to a question in the Commons only a few days later, when she claimed that I was 'not worthy' to have 'got through' recruitment to the Home Office.

A woman in the audience was brought in by Dimbleby: 'I agree you should resign … If you don't know what's going on; what else don't you know what's going on?' A man followed up:

How many people need to slip into this country because immigration checks are not done properly, before we turn on the television set and see trains blown up in London. How many can slip through … because it's your watch [Indeed it was: 'Minister for immigration, asylum and counter-terrorism.] … and you haven't answered the question about the e-mail. The e-mail lay in your box for a month … If Theresa May had an e-mail from one of her schools unopened for a month, I would expect her to resign.

Audience members came thick and fast denouncing Hughes. 'The Government has 700,000 new civil servants. How on earth don't you know what's going on?', one man disingenuously pointed out. The inevitable then came. 'President Truman had a sign on his desk saying 'the buck stops here'. Where in Whitehall does it stop?' Two others tried to chip in but Dimbleby concluded that Hughes had been roasted sufficiently for one night and moved to the next question.

Even before the show had ended I was chatting with friends and my brother on the phone about the surreal experience of being the main subject of the BBC's main weekly discussion programme. Then I was somewhat deflated when Mark Mardell — the BBC's chief political correspondent, of all people — on the This Week programme that followed Question Time, briefly and misleadingly summed up the week, saying that I had 'a bit of a bee in my bonnet about immigration' and referred to the Panorama e-mail in terms of 'nuking Islamic fundamentalists'. This was going further than the misrepresentation of the previous day. Mardell had actually stated that I was against immigration. This was untrue at the time he said it and is only true today in a qualified sense (see below). At the time (before I did the research that would lead to this book) I was not even against *mass net* immigration in principle. I was not the most enthusiastic supporter of it in practice, clearly, but that was because of what I had experienced in working 'on the inside' and seeing the maladministration of the system. If you take way the qualification, 'mass', then I would not even now have any problem with net immigration. Mardell claims that I opposed, even then, *all* immigration. His untenable claim was that because I had commented on a group of Arab Muslims, then this somehow made me think that an influx of East European Christians must be illegal when it was not. Bizarre. What made this so glaring a piece of poor journalism was that it was a day later and part of a weekly news review slot. It was supposed to be a considered summation and could not be excused as a rush job to get out on a news bulletin.

* * *

On the Friday, after David had worked until nine on the story, he came across to meet me in the hotel bar. Big enveloping chairs and vast tables right over the Thames; big glasses of wine and Leppard with a cigar. He seemed to have decided that I could cope with an honest appraisal of my 'Hash Wednesday'. We were lucky this had not broken at the very start of the week, he explained; or the whole story might have 'died on its arse'. He means: would Beverley Hughes have bothered to come to the Commons to concede I was right? That serious? Jesus.

He had ideas about my 'future', which seemed to be to do with persuading Whitehall civil servants to become a whistleblowing fraternity. They were opening an office in the West End, a Sunday Times outpost, where I'd be based. I had no idea what to make of this. Whistle-blowers could become a club, then a not-so-exclusive one; before you know it, we might be two-a-penny and regarded like school playground tale-tellers. I would have to reflect on it, but this felt far too distant in time compared to matters at hand. Leppard reckoned I could be suspended indefinitely; people had been kept in limbo for years, he pointed out. I might have to resign. The Sunday Times might have to bring an action to force a hearing.

I was thinking about how I got on with … how could I describe his function here? … well, Leppard's my whistle, I suppose — but I will stop the metaphor there. Me and Leppard got on OK, but we both communicated to some extent in ways the other didn't quite catch. That's to be expected though; we had been thrown together without the preliminaries you would have in a friendship. I quite liked him, but though relaxed I felt at sea.

I needed a drink and thought it about time that I bought for a change. At the bar I was recognized by some Italian chap. 'Mr Moxon!?', he exclaimed as he enquired. I thought better of starting a discussion. He had an accent like in a 1960s spy movie and I was paranoid about his interest in me. The night was starting to get weird.

Leppard's piece was shaping up nicely. We knew we had another killer lead story, and my worries shifted to the possibility of some enormous news event coming along that could knock us off the front page. But nothing did. (There was the Madrid bombing, but that wouldn't stretch to still being a main story by Sunday.) I was still in London on the Saturday, late in the afternoon when the paper was 'put to bed'. Counting down the hours, I passed some time in the Museum of London and then walked to Wapping and read the papers in a nearby bar while Leppard was ready for me to land. My life had become too much one of waiting for things to happen — and more waiting to see what bad things anything that did happen then led to. Eventually I got through security and was decanted somewhere on the vast newsfloor. Then a pre-print of the front page and page two landed on the desk in front of me. 'Can you check this for any inaccuracies?' One or two minor errors, one of which was deemed worth the trouble of correcting. Now the story would have new legs. I was in the news again — for the right reasons.

Having been shifted to another hotel, round the other side of the Tower of London — not in sight of Traitor's Gate this time — I woke up with a copy of the Sunday Times outside my door. On the front page it was; and page two; and two full pages further inside. Beverley Hughes would be livid, and Tony Blair would be livid with her. Blunkett would be in the middle in a game of blind man's buff, if you will forgive the mere allusion to his disability. I tuned in to the Sunday breakfast news shows and, as before, ITV covered the stories and had it as lead or next-to-lead story on their teletext, but by contrast there was no mention on Ceefax and again the ever nauseatingly deferential David Frost failed to pick out the headline as he surveyed the press and neither did any of his sycophantic guests. A soft news programme if ever there was one. For the second week running no mention of easily the biggest news story of the day. Suppression of debate? What else could it be? Sunday morning and a nasty story about immigrants: not in front of the children, please. And that includes all of us big kids, and especially granddad who will probably remember he's a racist if given half a prod. But this had been the pattern a week before. Slow to pick up, the BBC were bound to run with it later and prominently so. Feeling I could fully cope with the world, I made my way to St Pancras to travel back home.

* * *

Out of hotel protective custody, as you could describe it, no sooner had I got home than I got wind of a further mean trick by my erstwhile party. Not only had the Lib Dems denied even meeting me, despite my briefing of their Home Affairs spokesman, Mark Oaten, in full public view in the Portcullis foyer, but Charles Kennedy was going to allude to me in his forthcoming keynote leader's rant at the Lib Dem spring conference the next day. He was going to take a pot shot at Michael Howard for his 'opportunism', and his supposedly hasty hijacking of me was to be mentioned as a case in point. Once again I was to be caught in party-political crossfire. I was to be cited on the understanding that I was a person with such inappropriate opinions that not even the Prince of Darkness should risk being seen with me after midnight strolling in the graveyard.

I rang a friend who used to run election campaigns for the Lib Dems, and he rang people he knew who were at the conference. It came back that clumsy researchers were to blame (not having looked beyond the Indie story), but senior party figures were surprisingly thin on the ground at the late night Glee Club (the usual evening event at a Lib Dem conference) so no message could be got through to amend the speech. I then left a message pointing out the misrepresentation on their chief press officer's phone. No reply. No reply next morning. The speech went ahead unchanged.

I would never vote for the Lib Dems in any election ever again. The irony of Charles Kennedy having a go at another leader for opportunism, when in the process he took a cheap swipe at someone with no political power whatsoever (and who had long been approved as a candidate to stand for Kennedy's own party, in Muslim areas), on the basis of sloppy research ... this wannabe statesman had the gall in the very same speech to talk about 'honest politics'. The speech was not much reported, but I would have to get an apology.

Time was part of the offence. The longer the delay before the issue of an apology, the greater the offence was compounded, but delay works wonders in terms of 'news value' to ensure that any retraction would get next to no coverage in the media. This is just how Kennedy's office played it. But they hadn't done yet. The Lib Dem MP Vincent Cable stood up in the House to ask a 'helpful' question of none other than Beverley Hughes, who was up for a grilling — apparently this was far from the liking of the Lib Dems, who fancied a spot of time-wasting to prevent the Tories from embarrassing Labour on immigration; a policy with which the Lib Dems were in sympathy, if not still more out-of-touch with the reality.

Cable distorted my supposed views beyond anything so far. Apparently *all* Muslims, not just all fundamentalists, were now in my sights. Bev replied that I was not 'worthy' to have 'got through' the recruitment procedure at the Home Office. The audacity made the Lib Dem shower appear positively snub-nosed in the face of the ministerial Pinnochio, who had already shown herself to have serially 'misled the Commons'. Of course, both Hughes and Cable were safe under the protection of Parliamentary privilege, so their comments could not land them in court.

Her timing, let alone content, was rather unfortunate. The next day the Independent printed the retraction I had asked for. Not just regarding 'nuking fundie Muslims', but on all the other erroneous points they had made, bar that the Lib Dems had lied about not meeting me. I don't suppose it was my threat of the Press Complaints Commission, but more a case of someone putting in a word on my behalf. You do not need me to tell you that the retraction was a far smaller piece than the offending story, but it was as much as you can expect, and the press-savvy among those who saw it told me that it was as complete a capitulation as they had ever seen.

This was what I needed to finally drag an apology out of Charles Kennedy. I rang Richard Allan, my (Lib Dem) MP, and he said that he agreed that it was a misrepresentation. He alerted me to his website where he defended me. I was not so sure about how he described the full text of the web posting: a 'rivers of blood' type of argument. I seem to recall that this was how Enoch Powell's famous speech was described! My ex-Lib Dem election whiz kid friend told me of a piece that had appeared in The Guardian by Jonathan Calder which really hit the nail on the head in my defence. I had all the ammunition I could possibly need and sent copies to Kennedy. His office finally got round to apologizing, admitting that they had relied on the Independent as the source. The wording was careful: the minimum they could possibly get away with. As with newspapers this was how complete apologies were turned out by people with good reason to fear litigation. A similarly-worded admission arrived from Vincent Cable.

I sent a letter to the Home Office, citing the apologies from the Independent, Kennedy and Cable, asking them whether it was Beverley Hughes as the minister, or the Home Office as the Civil Service who was actually in charge of recruitment. In either case I demanded an apology for the repeated misrepresentation. I pointed out that I could hardly expect a fair hearing at any investigation by the Home Office. Hughes had inadvertently played into my lap. I added that should any disciplinary process be used against me, then I would have grounds for appeal on the basis of this ministerial faux pas alone. I followed up with another letter but this too was made into a paper aeroplane and flung into some long Whitehall grass. The top man, John Gieve, was to reply. Sometime next year, I supposed.

In the middle of all this I had a phone call from David Davis, the shadow Home Secretary. I had heard contrasting reactions to my 'Hash Wednesday': that Davis was annoyed, but also that he was not concerned. However miffed the Conservatives may have been over the media ambush of their PMQs set-piece, the appearance of the second Sunday Times story and intimations that further revelations were afoot, rendered my 'Hash Wednesday' subject to the law that 'a week is a long time in politics'. It was now ancient history. Davis rang to discuss possible future developments and, I suspect, to fish for what else the Sunday Times had up its sleeve. Apparently his staff had done a check on me before inviting me to the Commons and had found nothing adverse of any kind. It was interesting, therefore, that a three-year-old web posting in my name had suddenly appeared out of the blue just as the hordes were digging around for some dirt on me. The 'fundy' smear was taking a new turn.

At the bottom of why he rang me was that he had some revelations of his own – though he did not give any detail. It was obvious that something big was in the offing. What he had, of course, was the evidence of James Cameron, the Romanian consul, who declared that what I had said was only 'the tip of the iceberg'. This made me the Golden Boy again, and would soon absolve the Conservatives of the 'opportunism' jibe.

* * *

Well, my 'Hash' or 'Black Wednesday' turned out to be less black than shiny grey. A cloud very much with a silver lining. Chains of events are curious. Can you point to a definite causal link, like a line of dominoes? Would James Cameron have come forward if I had not first come forward myself? He e-mailed David Davis to say that what he had highlighted (not me, you understand) about Sheffield caseworking was just 'the tip of the iceberg'. So would Cameron have sent his e-mail if I had not responded to Michael Howard's invitation to the House of Commons? In retrospect, what I regretted having agreed to do at the time could have been my smartest move. Championing by the Tories — David Davis repeatedly calling for my reinstatement — may have been crucial to establishing my credibility. Even before Cameron's, there was a leak, to the Sunday Times, bolstering my story. Again, the material was sent to where I had made an earlier revelation. More leaks followed Cameron's identification. He was the Romanian consul after all; a man whose job title carried some clout, rather than a common caseworker like me. He was the man on the ground, at the other end of the process from where I was. Not being in contact with each other, we were mutual independent corroborators.

Chapter 14 — Analysis

Health Tourism, Settled Disease

A collision of the issues of immigration and health must sound the loudest alarm bells in any government with political sense, but the current administration manages to continue to completely foul up even here, despite supposedly having taken action. As I will explain, this is no remedy, and further half-hearted measures planned for the near future will prove just as ineffective; quite apart from the NHS being unmanageable in its current form. The problems have been exposed by Harriet Sergeant in her hard-hitting books, *Managing Not to Manage* and *No System to Abuse: Immigration and Health Care in the UK*:

> The Home Office and the Department of Health have ducked the issue. We lack an effective immigration policy and the result is seen every day in the A&E departments and on the hospital wards of our inner cities. We lack an effective method of checking entitlement to the NHS then wonder at its abuse. The Government threatens NHS staff who complain publicly with the loss of their job and everyone else with the stigma of racism. … We are finding it difficult enough to fund a National Health Service. Can we really afford an International Health Service? At present, little stops the one turning into the other.

Immigration causes major problems in the NHS on two fronts: the wholesale abuse by overseas visitors, and the unchecked permanent migration to the UK of those with serious health conditions; notably HIV, tuberculosis and hepatitis B. These diseases must be singled out because they are transmissible, intractable and, through their already high incidence compounded by accelerating spread, have become the most serious health problems in the very areas from which the UK receives most immigrants and most of those seeking settlement: sub-Saharan Africa, the Indian subcontinent and Eastern Europe. Alarming figures published in July 2004 show that in the aforesaid regions, those actually diagnosed as HIV+ number respectively: 25 million, 5–6 million, and almost 1.5 million. Furthermore, these are the very regions where AIDS diagnoses are most rapidly increasing, with new alarms for India and Eastern Europe that they are in the early stages of a pandemic set to be even more serious than the more established disaster in Africa. Estonia, one of the newly-acceded EU states, already has an HIV infection rate of 1 in every 100 persons. The country where the situation is worsening fastest of all is Russia, which is now only one very porous EU border away. Even the normally ultra tight-lipped Chinese premier has now admitted his country is being devastated by AIDS.

The great majority of HIV patients in Britain are not gay men, nor all of the people taken together who have contracted the virus through transmission on these shores, but recent heterosexual immigrants from Africa: 95 percent according to one estimate. A staggering 95 percent of all new hepatitis B cases and 60 percent of all tuberculosis patients are from abroad. TB is now more prevalent in London than in any other European capital, having doubled in little more than a decade, with some boroughs sustaining an incidence higher than in even the worst TB blackspot countries in the world. An increasing proportion of cases are multi-drug resistant, requiring up to two years to treat — it is difficult enough to ensure that patients see out their antibiotic courses for the six months plus it takes to treat ordinary TB, so MDR-TB will spread through the population even faster than TB is doing.

This is despite what is supposed to be checking at points of entry with x-ray machines, TB status forms and documents. But relying on spotting people who look sick is almost useless. There are only two x-ray machines in the whole country at entry points (at one of Heathrow's four terminals, and at Gatwick); where there are any there are not the staff, and when there is an officer available the process is usually held to be too time-consuming to bother with. TB forms carry a code which many find out and simply change to incorrectly show they are free of the disease; many Indians with what appear to be excellent medical references turn out to be infected; and where time-pressed staff ask for a contact address it has become almost the norm that letters are returned marked 'unknown'. People turning up with chest x-rays are let through on the presumption that they are actually theirs and not someone else's, and local health authorities don't follow up new arrivals because they wrongly assume they have been checked at the port/airport. There is no entry control on TB worth the name.

HIV, hepatitis B and tuberculosis are not even the most visible part of the costly iceberg. Many maternity cases are fly-by-nights from abroad, and one of the biggest sources of abuse: it is claimed by some psychiatrists that there are as many patients with acute mental illness ineligible for treatment because of their immigration status as there are those who are bona fide. Malaria is a long-term debilitating disease that is prevalent in the UK mainly through immigration rather than by travellers bringing it back from holiday.

The reason for these astounding realities is one of the greatest immigration and asylum abuses of all: *anyone who claims that they have a condition which cannot be treated in their home country must be allowed to stay in Britain to receive free treatment.* This confers an automatic right to UK asylum for any and every HIV sufferer from anywhere in the world, ditto insanity, courtesy of our signing up to international Human Rights legislation — or rather our strict interpretation of it and the almost unique British penchant for actually abiding by unwelcome and unreasonable law in practice. Precisely by virtue of their expense, it is of course the more costly treatments that are unavailable in poor countries, though arguments can be made that a vast range of diagnoses are inadequately dealt with by anything other than a health service of the standard to be found only in the developed world. In any case, all viral hepatitis and tuberculosis (and malaria and many other conditions) are illnesses that are deemed exempt from NHS charges for anyone, regardless of their immigration status — even if they are illegal economic migrants. This is a classic case of jeopardy: treating all-comers in the name of protecting the community from disease spread (and humanitarian concern) encourages others to travel here in large numbers for treatment, which thereby causes more disease spread than simply refusing treatment to all non-citizens; more than defeating the original objective.

The greatest threat to Britain is HIV because of all the virulent diseases we are now importing, as we know, HIV-AIDS is the most intractable. The epidemic is somewhat hidden by the effectiveness of drug cocktails in delaying the onset of AIDS, but delay is all that the treatment achieves, and a protracted multi-drug therapy is hugely expensive. What is more, during this long-term care the patient is usually fit and healthy enough to transmit the disease to others. In the countries where HIV is rife, there is poor HIV education, marked resistance to condom use, and often severe stigma for a HIV+ diagnosis, which is why AIDS is exploding in these regions and why importation of the epidemic to Britain is likely to escalate and then in turn drive an explosion within our own borders.

Not as impossible to effectively treat but a very serious problem nonetheless, tuberculosis thrives in the very kind of crowded housing conditions caused by large average family size, extended families under the same roof and relative poverty (often exacerbated by illegal immigration) that tend to prevail in Asian migrant enclaves. Indeed the disease is surprisingly prevalent in these communities, with MDR-TB a particular problem. MDR-TB is also common in some of the states newly acceded to the EU and especially in countries bordering these, between which there is little if any effective border controls. Likewise for HIV. As for hepatitis B: this is a far more common and a many times more communicable disease than is HIV so, despite a lower proportion of people developing serious long-term conditions compared to HIV, the health service is presented with a not dissimilar burden, albeit that there is a vaccine available for those most at risk that should help to check the spread.

The availability of high-quality treatment to stave off or to manage AIDS (and to cure MDR-TB or to deal with the consequences of hepatitis B), together with the non-existent checks on eligibility for treatment, makes the UK the premier attractive destination for sufferers. Given that HIV is a life sentence (as it is for many hepatitis B sufferers, and tuberculosis may require long and repeat treatments) then those who are infected will seek settlement and not just a protracted visit.

* * *

As with many aspects of immigration, Britain operates a uniquely open-door policy, but on what basis? The NHS is supposed to treat those other than British citizens (and those who have resided here legally for more than a year) only if the condition is an emergency or if it was contracted whilst in Britain. What is not supposed to be allowed is the arrival of people with pre-existing conditions who then present for treatment. But this is, of course, what is happening. At the initial point of contact with the NHS, the GP service estimates the proportion of patients who were not legally registered to range from 10 to 40 percent. This is not just a huge problem at the level of primary health care. The GP is the gateway to hospital referral. The problem was raised at the BMA's annual conference in June 2004.

Doctors described how visiting relatives of immigrants, especially those from Africa, Eastern Europe and the Indian subcontinent, were a particular problem. This is quite an admission by the BMA, which had been in general denying the impact of migration on the Health Service, complaining that there was no quantitative research.

This so-called 'health tourism' is policed neither by GPs nor the Home Office. There is no guidance to doctors from any level of the Health Service and simple proof of address is all that is needed to register with a GP. The position of the BMA's GP committee is that doctors should refuse to report cases of abuse. There is active pressure from primary healthcare trusts and health authorities not to deal with the abuse: Sergeant's investigations threw up some quite lurid tales on this score.

There are those who would see anything other than complete availability of free NHS treatment to all-comers as a 'human rights' issue, but the stated policy of the NHS is already more than sufficient to comply with international law and already more generous than anywhere else in the world. What about the interests of British society and British patients who are as a consequence pushed further back in the queue? The primary concern should be the prevention of the spread of infectious disease. There are laws of quarantine that compel individuals to be isolated should they contract certain illnesses. Albeit that such diseases are highly infectious by airborne particles, the mortality rates are invariably much less than for HIV. The more intimate mode of infection of HIV is the reason why such laws do not apply to HIV, but almost fifty countries stipulate that a HIV+ diagnosis prevents admittance, including all three of the other major Anglophone nations (USA, Canada and Australia). This makes perfect sense from a balanced human rights perspective. An analogy of our mistake would be the Fire of London, which consumed the whole city but could have been checked if the mayor had had the courage to create firebreaks by demolishing some houses in the path of the spreading flames. There is also an overwhelming economic case, with drug cocktail treatment increasingly available in poor countries by the use of generic drugs costing a mere dollar a day rather than the hundreds of pounds a week it costs using proprietary brands in the developed world. A fraction of the direct cost of importing HIV infection could treat most cases in the Third World.

Championing the individual rights of a few can have colossal adverse impact on the lives of the very many. That Britain is so out on a limb in itself is a major spur to importation of HIV and other diseases. As with any immigration and asylum policy, an aspect that is markedly more lenient than the norm around the world quickly becomes impossible to maintain. Free health care is almost unbelievable to foreigners and is the new version of the notion that the streets of London are paved with gold. Once again we are in the bizarre territory of the political Left whereby no distinction is made between citizens and foreigners, as if the stake and contribution made by people whose country it is counts for nothing. This was a conclusion made by Sergeant:

> States are necessarily inclusionary and democratic to its members, exclusionary and undemocratic to the outsider. That is a fact many in the present Government seem to be no longer comfortable with. They appear to believe that all individuals are invested with inalienable human rights, which must be protected. The NHS is where ideology crashes into reality. This Government is reluctant to appoint gatekeepers and give them powers. They seem unaware that in a society without gatekeepers, it is the weak, the inarticulate and the elderly — surely many of Labour's own natural constituents — who are the first to suffer.

There is an additional moral jeopardy aspect to a British haven for HIV sufferers. Why be quite so concerned about contracting the disease if an HIV+ status can be maintained without developing AIDS and at nil cost (and with subsistence payments to boot) simply by travelling to the UK? There is also a moral question of duty to British citizens, in that giving residence to overseas HIV patients is not a containable problem, because it creates not only the health risk of an extra potentially lethal sexual partner, but also the much greater risk of a person in circulation who tends to be considerably more likely than members of the indigenous population to practice unsafe sex, and therefore to have a predilection for transmitting this almost invariably terminal illness.

* * *

Sergeant's book is based on a large series of anecdotes — from doctors, consultants, nurses and NHS managers on the one hand, and on the other the illegal migrants and asylum seekers receiving treatment — collected on the promise of anonymity over two months of immersion in London hospitals and health clinics. Most consultants Sergeant spoke to were very angry, as were their managers. The report features many telling quotes from the capital's hospital A&E departments. Two managers put the situation in stark terms:

Relatives of families already living here fly over and use their uncle or cousin's address. Some with chronic conditions come backwards and forwards on six-month visas for treatment. Women are coming over all the time from the Third World to give birth on the NHS. The abuse is blatant.

If the English taxpayer knew how many overseas visitors we treated, they would be horrified. In my casualty department, one-in-20 people should not be there — and that does not include asylum seekers and refugees. I get no funding for them. We are very frightened to stand up and say that this is a fact.

(A senior consultant put the figure for his ward round at one-in-five, with asylum seekers and refugees included.) If management feel intimidated to speak up, then the health staff under them must feel even more intimidated; hence the importance of the study in not putting names to sources. At the other end of the foodchain the same picture emerged. A receptionist complained: 'We don't check anyone. How could we? You can call yourself Mickey Mouse and give an address in Disneyland.' Consultants were no less forthright, as in these two examples:

They arrive at Heathrow, take a taxi to my A&E and are referred to us with illnesses like chronic leukaemia, HIV infection or renal failure. They are coming here deliberately.

Today I am operating on a rich person from the Third World who has come through A&E as an emergency. I had to cancel the operation I was meant to perform on the poor, elderly Caribbean who has waited six months for his operation, is a citizen of this country and has paid taxes all his life. Tell me the morality in that.

This is a major source of sapped morale, in a service noted for morale problems. A system already stretched by over-bureaucratization taking money away from the actual work of healthcare itself, then wastes further very large amounts of money, and puts still more pressure on staff work load and patient waiting times, through a complete failure to provide even the simplest gate-keeping of patient access. London does seem to be where the problem is greatest, as you would expect — given the skewed distribution of recent migrants and proximity to major international airports. However, with migrant enclaves spread across the country and the dispersal of asylum seekers, the problem must be country-wide. (Sergeant cites major problems at the Royal Infirmaries of Doncaster and Leicester.) And this is apart from the problem of the burgeoning problem of the massively increasing numbers of Work Permit holders, students and other categories who are afforded NHS entitlement, together with all of the dependents of people in these immigration categories. This, of course, is another driver of illegal immigration: people secure student visas simply in order to bring in relatives for treatment.

Corruption within the NHS itself is also apparent. Sergeant found instances of doctors bringing over their own relatives from the Indian subcontinent, GPs conniving with patients, obtaining free treatments when it was private, and taking on patients temporarily then referring them to an NHS consultant without indicating their immigration status.

> Ali, a 28 year old Iranian married with three children was registering with his local GP when they discovered they were both Shia, the GP from Pakistan. The GP offered to coach Ali in the symptoms of epilepsy in order to claim a disability allowance when assessed by an independent doctor. 'My doctor said don't claim kidney pains or TB because they can test your urine or x-ray your lungs. But they can't test epilepsy because it's too expensive to send everyone for a CT scan.' The independent doctor declared Ali epileptic although he has never had epilepsy in his life. He now receives disability allowance. His wife gets attendance allowance for looking after him. He also gets income support and child benefit not to mention a flat from the council, free schooling and health care. He claims he is getting nearly £400 a week and has no intention of ever working. Social services say they have no idea of the maximum amount a claimant could receive. How much of this went to Ali's helpful GP? 'Purely kindness to a co-religionist,' was Ali's stern reply.

Certainly abuses by patients were apparent to me in the casework I handled myself when I was working at Managed Migration (up until March 2004). I had to deal with a countless number of applications from those wishing to extend their visit on the grounds of requiring medical treatment — and most appeared to have journeyed here expressly to illegally receive treatment — but there were few if any instances where the applicant could show payment for treatment received, nor even the financial resources that would enable him/her to pay for treatment. In many cases even the cost of day-to-day subsistence while over here, let alone the cost of treatment, was not shown to be capable of being met. I cannot recall any instance where I was advised that the applicant could be refused. As ever when I queried, I usually got the inevitable answer: 'it's none of our business'.

Astonishingly, for enquiring (or even for asking senior caseworkers about enquiring) I was reprimanded by management. They (deliberately?) misconstrued the information I was requesting and accused me of 'going out to check if a private medical patient had paid their fees'. It appears that anyone from abroad illegally receiving treatment on the NHS is classed as 'going private' and outside the remit of Managed Migration. It struck me at the time that given that the GMC also washes its hands of the problem, then just who is supposed to do anything about it? What more appropriate department could there be than Managed Migration for allocating staff to do this work?

I challenged my team leader over his reprimand, pointing out that I was merely attempting to implement immigration law. When a meeting was called with myself, my team leader and a senior caseworker; as with other points for which I had been taken to task and I had then rebuffed, I was told simply that I had answered by my 'improved performance' the point at issue and it was therefore not necessary to address my responses to the reprimand management had previously made. They would not allow me even to read out my answer to the bogus charges made against me. Instead, my supposed mis- behaviour regarding the questioning of NHS abuse was subsumed with other deemed misdemeanours under 'requesting further information when it isn't required'. The minute from the meeting made the assessment that: 'checking indicated that in all cases the inquiries were appropriate'. I had to make a fuss even to ensure that my replies were tagged on as an appendix in my performance file. At a stroke management pulled back from challenging me over my claim that we were failing to apply immigration rules. A handy dodge, it would appear, that put the problem in abeyance. Providing I did not push the issue, then they would not call further meetings to discuss my performance. It was a sort of unspoken truce.

This was a similar experience to that of health workers Sergeant spoke to. GPs who stood up to patients trying to work the system and were complained of to trusts received reprimands; staff from consultants down to receptionists feared accusations of racism. Some trusts actually wrote to staff warning of being charged with racism by the trust itself. Staff who asked for documentation were written to stating that this was contrary to guidance. As one GP said of the trusts: 'If they don't support us, who will?' 'Would you stand at Gatwick airport and hand out £1,000 to every visitor?'

* * *

The goings-on at Managed Migration are all the more surprising when you consider that this is one area of the immigration/asylum fiasco that the Government is supposed to be getting to grips with.

From April 2004, failed asylum seekers and heavily pregnant and other travellers together with their dependents were supposed to pay in advance for NHS treatment. Has this been put into effect? There is no research thus far, and if there are any systems in place then there is ample evidence that there is no will to implement reform. Dr Edwin Borman, the chairman of the BMA's international committee said: 'it is incorrect and inappropriate for the state, if it is unable to deal with its own particular Home Office-related proce-dures, to then call on the NHS to withdraw treatment'. Regarding the denial of care for failed asylum seekers he described this as 'utterly unacceptable'. The RCN voiced concerns about trust between patient and carer that could endanger the patient's health.

Health Service professionals do not see why government failure at the Home Office should be off-loaded on to them, but no scheme can work unless there is checking at the point at which the service is/would be supplied. The same impasse looks set to scupper the next set of proposals: to limit access to GPs. The consultation docu-ment on this was put out in May 2004, with a deadline for feedback in August. The problem was identified that many GP practices allow patients to register without producing their NHS card or passport. But so what if it is made mandatory to show your medical card and doctors and receptionists comply? It is no answer to the abuse, because the root of the problem is that little or no evidence is required to get an NHS card. That is one reason why surgeries show little interest in asking new patients to show them. In any case, the Government's proposals exclude infectious diseases — specifically, tuberculosis and all forms of viral hepatitis (and also malaria) — which as we have seen afflict a large proportion of asylum seekers, because their illness is the basis of their asylum claim.

The consultation paper 'Proposals to Exclude Overseas Visitors from Primary Medical Services' shows that the Government's pro-posals are useless. The idea turns out to be self-certification, with the NHS merely checking a sample of claims — what proportion of the patient total the sample is to represent is not given — and then ask-ing patients who are found to have lied to pay, and then to chase them up when they don't; which is what is supposed to happen already, but for everyone, not just a sample of patients. This could be even worse than the system which doesn't work that we have now. Just to make sure it won't work, not only will patients requiring emergency treatment be exempted, but so will those needing 'imme-diately necessary treatment', which is, of course, anything the GP deems it to be. Worse still: 'immediately necessary treatment will also include treatment that, in the clinical judgement of a health care professional, is required to treat a pre-existing condition that has become exacerbated during the period of a person's stay in the UK.' So if you just tell the doctor that your bunions got worse walking from your 'health tourism' charter flight to the arrivals lounge, that would be all you need to do to still get free treatment. The proposals seem to be little better than a farce; a fudge to placate the BMA.

Quite how useless are the Government's reforms already in place (from 1 April, 2004) is revealed by the Department of Health document, 'Implementing Hospital Charging Regulations: Guidance for NHS Trust Hospitals in England', which is not about laying down the law but empty cajoling and a big wink that exemptions allow hospitals to carry on as usual. Trusts are merely 'strongly advised' to make changes, such as appointing a dedicated Overseas Visitors Manager. This is then qualified with the suggestion that the post could be linked. So, no 'dedicated' officer at all then: just added duties to that of an existing manager. Trusts are 'strongly advised to seek deposits equivalent to the estimated full cost of treatment in advance of providing any treatment' from patients needing urgent care, and otherwise that they should pay up-front. That this won't happen is conceded when the advice goes on: 'to make use of a debt recovery agency that is experienced in handling the recovery of overseas debt'. As for the evidence patients are supposed to provide of UK residence, 'one or two pieces' is sufficient, and can include things like utility bills and bank statements. Not only are these child's play to forge, but patients could simply bring along those of someone they know who is resident in Britain. It seems that nobody is going to bother to check that the bills are actually those of the patient. And how about this:

> Being unable to provide evidence does not mean that someone can or should be denied treatment, only that they should be referred to the Overseas Visitors team for further investigation. … Patients may provide other evidence that is equally valid, and interviewers should be prepared to be flexible. … Where, however, the patient does not have the evidence to hand, an interviewer may be asked to … accept the word of the patient without supporting evidence. What level of evidence is acceptable is entirely a matter for the trust in the light of an individual patient's circumstances.

Amazingly the guidance stipulates that: 'interviewers should avoid questions relating to immigration status'. An IND (Immigration &

Nationality Directorate) helpline number is provided but: 'This service will not provide trusts with details of a specific individual's immigration status.' The number is merely for help with identifying different types of visas and stamps.

This hopeless fudge appears to be a combination of the Government refusing to accept the scale of the problem and kow-towing to the BMA and the GMC. A tussle between ethics and cost leaves a stalemate. And you can see the doctors' point. As Harriet Sergeant pointed out to me (personal communication), the Government just doesn't deport people. That is the root of the problem. As I have previously explained, even the worst abuses of immigration and asylum are rarely rewarded with 'removal', and these people can simply return as if nothing had happened. Deportation, which expressly rules out re-entry for some considerable time, is almost unheard of. As Sergeant sees it:

> Individuals cannot be blamed for abusing the system. There is no system to abuse. Once migrants are in this country, it is too late to withhold health care. ... Far better to have an immigration policy that restricts the numbers who come here but treats those that are chosen properly. The Government does the opposite. It allows in unlimited numbers but then fails to provide the extra services required.

Doctors put in a nutshell the problem as they saw it:

> 'We are doctors not policemen.' As one explained, 'By training and by inclination our job is to treat the sick person in front of us. ... 'Once a doctor is in contact with a patient, it is too late. You have listened to a story of distress. You have a contract of care towards that patient. You must treat them to the best of your ability. You can not consign a gate-keeping role to those who are carrying out care.' The two roles are in conflict. He went on, 'Who is entitled to care must be decided before a nurse, doctor or porter steps forward and says, "How can I help you." '

The costs to the taxpayer must be colossal. There are no estimates, not even a guess by the Department of Health. The only figure that is discussed is the £50–£200 million that CCI Legal Services, which is a debt recovery agency, reckoned was lost to the NHS every year through the non-recovery of charges. But this is merely the amount of money that chasing up still fails to recoup. It bears no relation to the astronomical figure for the total spent on ineligible patients, the vast majority of whom are never invoiced in the first place. This must run into not hundreds of millions but many billions of pounds. Just how many billions no one is guessing.

Why the figure must be so vast is easy to explain. The HIV/AIDS caseload alone is already of the order of half a billion pounds, and the rise is not just rapid but accelerating. Over the lifetime of currently diagnosed sufferers the figure will be between £5 billion and £10 billion. And that does not even include the benefits bill. Just a single case of drug resistant TB can cost £250,000. Hepatatis B often leads to liver failure and cancer, with the need for very expensive transplantation. These are just the headline diseases. To keep one patient in a bed on an acute psychiatric ward costs the best part of £2,000 every week of what is often a stay of several months. Harriet Sergeant's book is full of anecdotes of overseas patients clocking up tens of thousands or hundreds of thousands of pounds worth of unpaid-for treatment *each*. One Overseas Visitors Manager said: 'In my trust once the sum goes over £20,000, I am told not to issue any more invoices. The figures look so terrible on the books.'

No wonder nobody in government is prepared to hazard a guess at the scale of this economic disaster. It is no exaggeration to worry that the use of the NHS by ineligible patients is destroying the whole service, even without help from the hopeless administration that completely fails to manage and drains resources from the healthcare front line. If you put the two together, then in commercial terms the NHS has been bankrupt for some time and resembles unscrupulous companies that repeatedly go bust and recommence trading every new financial year under a different name.

Bev Gets Knotted

At the end of March, while I was gearing up to the hearing by the Home Office's top HR official as part of the investigation into my 'disclosure', I had been banging off press releases every other day or so to put on the Press Association newswire for journalists to pick up; unpicking the increasingly advanced knots that Beverley Hughes had been tying herself in since the beginning, but particularly since she had seriously and personally maligned me in the House of Commons the previous Monday. It was a day of yet another story in The Sunday Times, the fourth in a row, making March a complete month of misery for the immigration minister. Given the open season she had declared, I was in an almost cheeky mood, as you can see from this latest missive I rattled off, titled 'Never in a Month of Sundays', after the saying my mum used to come out with as an epithet for extreme unlikelihood:

> In a month of similar Sundays, today's revelations regarding an Immigration Service HQ memo conclusively prove that Beverley Hughes, the immigration minister, has serially and seriously misled the House of Commons — every time she has spoken — and on a number of points. What we now know for certain is that she personally approved the granting of tens of thousands of cases — likely well over 100,000 in all — with no checks whatsoever: exactly the same as happened more recently at Sheffield but now across all case types (including students and marriages) and at both Sheffield and the Croydon HQ. It could not be more damning.
>
> There appears to be a last ditch defence by Beverley Hughes to the cumulative revelations about her role in the immigration scandal, amounting to throwing sand in the eyes of her assailants.
>
> The Home Office has accepted as accurate the Sunday Times story regarding a leaked memo from senior staff at the Croydon HQ. Subsequently it was stated that the 'no checks' policy across all workstreams dating back to July 2003 was in respect of cases over three months old only. But when I started work several weeks later, all cases were over

three months old, such was the massive backlog of applications and the inadequate resources to deal with them. The qualification of 'three months' is, therefore, meaningless.

Just hours later the position had changed to a defence that a 'no checks' policy had been running for many years. But there is no excuse for the crimes of, for example, national leaders, on the grounds that previous leaders had behaved in the same way. This claim is a distraction to take the shine off the news value and, presumably to divert attention to the origin of the policy under a different government. Even if this turned out to be true, Beverley Hughes would still be responsible for unacceptable behaviour by her department.

It was also claimed tonight — another backtrack — that the procedure was 'not secret'. This contradicts the words of the Home Office official who was telephoned by the Sunday Times, and said '… there's no way the press should have seen it unless someone has leaked it.' Clearly, it was secret.

Originally too (earlier today), the position was that the July 2003 instructions were different from those more recently given at Sheffield, but the words of the official who leaked the memo as well as the wording of the memo itself show that the instruction was 'no checks' and this is exactly what was happening at Sheffield. The memo reads: 'All applications … should be granted unless the information on file is such that it can properly and defensibly support a refusal. Where a case will result in a refusal, the case must be cleared by a senior caseworker. No further inquiries should be made.' The official who leaked it remarks '… be in no doubt that this instruction means grant every application without enquiry unless you absolutely have to refuse.' As a caseworker myself, I know this means in practice not to refuse unless the applicant is a long-standing overstayer as well as not meeting conditions in other very substantive ways. In just the same way, more recently at Sheffield, the instruction was to check the passport to see if the applicant was a significant overstayer.

It is interesting that the Home Office line changed from first trying to maintain that the July 2003 HQ instruction was of a different nature to the 2004 Sheffield instruction, to one that they were the same, and that furthermore this instruction was a repeat of those issued over many years. Obviously, when it became no longer tenable to blame Sheffield, the only way out was to deny there is a real problem at all. But this completely contradicts Beverley Hughes' reaction to her 'discovery' of the 2004 practice at Sheffield re ECAA cases that this was 'quite, quite unacceptable' — her own words in the House of Commons.

Another positional change, and one argued before in connection with ECAA cases, is that applicants were mostly 'already here' in the UK and were not gaining entry as a result of lax decision-making. This is a false distinction and another empty distraction. Anyone can arrive in the UK ostensibly as a visitor — literally waived through as a tourist — and then apply in another category. Very large numbers of applicants in many categories do this, and apply to Managed Migration with just a visitor's stamp in their passport. Yes, they are already in the country, but it is not true to infer that they have been in any way subject to checks of any kind, let alone in regard to the category under which they are now applying. And even if an applicant is re-applying — when checks in the relevant category have previously been done — first stage checks in a category are usually laxer than subsequent ones and are often of the nature of a provisional, 'given the benefit of the doubt' nature, pending proper checks on re-submission. Therefore, to claim that large numbers of applicants who get 'no checks' automatic grants are somehow not a threat in terms of abuse through illegal working, benefit fraud, security risk, etc; is simply untrue.

It is clear that Beverley Hughes has clean run out of excuses and is clutching at straws to try to hang on. The defence in the wake of today's revelations is substantively non-existent. Hughes' position is no longer just a question of her resignation as a minister but also should be one of the removal of the Labour whip and deselection by her constituency party.

On Monday the minister abused parliamentary privilege (and put the Home Office in a difficult situation regarding my hearing this Thursday) in stating that I was not 'worthy' of having 'got through' Home Office recruitment. This was based on a bogus story about my supposed view — which I do not hold — of advocating use of nuclear weapons against Islamic fundamentalists. This story was retracted by The Independent newspaper the following day, and I have now had a letter of apology from Charles Kennedy for his reference in his leader's speech a week ago today. Clearly, the person who is not worthy is Beverley Hughes. Her behaviour throughout this month of Sunday disclosures would have got her sacked as milk monitor in my old junior school.

My disclosures to The Sunday Times had already been fully validated, but now my suspicions have also been shown to be spot on.

Hughes apparently enjoys special Prime Ministerial protection: queen of the Blair babes. But the survival of a minister under such dire circumstances as these would set a new precedent for ministerial non-accountability, even by the standards of the present Government. Tony Blair has the choice of ditching his babe or enduring lasting damage to his own credibility. The old saying, 'never in a month of Sundays', may well acquire new meaning.

Not too many points for prescience here: it was getting only too obvious that Hughes' days were numbered. Only three days it was, in fact, before the hapless minister resigned; before another Sunday could arrive. The month of March was but a few hours old. The morning of April 1st is usually reserved for making fools of others, but Beverley had, by a convoluted series of 'misleadings' and inaction, made a fool of herself. I was wondering whether it was going to be me or the Home Office who might be looking like prats this morning. I hadn't got Beverley Hughes in the frame. My mind was on being interviewed by the Home Office's head of HR (Operations), Rosalind McCool, here in Sheffield, within the aforenoon April Fool's window at 11.00am, to decide whether or not my coming forward fell within the terms of the Public Interest Disclosure Act.

The BBC had arrived as scheduled at my flat at 8.30am to do an interview and to run with correspondents' voiceovers background visuals of me ... washing the dishes as it turned out and opening mail which just happened to be my payslip from the Home Office. All of about £850. The BBC left, ITV didn't show and at 9.00am it was Channel 4's turn. Another interview and background footage. As they were shooting me sitting on my lounge sofa, the phone rang: it was an on-air BBC Radio 5 Live presenter — she was broadcasting the call. Do you have any reaction to Beverley Hughes' resignation? Bit of a pause ...what? She's resigned? No, I had not heard. I think I should have heard, because the news guys are here in my lounge filming as I'm talking to you!

This was supposed to be my media day — Bev was stealing my show! TV and press had been ringing me for days confirming where I would be. They would all be outside Milton House, the Home Office building on Charter Row in central Sheffield from half-an-hour before the meeting. They were now going to get two stories for the price of one — and I was going to get, in effect, only half the expected coverage for each story! But hang on a minute: what have I turned into to think this way?! An over-optimist: what happens to me might have next to no news value. Well, there is no question now that the story is going to be at the top of the news bulletins.

I didn't have a reaction for the R5 Live presenter. I wasn't glad and I wasn't stunned particularly (though not too far short of gob-smacked). The resignation was unexpected. I said that I could not understand why, after all the effort she put in to defend herself, she suddenly decided to resign. There must be something else to this. You don't think she was trying to cut my sympathy vote and paving the way for my 'resignation'?! I couldn't find out what had made her cut loose because I was in the hiatus of a media scrum before and after the interview and I wouldn't be out of it all until tea-time, if then. After the news sank in I didn't feel any different, though if I'd have been on my own I might have jumped up and down a bit and excitedly rung friends. I realized that was the worst thing I could do. Quite truthfully I said that I didn't feel any more vindicated now than I did at the beginning of the week when all the revelations emerged backing up my story. I repeated this throughout the day, and carefully; only to find that in more than one of the following day's newspapers I had been misquoted: 'Steve Moxon said he felt vindicated ...'. The press can even turn a negative into a positive.

Channel 4 took me to the interview in their big van, even filming me from behind as we went until I asked them to turn it off. It only takes an unguarded moment to do or say something and it's there in a vision/soundbite on the main evening news contradicting how you seem and what you said for the other 99 percent of the time. I was getting wiser. They had taken too long at my flat and we were in danger of being late; something I hate, let alone when I'm on TV and up before a major hearing.

Stepping out of the van, the biggest crowd of journalists I had ever seen paused while they looked across to see if it was me, hesitated and then sort of rushed me. I said the stuff I had said to R5 and C4, as if they had been rehearsals. Do I expect to lose my job? No, that is not what the interview today is about. Was that for the benefit of uninformed viewers, or a question from a journalist who doesn't do his research? None of this irritated me, because I need the media and this day was a good day whatever happened.

On the pavement I managed to find Martin Kelsey, my PCS union rep, who I'd never more than chatted to over the phone until now, and we escaped inside to be met by a very friendly Home Office official who would be taking the notes in the meeting. (No tape recording is allowed in Home Office investigatory or disciplinary hearings. The minimal notes the scribe takes can leave out anything not useful to the Home Office and can include distortions of what the interviewee says to contradict his properly considered written submissions.) Martin was very confident that we would sail the interview — as well he should be, with good legal advice that I was fully above-board regarding the Act. We went up in the lift and through an L-shaped office to a side room to meet Rosalind McCool. And that's as much as I was going to say about the meeting, because I was now back at work, you could say. On suspension with full pay, for the next two hours I would be doing the nearest thing to earning my pay as I had got for several weeks. If I revealed the proceedings of the meeting I would be in breach of confidence and making a further and possibly substantive disclosure to the one I made to the Sunday Times, and therefore potentially in breach of the terms of the Public Interest Disclosure Act.

Or would I be? Haven't I got the right to bring out details of action against me in the wake of my coming forward? Suffice it to say that both myself and my adviser were even happier after the meeting than before it. Nothing unexpected came up to trip me up and I managed to put over all my points in reasonable detail. The truth is that nothing of especial interest happened in the meeting for me to disclose! McCool was fairly cool; Kelsey didn't say much at all. McCool was a middle-aged soft-spoken woman with the gentle remains of an accent, Irish, I think. Over about ninety minutes she asked each of a small group of questions in almost every conceivable way. The main focus was on whether or not I had followed laid- down internal procedures — that I argued were irrelevant anyway, in that I had done more than I needed to as set out by the Act. McCool seemed not to want to hear that I had deposited with Leppard all the material on Home Office equal opportunities abuses as part and parcel of my 'disclosure'. Slightly taken aback she was. It was all surprisingly polite, with handshakes and 'pleased to have met you' greetings and farewells.

The scrum outside was even worse upon leaving than it had been when I arrived. Lots more questions, then round the side to the BBC van to do a feed for Radio 4's The World At One, then to ITV at their Charter Square studio, via a Channel 5 crew who intercepted me in a square en route. 'Do you want your job back?', the interviewer cannily asked me. I was a little stumped. You would think this a question for which I would have rehearsed. I gave a politician's answer, deeming the question hypothetical, since nobody I have talked to thinks there is the remote possibility that I will be reinstated. After ITV I had promised to go into Radio Sheffield, but I was too knackered and cried off, doing it over the phone later. A taxi was coming to take me to Leeds to do the two main local TV evening news shows, BBC Look North and ITV Calendar. This was getting to be old hat.

At some point I hoped to snatch some time to find out why Hughes had done an about-turn and resigned. I got garbled accounts and I might have glimpsed an evening newspaper, but really it was only when I got back from Leeds and slumped in front of the TV that I got any detail. Nobody had bothered to brief me, so I was being interviewed all day blind. But no problem: it meant that the soundbites they would use must contain reasons why *I* thought she should resign, rather than just my reaction to the reason why, finally, she had to go.

Still few if anybody, bar certain newspapers, used the word 'lie' and stuck with 'misleading the House'; as I had done. I was going to call a spade a spade on Look North, but in chatting beforehand to Christa Ackroyd, who was going to interview me, she reckoned that sticking with the accepted phrase was best. The next day's press was fearsome and some dropped the niceties. The Daily Mail's front page read: 'Why Do They Keep Lying?'

What had happened became clear. Hughes went into the Channel 4 News and BBC Newsnight studios on Monday March 29, to insist that the Government knew nothing about the latest revelations about ECAA scams in Romania and Bulgaria until David Davis, the shadow Home Secretary, had presented them earlier the same day. But Labour's deputy chief whip, Bob Ainsworth, met her in the Commons corridors between the two broadcasts and reminded her that they had an exchange of letters on this very subject more than a year before: on March 4, 2003, when he wrote to her, and she responded — twice (on March 17 and April 10). At the time he was himself a junior minister in the Home Office and he had been told of serious fraud and abuse of immigration procedures on a visit to Romania and Bulgaria. He pointed out that the game was up, because with an investigation in progress the letters were bound to come out. What is interesting here is that Bob Ainsworth had collared her after her Channel 4 appearance but before Newsnight. But she still kept to the same line!

It's worth reproducing the letters in full:

Dear Beverley

During our visit, the week before last, to Romania and Bulgaria, both posts raised with me claims of abuse of immigration arrangements under the European Community Association Agreement (ECAA).

You may want to follow this up with IND [Immigration and Nationality Directorate].

Applications for admission under the ECAA are routinely facilitated by UK solicitors who provide pro-forma business plans. Cases are required to be referred to IND for decision by the Business Casework Unit which invariably grants them, despite post's reservations about the individual on the basis of both the business plan and history.

Posts are understandably demoralised by having their recommendations routinely overturned, which they see as a weakening of the immigration control.

Regards, Bob

Dear Bob

Thank you very much for your note of 4 March. You have raised some important issues which I will raise with IND and I will let you know the outcome as soon as possible.

Best wishes, Bev

Dear Bob

Following my note to you on March 17, I have discussed the points raised during your visit to Bulgaria and Romania with IND.

On handling the ECAA applications, there have been a number of discussions between the IND and UKVisas and, indeed, the senior case-worker from the Business Case Unit visited Bulgaria last month to pursue these with the ECOs (Entry Clearance Officers). We are aware of concerns about possible abuse of the arrangements but we also have to recognise that these agreements do provide entitlements. We cannot refuse applications unless we have the evidence to sustain those decisions. The proposal that cases should be decided locally is still being considered.

Regards, Bev

The next day, she fielded questions in the Commons as if nothing was amiss. The day after that, Blair also went to do battle in that week's PMQs in full knowledge that Hughes was doomed but never let on (though suspiciously not mouthing support for either Hughes or Blunkett). That night she had a meeting with Blunkett and Blair to see if there was any way out. Blunkett was staunch in her defence, as well he would be given his various 'over my dead body' comments of late, but Blair overruled him. She gave her resignation to Blair at 8.15 am on April Fool's Day. At 12.30 in the afternoon — half-an-hour earlier and she could have been accused of perpetrating an April Fool's swansong deception — Hughes stood up in the Commons, doughnutted by as ugly a bunch of sad or scowling Blair babes as you could gather. Quite unbelievable though it was, she had the brass neck to spend the next six minutes still denying she had lied. For giving a 'misleading impression, albeit unwittingly', she said, was why she was stepping down. Perhaps she thought that we would be thankful that at least she was not still trying to pass the buck to her staff.

The next morning's press was merciless — even the Independent pulled no punches. Steve Bell, the Guardian cartoonist, who readily obliges to 'pull the other one', had Tony in his bed scared out of his wits pulling up the sheets as some ghoul asked him what he would do about all these bogus Transylvanians. The adjacent frame had our Bev bloodstained with the same ghoul standing over her saying: 'Welcome to firm-but-fair heaven, Beverley!' The Daily Telegraph sketch writer, Andrew Gimson, was skilfully savage, giving an account as if an inquest in to her 'death in suspicious circumstances'. Tony Blair and the Blair babes became: 'Miss Hughes' family, who are still struggling to come to terms with her loss, said they could not begin to understand why anyone should want to harm such a lovely girl.' Gimson explains that:

> at an hour when normal children had been read a story and safely tucked in bed, Miss Hughes was seen entering a Newsnight studio, where Kirsty Wark instead tried to get a story out of her. Some will blame Miss Wark for not sending her home, but others may question why Miss Hughes was allowed by her family, which has long trumpeted its commitment to high-quality childcare, to wander all alone around a television studio of all places, where she might at any moment be molested by some passing journalist with an unhealthy interest in attractive young politicians. …The New Labour family should be left to grieve for a day or two before social workers start considering whether the surviving Blair babes need taking into care.

Ouch!

It was widely remarked that after all of Hughes' sins it seemed that misleading a Newsnight presenter ultimately was what was deemed beyond the pale rather than repeatedly 'misleading' all of our MPs. The punishment for this, Gimson quipped, should be known as 'Warking the plank'. What would be more apposite is the use of the term 'doing a Beverley' to describe habitual 'misleading', the author of which refuses to come clean regardless of the evidence.

Beverley Hughes, even by the standard of contemporary government, set a new low standard in ministerial behaviour. Quite some achievement. That she stayed as long as she did was because David Blunkett was so determined in her defence. In the end she was the fall guy for the Home Secretary, who has been severely damaged nevertheless. As press and TV noted, Beverley was the monkey supposedly dancing to the tune, but responsibility for the policy rested squarely with the organ grinder, Blunkett himself.

Who Feels Aggrieved?

Even before immigration started to hog the news from March 7, 2004, polls had shown that the majority of people opposed immigration policy and thought that there were too many immigrants in Britain already. Among 'poor whites' the opposition was overwhelming at a whopping 90 percent. When the immigration scandal burst upon the scene the issue rose to be the number one priority with the electorate and stayed there, though it had always been at or near the very top of many or most people's concerns. Even a large proportion of people from ethnic minorities think that the large scale of immigration is a problem. And there does not seem to be much difference between those who live near or are familiar with people from ethnic minorities and those who have had little if any contact.

The mainstream idea foisted by the intelligentsia is that all criticism of immigration policy is really an attack on immigrants and that this is down to racism. The knee-jerk racism charge is allied with the idea that Union Jack-waving patriotism is proportional to an indiscriminate xenophobia against all non-whites. Research into 'ethnocentrism' (sociological jargon: it means favouring your own ethnic group) by community survey and laboratory study over many years proves this completely wrong. It turns out that thinking well of your own ethnic group does not correlate with looking down on other ethnic groups; and if you do look ill on a particular ethnic group it may or may not say anything about how you view other ethnic groups. You can be an extreme patriot without being a 'racist', and conversely you can strongly dislike one particular kind of foreigner and feel little identification with your own kind. This is a perhaps surprising but constructively interesting qualification to a simple theory of 'in-group'/'out-group'.

The theory of 'ethnocentrism' dates back to 1906 (Sumner), and its tenets that nationalism, authoritarianism and cognitive rigidity are all related has long been accepted wisdom. But it has been challenged by several notable studies. Doob (1964) denied the connection between nationalism and authoritarianism and Ray (1974) found that patriotism bore little relationship to racial attitudes. Specifically, Ray & Furnham (1984) reported no significant correlation in a British sample between patriotism and attitude to blacks. More recent work demonstrates that patriots are at worst no more 'racist' than most people, nor more conformist or authoritarian — traits that might be expected to be associated with 'out-group' hostility. The upshot is that people see each other in complex ways and it turns the spotlight on the Left's hatred for anyone who detracts from people who happen to be non-white — this Leftist view being the real prejudice. In the absence of systemic automatic 'in-group'/out-group' hostility simply on the grounds of race, it begs the question of how such situations arise. Whether or not mutual hostility ensues depends on 'rule-of-thumb' reasons grounded in real experience and the dynamic of group-to-group interaction, where several factors come to play. Antagonism between groups is a human predilection, not an inevitability. The problem is that there are indeed the right conditions for antagonism in Britain today between migrant enclaves and the host community. It has little to do with 'racism' or xenophobia.

The degree of concern about immigration varies, of course, and the assumption might be that the people who grumble the loudest about immigration policy are those who bear the brunt of the wage cuts and unemployment that are the indirect consequence of immigration. These are low paid workers, the unemployed and those who have 'given-up' — i.e. those who cannot (or can only with great difficulty) find work that pays at or above the 'reservation wage' (the level of wage that is in their estimation sufficiently above what they would receive in total from benefits to make work worthwhile.) Certainly these people are disaffected, but if they are out of work then they are takers from the system in that they get benefits. People on benefits might grumble about having to scrape by but they are aware that they are taking without giving and often to some degree keep their heads down and some indeed may have little interest at all in issues concerning the society from which they may well feel excluded or even from which they have excluded themselves. Alternatively, if they do not actually lose their jobs then they are likely to be in receipt of tax credits and in-work benefits, and lower rates of pay will often be compensated by increases in these. (Though it is the chronic widespread low pay exacerbated by immigration that has

forced the Government's hand in introducing expensive tax redistri-
bution as in-work benefits in the first place.)

Don't get me wrong — poor whites at all levels strongly dislike
immigration; but though the difference may not be large, there is
another section of the population that consistently feels most antagonized of all. These are the people in an economic strata above the
underclass and above the poorest of the working poor. Not those at
the top (who have enough money not to care and probably gain indirectly or even directly by the work of low-paid immigrants) but the
famous 'Middle Englanders', who are neither poor nor well-off.
These are the people who's earned income takes them just above
equivalent benefit levels and see very little of the several hundred
pounds per month of tax coming back to them in some form. They
may perceive themselves to some extent as being taxed so heavily
that they are being pushed in the direction of the 'reservation wage'.
They are most hostile to waste and those who allow waste to go on
unchecked, and to those perceived as 'free riders' of the system and
those who allow such abuse to go unchecked.

Mr & Mrs Middle England are the crucial, major part of the electorate (as New Labour very well knows) in that their discontent
makes them politically volatile and so more likely to be the 'swing'
voters that are the deciders of elections. It was in areas of Burnley
where these sort of people lived rather than 'sink estates', where
BNP candidates have done especially well or even got elected.

The frustration of the Middle Englander is rooted in a radical shift
towards inequality through a combination of changes in the global
economy and the shifting of the tax burden specifically in Britain
towards poorer workers. David Donnison, in his book, *Policies For a
Just Society*, charts this conspiracy against ordinary people as beginning in the early 1970s but then really gathering pace in the late
1980s. The coup de grace was delivered by tighter means tests on
benefits that denied more and more of those at the 'working poor'
end of Middle England. And I would argue that the more recently
introduced tax credits and in-work benefits have not much helped
this state of affairs, because they especially reward non-traditional
families and non-families (single parents); even those in households
where the hours worked per week total just sixteen. The effect may
be that although some of the 'working poor' have been alleviated, it
has left the core of Middle England still more aggrieved than ever.

Another factor should be put into the equation here; and that is
Robert Putnam's findings on social capital. As he described in his

book, *Bowling Alone*, there has been a profound general progressive civic disengagement in all developed countries starting some time after World War II. By 'civic engagement' he means all forms of community involvement, from visiting friends through membership of clubs to standing for the city council. He analyses this as principally a 'generational change': those who lived through or grew up in the Second World War garnered and retained a sense of social solidarity that has been progressively lost and quite sharply so by succeeding generations and age cohorts. He cites other factors: TV, commuting, urban sprawl, time pressures, etc; but 'generational change' accounts for about half of the effect.

Civic disengagement perhaps can be viewed from a different angle. The most powerful force in society after sex (or alongside it) is status competition and this has become a more obvious feature of our lives, to the detriment of other aspects. Wealth is both a manifestation and a driver in this regard. As Oliver James remarked (in his book, *Britain On the Couch*): 'modern life makes us feel like losers even if we are winners', as we experience 'death by a thousand comparisons'. Mass media, higher education and general social mobility have extended the horizons of life out of all recognition. We can have expectations of wealth, social standing, attractiveness of partners, etc., out of kilter with what is reasonably possible. The plethora of successful people who have become salient to ordinary folk as competitors has become unmanageable. Instead of striving to get in the second team of your local works football club, it's premier soccer or forget it. Patience and fun in the process of doing something that may or may not lead to something bigger is replaced by the frustration of battling with a winner-takes-all scenario. Everyone is looking up and not down or sideways, so it is not surprising that the 'grass roots' of civic engagement has declined. We all suffer 'status anxiety', as Alain de Botton titled his new book.

This in itself cannot but weaken the social contract underlying acceptance of the welfare state and is the background to the Middle Englander's resentment. The object of greatest resentment, and not just by Middle Englanders, is the welfare 'scrounger', and this is where the immigration issue comes in with a vengeance — not that all immigrants are on benefit, of course. It is one thing to have to support someone who has a cultural background in Britain and can show — by a visit to the graveyard — that he most certainly belongs to the country; but many feel that it is quite another when it comes to a recent immigrant to whom they have no cultural affinity and who can demonstrate no prior investment or connection of any kind to the nation he/she has only just begun to reside in.

The problem is that the very sort of immigrant who is, through cultural alienation from their new host country, most likely to gather in enclaves with others of their (former) nationality, is the very sort of immigrant who is likely to be unemployed. Pakistanis and Bangladeshis, for example, have unemployment rates several times that of the average (around 20 percent). Their work participation rates are of the order of just 50 percent, because the great majority of Pakistani and Bangladeshi women do not work — for cultural reasons and because they tend to have large families. The standard pattern in these communities is of the single-earner family household, and although many will find this a commendable traditional family set-up, offering the best situation for rearing children, it is despite often very low wages and larger than average families to support. Most of these workers then have to claim in-work benefits and frequently at or towards the maximum levels available. The perception of this 'out-group' of work- and pay-poor, benefits-rich recent immigrants causes resentment in the wider community about taxation to pay for their benefits.

It would do no good sending economists round to tell the white neighbours of these enclaves that the average subsidy a taxpayer pays in respect of this is perhaps smaller than they might imagine. It is the principal of the thing. For social comparison, people have their neighbours and near neighbours to the fore of their minds, and an entire neighbouring enclave being seen to have unfairly favourable treatment is galling. People feel resentment even if they are paying no tax themselves, partly because they will imagine that but for such (what they would consider) squandering, more would be available to be shared among those with a more (what they would consider) deserving claim: not least themselves. But it is also as if they set themselves up as representatives of the wider population with responsibility to arbitrate over the destination of large portions of public expenditure. This civic responsibility can assert itself in unexpected quarters. Just because people feel utter contempt for elected representatives at all levels, it does not mean that they could not care less — even about the 'waste' of other people's taxed income. Such is the power of our evolved 'cheater detection mechanisms'.

This scenario is just the same as resentment towards inhabitants of 'sink estates', and some politicians may be tempted to restrict who is entitled to benefits by more stringent means tests to try to damp down these sort of enmities. But because the very poorest tend disproportionately to belong to an ethnic minority, the result would be an even bigger slice of the welfare cake going to ethnic minorities. Further resentment against taxation and the welfare state is thereby fuelled. The 'cure' and the 'cause' are not independent of each other, but mutually exacerbating. This has been the lesson from the USA.

It is an irresolvable political dilemma, because it is a vicious spiral that is a reflection of a real problem rather than a phenomenon that can be portrayed as an unfair perception. The problem cannot be blamed generally on the unskilled immigrants themselves, though no doubt abuse goes on as it does in other communities, and for various reasons likely more so; but there are special factors. People are bound to question the morality of large families that cannot be supported on available incomes, just as they question government policy that supports never-married single parents. There is the view that the absence of integration into the mainstream is bound to foster the acceptance of benefit fraud and of receiving benefits as a long-term lifestyle and to a greater extent than in the wider community; just as people criticize 'benefit scroungers' living in white 'sink estates'. On the other hand, there is not an unambiguous view that immigrants are workshy. By and large the ire of Middle Englanders is directed not so much at immigrants themselves as at those who make the policy of dumping the problem of ethnic minority enclaves on the wider community without ever themselves having to witness and live near the consequences — or even present this policy to the electorate.

The consequences can include: housing blight for home owners; rented housing shortages for poor whites; school standards falling and indigenous pupils needing special attention being neglected, as attention is transferred to language difficulties and other problems of ethnic minority pupils; street crime by ethnic minority youths and young men disaffected both from their own community and from wider society; and undercutting of bona fide workers and firms by an ethnic minority workforce in both the legal and black economies. This is nothing to do with racism, though of course racism by a small minority can compound the perception of a serious problem.

There is research evidence of a detectable gross effect of 'ethnic fragmentation' or 'ethnic fractionalism'. Mori found that satisfaction with local government had a very strong inverse relation to the proportion of ethnic minorities in an area, even when the results were controlled for the confounding variable of poverty (because it may be expected that poor people feel more than average dissatisfaction with their local council). Robert Putnam has found that social capital declines in areas with a high ethnic mix.

The only way the overall problem can be countered is by addressing the root cause: by curtailing mass net immigration and in particular the uncontrolled chain migration into ethnic minority enclaves.

* * *

The other source of real annoyance about immigration concerns democracy and identity. Never has any immigration policy been put to a vote in Britain. It is usually absent from the headlines of party manifestos, despite being one of, if not the most important, issue for many electors. If immigration policy is in a party manifesto at all, it is not put in meaningful detail and, in any case, the policy outcome often bears little relation to stated policy: that of the current administration being a glaring example of this. This gets to the very heart of the most salient gut-political feelings of everyone: the right to self-determination. It is axiomatic that citizens of a country must feel that they have, albeit nominally, a part to play in a collective say about the future. Everyone knows that their individual part in the process is so marginal as to be completely off the scale, but nonetheless there is a principle that matters to people, including most of those who have given up bothering to vote.

Mass net immigration begat a social policy of multiculturalism. Nobody has ever had a vote on this either. At first more implied than overtly stated, multiculturalism has become not just policy but something of a mantra. The problem is that it has outgrown its boots. One reading of the notion of multiculturalism is an avowed celebration of difference. We are all different, so what could be wrong with that? What is wrong with it is what it then became. By extension, a celebration of difference transmuted into the insistence that cultural variety should take precedence over the mainstream culture that by overwhelming numbers of people and their common history had always been dominant. The mission became one of eradicating a society-wide identity as a supposedly necessary part of the process. What for? Nobody questioned the negative motives of those in favour of this. Display of the Union Jack was in many official quarters actually deemed offensive and tantamount to support for extreme right-wing political parties or as championing thuggery. The Commission for Racial Equality openly challenged the very notion of 'Britishness' and wanted an official declaration that Britain was a multicultural society. Naturally the majority of the population rejected the attempt to impose what was a denial of an obvious reality. This was something worse than the usual arrogance of the intelligentsia telling everyone else what they should think. It was tantamount to telling everyone that in the way in which they see themselves they should not exist. This was the revenge of the defeated socialist. Multiculturalism was supposed to be a policy of inclusion but instead it had been reborn as a monster mutant policy of exclusion towards the majority. It was an idea heading in only one direction: towards very serious trouble.

Just as those most aggrieved on the economic front tended to be in the lower ranks of society (though not at the bottom), the same tends to be true regarding questions of general identity and democracy. Those 'higher up' are to varying degrees insulated from such concerns by their far-reaching interlocking orbits of social status and buying power. If, on the other hand, you have less of what makes you stand out from the crowd, then you have more to gain through the solidarity of mass identity and democracy. Of course, this presupposes some engagement in the first place, so we are not talking so much about those who are struggling to run with the crowd — the poorest of the working poor — and still less are we talking about the underclass here. We are back with Mr & Mrs Middle England.

But there is no reason why you cannot have both multiculturalism and a mainstream dominant culture. If you can have both, then why bang on about multiculturalism in its extreme version and so jam immigration policy full in people's faces? The penny dropped and there was, in the middle of the immigration furore, the startling proclamation by Trevor Phillips, the chair of the CRE, that multiculturalism must be abandoned. Of course, he did not mean this literally, but that the stronger form of the concept must retreat in favour of the original notion of multiculturalism. To prove he meant what he said, the CRE almost immediately announced that it would no longer fund projects that primarily were concerned with promoting a sense of separatism. As was remarked upon by commentators, this move by Phillips was profound not just in itself but because he is so close to Tony Blair. It was tantamount to a statement from Blair himself.

How much ice this will cut with the electorate is uncertain but it is unlikely to make much difference. As I point out in Chapter 8, Phillips' seeming conversion appears to be a prelude to Government plans for pouring money into Muslim enclaves. The public is fairly convinced that what the Government (any government) says about immigration is not the same as what it does — or rather does not do. This is the common attitude to all government policy but perhaps has applied to immigration policy more than to any other. Given the recent events sparked by my disclosure, if there was any doubt about this then there is doubt no longer.

* * *

The combination of these two strands of opposition to immigration policy — economics magnified by human psychology, and the attack on basic democracy and social identity — is so powerful that racism barely registers as a component. Few people take the natural social-psychological behaviour of experiencing their 'in-group' vis-à-vis an 'out-group' and develop this into a near pathological detestation of people as individuals from the particular 'out-group' of ethnic minorities. If someone reacts in such an extreme way to ethnic minorities then, notwithstanding varied attitude to other 'out-groups', it is likely that he/she will react strongly whenever an in-/out-group scenario becomes salient. Such a person is not so much racist as 'out-groupist', showing unusual hostility to any unfamiliar group. Almost everyone is fully aware that they react differently to individuals compared to how they react to groups of those same individuals. Almost without exception white people, in common with all people throughout the world, are spontaneously hospitable to an individual, regardless of his ethnic origin. The average white person is friendly even if that individual belongs to an ethnic minority enclave that he feels hostile towards. In any one-on-one meeting, the groups to which both parties belong cease to be salient. Nobody needs some expert race relations mediator to show them the truth of this. And race relations experts have been telling us all that we behave in ways we know we do not.

Everywhere there is now retreat from the obviously false and deeply insulting charge of common racism as the principal basis of opposition to immigration policy. The contention was that it is an objection to visible ethnic minority individuals rather than to immigration per se; but in fact the opposition is broad and deep, against the imposition of ethnic minority enclaves in particular and the imposition of the very large numbers involved wherever they live within the country. The popular view is very far from unreasonable.

Not only is the problem not going to go away but it will get progressively worse over the longer term. As Prospect editor David

Goodhart pointed out in his article, 'Too Diverse?', those who do not see a serious problem '… assume too swift a reaction to growing diversity — these are forces that take effect over decades, if not generations.' Government cannot know what the damage to the social fabric its policies (or lack of them) on immigration will be ultimately. It needs to emulate the reaction by the general public that unlike the Government's is astute and suitably cautionary.

An African refugee summed up the problem for Harriet Sergeant in her book, *Welcome to the Asylum*:

> 'When you are the first refugee to enter a village', he explained, 'they see you as an individual. They help you. They invite you into their homes and ask about your family.' But then more arrived and even more. The villagers turned surly. 'They refused to give the bread they had offered me with a smile.' They forced the refugees to camp outside the village. 'Finally they pelted us with stones.'

U-turn, Migration Mayday

Dubbed 'Tony Blair's great U-turn on immigration', the not-so-great leader's speech at the London Business School on Tuesday April 27 was a significant admission. It was 'crunch time', requiring a 'top-to-bottom' review of the whole of immigration policy. This was less a U-turn than a necessary admission of the obvious, but just long enough after the Beverley Hughes debacle and Blunkett's restatements on supposedly tackling abuses so as not to appear an absolute capitulation. A badly-executed attempt at a three-point turn, perhaps. Laziness may explain journalists' description of the speech as a U-turn. Coming only days after blasting through the central reservation crash barriers on the European constitution referendum, the belated admission of the seriousness of the immigration debacle could be portrayed as part of a pattern. Sure enough, immigration and Europe — along with terrorism — is a lethal political package.

Yet again I tried without success to be allowed to comment on air, so I waited for the inevitably inaccurate TV coverage. Both BBC and ITV early-evening bulletins led with the notion that 'quotas' of non-EU migrants would be reduced to try to balance the increased inflow from nationals of the EU accession states. I rang the Millbank (Westminster) desks of the main channels to point out that there could be no question of reducing quotas because *there were no quotas of any kind in Managed Migration* (see below).

I looked in vain for reference to quotas in reports of the PM's speech. Perhaps reporters were misled by briefings aside from the speech? It looks as though once again the lack of an elementary grasp of even the basic structure of immigration procedures led to serious misreporting and/or the usual failure to challenge the sense of Government policy — or even if members of the Government understand the issues themselves. Of course, Blair's advisers know how to mislead by conflation. This would not be the first time that Government spokesmen have deliberately obfuscated by passing off uncontrollable 'Managed Migration' as subsumed by the rules for Work Permits. Sir Bernard Crick had done this blatantly on a Newsnight discussion. He had actually said that all migrants have Work Permits: a transparent untruth that nobody in the studio challenged. As usual the BBC didn't have anyone competent to act as counterbalance on the discussion panel. Just the political editor of the Daily Express: someone who would not know, and in any case was easily discountable as partisan.

True to form, when I rang Newsnight I was told that Blair's speech was not going to be an item on that night's show. I tuned in to check, and sure enough, several items, including a long feature on an obscure novelist, but nothing on immigration. Yet another instance of the BBC burying the immigration story. Channel 4 also placed the story well down the order in their bulletin that evening. Given that Blair's 'U-turn' was the top story all day on all teletext news services and on the BBC evening broadcasts (and the second item on ITV) then how is it that 'news values' preclude getting to the heart of the day's main story? Consistently the BBC did not interview anyone with the knowledge to contradict the Government's line, and I am not exaggerating to claim that on operational matters I was the only player on the bench: the one person who could usefully comment and is fully free to do so. Instead, the BBC were regularly interviewing Keith Best, the chief executive of the Immigration Advisory Service, a body that provides free legal assistance to immigrants that functions as an advocacy pressure group and an enthusiastic supporter of the Government line when not in conflict over what it perceives to be its illiberality.

I took the opportunity, while I was correcting newsmen on the quota question, to also point out that there was no mechanism to prevent East European incomers from claiming benefits, and no economic case for mass net immigration. A business conference was an especially good place to repeat the untruth that immigration as a whole was of economic benefit to the country and Blair did not miss the opportunity. Needless to say, no reference was made in TV broadcasts to the research which clearly contradicts this Government mantra.

Why Tony Blair delivered his immigration speech when he did is clear. It was a few days before May 1, the day that nationals from the

EU accession states could start to move freely throughout the EU (but are free to work only in the UK and Ireland). So now that Migration Mayday, as we might dub it, has arrived and passed, just where has the Government progressed to in the great immigration debacle? Somewhere between not very far and nowhere. We began with David Blunkett's restatement after restatement that he would tackle bogus marriages and bogus students and colleges. These failed to address the core of the problem and to make the necessary fundamental changes to procedures required. That Blair's speech was also restatement of what had been previously announced was hidden by being made newsworthy through the 'top-to-bottom' review promise, the 'crunch time' admission and the ditching of the policy of smearing critics as racist. The other novel aspect was that it was the PM rather than David Blunkett or an immigration minister giving a speech on immigration: the first since Blair came to office seven years before. Yet still he did not admit the extent of the problem: of an across-the-board and in-depth major Government failure.

The new EU migrants would not get benefits, Blair reiterated. Oh yes? So by whom and by what system will this ever be checked and enforced? There is no method whereby staff at any Job Centre or Benefits Agency office can check if someone is not entitled to benefits by virtue of their immigration status. Likewise, at Managed Migration there is no routine procedure. A caseworker has to go through two layers of management to get approval to fax to a central checking facility at a place called Longbenton. Hours, or a day or two later, you might get a response. I managed to get approval for only two benefits checks in the whole of the six months I worked there.

The PM was reported to be planning to cut quotas of non-EU migrants to try to balance the increased inflow from nationals of the EU accession states. This is either obfuscation or misreporting: as I said, there are no quotas of any kind in Managed Migration. We responded to whatever volume of applications were received. Quotas exist only in the much smaller Work Permits division of the Home Office. Well over half a million people apply to Managed Migration every year and none of those receive Work Permits, even though the great majority are allowed to work. If the Government is intending to reduce Work Permit allocations then this would be in the very area of immigration where incomers are more likely to make a genuine contribution to the economy — or so we thought (see Chapter 4). Of all the migrants who achieved permanent settlement in 2002, only one in five actually came here to work.

The PM was also still peddling the line of some supposed economic benefit to Britain overall of mass net inward migration, when the most recent research shows precisely the opposite. What about the eight million people in Britain of working age who are not working? Unemployment stands at a million and a half, with over two million on top of that who want to work but can't find any (they are unemployed in every sense but that they can't claim benefits), then the millions upon millions of the under-employed, forced to take part- time and/or temporary work or in jobs that don't pay enough to support the family they would like to have.

So what of Mr Blunkett's announcements? Regarding bogus marriages, most applicants marry abroad, where of course no UK registrar's report could alert a caseworker to an obviously suspect ceremony. So placing Immigration Service staff in a select few registry offices will not solve the problem. That's a half-hearted sticking plaster across a gaping wound ploy. Where is Mr Blunkett on the ridiculous state of affairs whereby a single gas bill or the like is all that someone requires to supposedly confirm a continuous two-year subsisting relationship to gain permanent UK settlement under the marriage rules? Where is he on the similarly lax consideration of what counts as sufficient income in this regard? And as with EU accession state nationals, what about the absence of benefits checks?

On bogus students and colleges, the Home Secretary has also yet to discover the plot. The point of bogus application is to get a stamp in your passport allowing you to work legally, though supposedly only part-time. So why not check that ostensible students are indeed students and not in fact workers? Most fraudulent applications are in respect of minimum-contact-time (fifteen hours per week) courses which someone could partially (or fully) attend and easily manage to do full-time work. What about the almost non-existent checking of a student's source of funding? Income is usually simply assumed to be as declared and not from work. And if, at long last, colleges are going to be checked that they are bona fide, then where are the staff coming from to do this and what aspect of the Immigration Service, already cut to the bone, will be denuded as a result? What of those colleges that function legitimately but in addition take fees from students in full cognisance that they will never turn up?

When will Managed Migration staff be properly trained so that some real effort can be made to spot forgeries? Training in what foreign passports actually look like (rather than just learning on the job) would be a start.

The wider issues are even more urgent. The re-instatement of embarkation controls so that we can know who and how many of the ninety million UK entrants annually (fail to) leave the country. Proper coverage of points of entry, so we do not have the scandal of ports unmanned at weekends — as complained of by Immigration Service unions in May. Only one in every hundred lorries is checked at Dover and planeloads of people pass through airports without even having to wave the outer covers of their passports. How about more than a token staff to actually find and deport (and not just 'remove') overstayers? Immigration and asylum are related issues, with migrants being able to switch from one status to the other: the 1951 asylum agreement was drawn up in an entirely different age to deal with handfuls of defectors who had managed to cross the Berlin Wall. So tear it up and negotiate something sensible.

The most important development, according to Tony Blair, is the ID card. Oh yes? ID cards, or rather the database behind them, could be the way to go forward but they are many years away. Not until 2013, and there is no decision anytime soon as to compulsion. It's another case of eyes not being on the ball. It is the procedures which would allow people to obtain the ID cards where the weak link lies. If, for example, you could get through MI5 recruitment by posing in a bushy black beard and a white frock with a name that was an anagram of Osama Bin Laden, then giving ID cards to all MI5 employees would be less than useless. The same rationale goes for the UK as a whole re immigration.

David Blunkett had announced his ID card proposals just the day before, and I was telephoned by the producer of a proposed half-hour slot to grill the bright spark of Brightside on that morning's BBC Breakfast programme. I was 'not the Home Office's favourite person', she told me. She was looking for someone to take part in the panel of questioners, but since I had 'baggage' (yes, I thought, like the only person to have told the truth in the immigration debacle), rather than me, could I suggest anyone else who had experience of working in the Immigration Service? I said I could not. Obviously, I am the only person who has come forward from the Home Office and I remain the only one with current work experience there and so there's only me with qualification to speak. The panel was to consist of people with a particular expertise. There was, for example, a forgery expert. I watched the broadcast and all the questioners were experts of one kind or another. But in the phone call I took, the producer completely changed tack. She now said that the panel was not of 'experts' but of 'ordinary people'; and that, of course, I was not an ordinary person in this regard.

I said that if I could not appear then could she ensure that the substantive point I would have made is made by someone to Blunkett? This (which I e-mailed to her) was that ID cards are not an answer to any aspect of the immigration fiasco – I gave the analogy of ID cards for MI5 recruits. Before the Blunkett section there were on-air invitations to viewers to send their points which may then be put to the minister, but my point was not put to him. I guessed that the Home Secretary was not willing to appear in my presence. I rang the producer afterwards to ask her if the BBC normally bow to this sort of pressure. Why, I asked her to explain, yet again was the issue of immigration not properly discussed on a BBC programme?

The anchorman at Westminster asked Blunkett about deportation of illegal entrants/overstayers, and Blunkett clearly dodged the question – answering that Britain would become a less attractive place for illegal migrants. Oh yes? Like the potential supply of several billion people is just going to dry up. An open goal, but the question was not followed up. Once again the BBC let Blunkett off with an easy ride. When does an easy ride becomes collusion with deliberate obfuscation?

* * *

Mayday 2004 was a good day for Europe in that the ghost of a Europe split by the empty but highly dangerous fascist ideology of Stalinism has been firmly laid to rest, but regarding migration it is a Mayday in the sense of 'Mayday!' – the coded alarm that crackles over the airwaves from pilots alerting air traffic control to the imminent disaster of their flight. The flight over our borders by EU accession state nationals – and those using forged documents to masquerade as such – cannot be other than a disaster, but if it turns out to be only a minor one, then it would be no thanks at all to the Government. We won't know about the scale because the Government is refusing to count those coming in: just those few volunteering to be put on the Government's special register! But this is only a small part of the picture. It is important not to be distracted by the focus on the one-legged Romanian roof-tiler and his ilk, because their numbers are dwarfed by other immigration routes and from other countries. It is the wider, deeper maladministration that we should be keeping in frame.

The entire way of working in Managed Migration needs to be re-organized. The emphasis on handling at least a certain number of cases daily (fifteen) and deciding — almost always granting — twelve of these, leaves little time for more than the most cursory scrutiny. The ethos of Managed Migration is that the Home Office is providing a service for would-be migrants, instead of the onus being on those who would wish to be here and to settle to responsibly provide everything required. Obviously, the latter was the intention of Parliament. The Government is not willing to listen to MPs and its understanding of its obligation to the electorate seems to be merely to alter the presentation. Don't hold your breath for any meaningful Government action.

* * *

A response to Blair's speech was prepared by Anthony Browne for the think-tank Civitas. Much of it was retreading arguments Browne had made before, and which I have alluded to above, but he made a couple of points I had not thus far realized. Browne now questions even the basic tenet that advanced nations all necessarily have inflow and outflow of people (whether in balance or not). Japan, Norway, China and South Korea he points to as examples of countries with virtually nil inward migration, and these are all notably highly successful economies. There is no a priori reason, therefore, that Britain requires any immigration at all.

Britain is alone, Browne shows, among the very small group of nations (USA, Canada, Australia, New Zealand, Israel and the UK) that actively encourage primary immigration as government policy . The UK is the only country that is both mature and densely populated. Israel is an anomaly, obviously, because of the special situation of the Jews and accepting only Jews as immigrants. Active promotion of mass net immigration into an already crowded and fully developed economy is unique to Britain.

Crowding Stress

You do not have to be a Greenpeace or Earth First! supporter to be concerned about the carrying capacity of the planet and that tiny portion of it that is Britain. Amenities become more expensive, scarcer and trickier to access as population rises in a fixed amount of space. Not many people want to live somewhere as crowded as Hong Kong, or Holland, even — where immigration is the hottest of political issues for this very reason. The presentation of the problem as potential conflict and mutual alienation occasioned by the influx of obviously foreign groups, is the other way of looking at it, but the size of the country in comparison to the volume of immigration is key. There is nothing like so much of a problem in a large country such as the USA, which is why America can handle immigration on a large scale and sustain having a population with such a large proportion of recent migrants — though even here there are limits. Small European countries are a different matter.

The more the natural carrying capacity is stretched, the more we become reliant on economic growth, and the greater the adverse impact would be of any future forced change to more nearly meet the reality of environmental constraints. There are many such changes that may be in the offing; for example: transport reappraisal through increasingly scarce and expensive oil, a retreat from industrial intensive farming, an energy crisis because of the exhaustion of gas supplies, and stretched water resources. Even the USA — particularly the USA — is vulnerable on all these.

The impact is not just at the macro level, and is not so much a sociological phenomenon as a psychological one. The *Journal of Social Issues* published back in 1981 an article, 'Crowding Stress In Human Behaviour' by Y.M. Epstein, that explains what 'crowding stress' is:

> The task of managing one's environment becomes increasingly more difficult as that environment becomes more populated. Attention and energy ordinarily available for doing work must be diverted to the

crowded situation. Resources typically become scarce. Other people's activities begin to interfere with one's own. Unavoidable and often undesirable interaction with others distracts the individual from work tasks. Violations of personal space cause discomfort. It is through such a process that crowding causes stress. It is not simple density that produces the stress reaction. Feeling crowded is different from feeling cramped. Cramping results when there is too little physical space. Crowding is a psychological phenomenon resulting from group processes. You feel cramped when your office is overfilled with furniture, file cabinets, and boxes of stuff on the floor. You feel crowded when you share a small office with several other people. One factor that mediates stress induced by crowding is the relationship between the crowded individuals. If this relationship is communal or co-operative, as it often is in families, then high density will not necessarily provoke stress reactions. However, in residential settings other than homes, such as dormitories, the orientation of residents is likely to be more individualistic than communal, and crowding is likely to result in stress.'

This is the social psychological level, but what has been recently studied are the effects at the next level down: at the physiological level the principal effect appears to be lowered fertility. Birth rates have fallen across the developed world, and there is an intriguing possibility that this is not a surface cultural trend but akin to the phenomenon of 'crowding stress' as physiologically manifested, as research has shown, in many animals. Do humans respond to aspects of their environment — especially their social environment — by hormonally mediated (and unconscious, obviously) bodily processes that actually depress their own fertility?

Logically, in a pre-modern, unsafe world (the one to which we are genetically adapted), if we encounter many people who are non-kin and unfamiliar strangers, then there would be more risks in trying to raise children than in the social environment we are born to expect, of a sub-tribal group. Higher investment in offspring, and fewer of them, and more careful choice of a partner would be the best strategy to deal with such an unusual social milieu. This chimes with what we see today. Most people have children, still; but until recently an unheard of large minority now live in childless long-term partnerships, while many others practise late motherhood, procrastinate almost to the end of, if not beyond, child-bearing age; and a substantial minority fail to (or choose not to) be in a long-term partnership at all. But these are behavioural changes. Are there physiological ones?

We know that almost all biology is pretty much the same, from lowly mammals up to advanced primates. It is more likely than not that the same mechanisms are in play in ourselves as in 'crowding

stress'-afflicted animals. It may be that the response has a more complex mediation in our case (for instance, specific facial-recognition
neural structures, more than pheromone receptors), but they would
be merely a case of sophistication rather than of a fundamental func-
tionally-distinct apparatus.

There is some evidence that fertility depression through crowding
stress does occur in humans. Sam Wasser of the University of Washington, as well as demonstrating the effect in captive lowland goril-
las, has identified it in women − at least when crowding stress is
persistent − with decreasing fertility of up to 10 percent (and also
accounting for 25 percent of habitual abortion). The yellow baboon is
another primate shown to be susceptible, and in its natural wild hab-
itat. Here the hormone regulation of the process was detected. The
same but more pronounced hormonal patterns are apparent in all
sorts of other mammal species, especially snowshoe hares, lem-
mings, voles, rats, mice, and tree shrews. What is more, it can be
shown that what the physiology in these animals is responding to is
social rather than environmental stress, and specifically population
density. It kicks in even though there is no restriction at all in the
availability of food. This is the important factor, because it is well
known that across the animal kingdom pronounced food shortage
can lead to the activation of various conservation mechanisms of
which reproduction − being the least necessary bodily function
when it comes to short-term survival − is often the first function to
be shut down. The reproductive shutdown, in reaction not to food
shortage but to population density, is different in a surprising way.
It can go far beyond just a lowering of fertility; in some cases reproduction stops altogether and, occasionally this can actually lead to
the complete decimation of the local population. The trend can go
beyond the point of no return, so that even if there has been a population collapse to the point that social stress has been completely
alleviated, instead of this feeding back to produce a recovery the
decline becomes precipitous.

Research on this weird feature of nature originated quite some
time ago. Back in 1936, Hans Selye discovered what he called 'the
general adaptive syndrome', and this was confirmed in various wild
rodent species and in laboratory rats. Laboratory manipulation of
the environment to produce conditions of high population density
but no food shortage gives rise to a suite of social aberrations − such
as higher levels of unusual and unproductive sexual behaviour
(notably homosexuality and paedophilia), aggression, infanticide

and cannibalism, reduced reproduction, abandonment of infants even before weaning — and a wide range of physiological abnormalities — like delayed sexual maturation, suppression of ovulation and implantation, insufficient lactation, susceptibility to disease and a big jump in infant mortality — to list but some.

The reason this strange behaviour is called 'the general adaptive syndrome' is that it is thought indeed to be an adaptation: to the threat of the wholesale degradation of the species' environment by unregulated population growth completely exhausting food supplies. By self-induced non-reproduction, extinction through the collapse of environmental support is avoided. Thus it is that when a mammal plague collapse is investigated the corpses appear well-fed and there is no evident problem with the supply of food. If it is an adaptation it seems not a very good one. There is little point in saving yourself from partaking in mass starvation if the process overruns and you end up leaving no offspring behind. Presumably then, the process works more often than it fails: reproduction resumes before all the animals are past reproductive age in most cases. The problem with the theory is that the mechanism would appear to have to operate at group level, and for this to happen there would have to be selective pressures that overcame those at the level of the individual, and in a situation of still ample food supply there is obvious advantage to any individual who breaks ranks and reproduces — a free-rider. However, there are evolutionary models that demonstrate that apparent group selection that is really to each individual's advantage is the correct analysis.

* * *

Somewhat spoiled by what would appear to be an extreme doom-laden prediction, the most well-known exposition of the problem at the macro level is that by Reg Morrison in his book, *The Spirit of the Gene*. His thesis is that the human species, being a global village rather than a collection of quite separate local populations, is on the path to possible extinction and certainly to ultimate decline, because we are following the usual patterns that have characterized the extinctions of species when they go into what is known as 'plague mode'. That we are in 'plague mode' supposedly is indicated by the declining fertility rate across the past two decades, which is set to slow population growth to zero roughly by mid-century, after which, Morrison predicts, population will plummet.

The problem with Morrison's Armageddon thesis is that there is no evidence of the susceptibility of women to devastating fertility collapses. Wasser found up to a 10 percent fall only, and there is no anthropological evidence (that I have come across) of any isolated communities suffering 'plague mode'. Morrison proceeds to look at the effects not on female but on male fertility, but are there analogous impacts on males rather than females in other species? He cites the well-documented fall in sperm counts, but admits this could be due entirely to pollution by man-made chemicals acting as 'endocrine disruptors', potent enough to have effects even at massive dilutions. He mentions Gunter Dorner's surveys showing a substantial increase in the incidence of male homosexuals born during or shortly after the extreme stress their mother's endured in the very last stages of World War II and its immediate aftermath; this echoing similar findings of male offspring of highly stressed female rats being attracted only to other males. This is evidence, but there could be cultural explanations, and it is a rather indirect expression of reduced fertility in females, which is where, logically, the adaptation would lie, since women and not men are the limiting factor in human reproduction (females being so in all animal species).

A problem with Morrison's theory is that demographers dispute the significance of the decline in fertility over the past two decades. I have rehearsed this argument above when I examined the economic arguments for mass net immigration. The recorded falls in fertility are apparent only: an artefact of a mistake in how fertility levels are measured (see the second page of Chapter 4).

So citing recent, albeit consistent, sharp fertility decline may not support the notion of the onset of 'plague mode'. I should emphasise, therefore, that a very serious impact of 'crowding stress' on human fertility is speculation. The theory has not been tested. It may be that it would be hard to get data unconfounded by other variables. As in many areas where social science would like to research, it could be that in this area too there are as yet no statistical models that have been devised that can address sufficiently complex interactions; in which case, for the foreseeable future, we will not be able to find out. Nevertheless, it should be something to always bear in mind, in just the same way that for many years the debate about global warming led to (albeit trivial) measures to combat greenhouse gas emissions, despite controversy as to whether or not the phenomenon of global warming could be shown actually to exist.

* * *

If such mechanisms really do account for a large element of the declining human fertility and associated reproductive behaviour, then this raises a profound question regarding immigration. A population increase, when it is an increase of people without any family or social connection with the indigenous UK community, and with not even a cultural connection to Britain; is likely to disproportionately increase social stress, and presumably there will be a commensurate effect on individuals of psychological 'crowding stress'. This could produce a positive feedback loop exacerbating the various problems causing declining rates of reproduction.

As I have already explained, immigration is no solution to the support ratio of workers to pensioners, and neither will it have any significant impact on any population decline — should that be seen as a problem rather than as a relief. But we may have a situation that by the very policy of bringing in more people who are perceived as alien to the bulk of the population, we bring about an accelerated decline in the British population. Furthermore, it is one thing to look at impersonal demographics, but if you consider the psychological impact on individuals then this could be extremely serious. Forgoing the personal fulfilment of raising a family is the greatest imaginable difference to how your life turns out. The vast majority of people under normal circumstances have a very strong desire, if not an overwhelming need, to raise a family. It is not good enough to say that if people have good reasons for not opting for this path through life then that must be good for society because people are now expressing such a free choice, whereas in times past they may have felt no option. Notwithstanding that almost infallible free prescription contraception has availed everyone of the choice, the increasing proportion of those 'voluntarily' childless should instead alert us to the distinct possibility that something very serious is wrong.

Of course, we might take the view that at a national policy level this is good for the country, because over time the population will fall to a more natural density. I imagine that many in the Green Party and those belonging to Friends of the Earth would tend to see it this way. I wholeheartedly agree, as I suspect the great majority see lots of benefits in a lower population, and Margaret Beckett's claim not to see any ceiling to the sustainable population is an extremely worrying notion for a senior politician to have. So why then try to nullify this trend by replacing lost population with immigrants? From the 'green' perspective again, taking people away from a relatively low-impact lifestyle in the third world and adding them to the population of a developed country like ours, where per capita impact on the Earth's carrying capacity is many times greater, is creating a problem for the global environmental balance sheet to compound global population growth. It serves unhelpfully to damp down the negative feedback loop that would slow and then eventually reverse unsustainable numbers of people in third world regions, which were often the very areas of greatest environmental stress to start with. That migration from third to first world really does have this effect has been shown in studies conducted in the Caribbean. Sustained high birth rates attended areas where there were high rates of emigration and conversely, in places where emigration was low, birth rates were low. Birth rates tracked changes in emigration: an increase in emigration was followed five years later by a commensurate rise in the birth rate.

Mass net immigration is a problem however you look at it.

Whistling in the Wind

What hope I had of getting a response and action out of the Home Office on the concerns I had about immigration procedures was coloured by my experience of the department's obstruction of my complaints and observations on a different set of abuses: of equal opportunities. So I will outline these parallel goings-on to illuminate the sort of tactics the Home Office arrogantly and contemptuously employs to try to shut up what it perceives as awkward oiks like me, and so cover up wilful ignorance, unacceptable practice and policy vacuum. Though the threads entwine interestingly, as I explain, this chapter is mostly not about immigration (which is why it appears as an appendix), so some readers may wish to pass it by and go straight to the epilogue. But they will miss an explanation of the timing of when I came forward: pieces of the jigsaw and important background.

That my concerns over equal opportunities abuses was treated in the same way as my alerts on the immigration work further bolsters my case that it was futile to continue to try the internal route before going public. This should be held in mind for the 'epilogue' that follows, looking at the Home Office's denial that I was acting within the Government's recently introduced law to cater for just the situation in which I found myself. What will be of further interest to those who reflect on such things is that the issues of immigration and equal opportunities are not at all as unconnected as they might first appear. They are both aspects of the moral totalitarianism of the political Left and its vehement denial of its own heritage ultimately in both Stalin and Hitler — all of the totalitarian evil of the previous century. As with the unravelling of the truth behind the bizarre stance on immigration, a similar dissection of the repressive zealousness of bogus notions about equal opportunities is also set ultimately to contribute to the electoral annihilation of the political Left, however their policies are masked. But that is the subject of my next book, though it shares with this one the root of challenging the current unquestioning, quasi-religious allegiance to the untenable idea of universal equality.

* * *

My first brush with authority came even before I had finished being mentored. I was briefly interviewed by a young woman I had never met, who did not make clear to me what her position was within the managerial foodchain. It was a routine quick check on progress with a sting in the tail. Several members of staff, she told me, had complained about my 'inappropriate language'. She played it down, just pointing out equal opportunities rules. I knew I had not spoken in any way that could be so construed, so I knew what this was about: I was the only person to complain about the very poor quality of the initial training. Deciding I was a trouble-maker, or one in the making, they placed a shot across my bows.

I sternly stood up to this. 'In writing please: I want full details of exactly what I am supposed to have said, in what context; and the names of the person or persons making allegations.' My chastiser was pulled up sharp. She started backtracking but I was having none of it. Nothing happened for several days so I e-mailed her to repeat my request. As elsewhere in today's world of work, everything that could be done by e-mail rather than crossing the office floor and doing it face-to-face was done in this tedious electronic fashion. It did have the advantage that you had a record, just in case of future denials. Being sent an e-mail obliged her to respond also by e-mail. She feigned innocent misinterpretation and responded with what she had said in our brief meeting, as if that is what I wanted her to put in writing. This stalemate went on and I started work proper in another building. Eventually, at my request, she came across to meet me and was disarmingly persuasive that the matter was dropped, of no consequence, and not put on record. Later in the week I thought better of it. Another meeting was set up through my team leader who pressured me to drop the whole thing. The reason I fell into line this time was that by now I had bigger fish to fry.

I had put in a request to be allowed to do a presentation on equal opportunities — I had researched for five years male/female differences and I could show that not women but lower status men were the major disadvantaged sub-group in society. There were major implications for assumptions about men–women prevalent among opinion formers that had now firmly taken hold in places like the

Home Office. Current equal opps, or how it was implemented, had got it badly wrong. For weeks, for months, I tried to meet an 'equal opportunities and diversity' officer, who always managed to find some excuse to cry off from an arrangement. He was too preoccupied with 'Diversity Week' to talk for a few minutes about fundamental equal opportunities issues.

'Diversity' was a hot button at the Home Office. I signed up to a session on 'gender' (or sex, as normal people would say). I then found out that it was a discussion about 'transgendered persons' (that's trans-sexuals to you and me). Now this may look like the Home Office taking the Michael out of the staff when you consider that there are something like only one in 12,000 men and one in 30,000 women who are in this category, so you are extremely unlikely ever to meet one in your office. Those running 'Diversity Week' may be the very first place to start when it comes to staff cuts, but the Home Office was perfectly serious that we should down tools in order to receive this invaluable training at taxpayers' expense. Hardly anyone turned up, I later heard, despite the chance of skiving with free snacks. I imagine they thought as I did, that we should not humour such an abuse of resources when apparently there was not the wherewithall to train us in what different countries' passports looked like.

In the first weeks, months even, equal opps was the focus of my dissent and I made attempts to constructively engage with the Home Office to bring about a debate. It may be that this distracted me from having serious concerns about the work itself; or if I was already aware of serious problems then perhaps I sublimated them in this way. It was one thing to be a rebel about meta-issues at work, but calling into question the work itself, about which as yet I did not know too much, would be more nearly a hanging offence. Nobody else had spilled the beans about Managed Migration, and this must be because everyone else lacked the something inside them that so completely distances you from the usual 'oh it must be right because everyone else is happy doing it'. It is not so usual to be able to stand apart from the imperative of social acceptance and blow a great big raspberry in everybody's faces — or a whistle, indeed.

* * *

Suspension from work at Managed Migration is not unique to my case. The one person I had met in initial training who seemed on my wavelength, a man in his late thirties named Adrian McKenzie, beat me to it. The strange circumstances opened further windows on to the Home Office parallel universe of equal opportunities, and shows the opacity of the department to fairness and common sense.

McKenzie wanted to do something a bit elaborate for the leaving do of a friend of his called Peter, and rather than take up work time as some staff were wont to do, he used his home PC. He set up a website spoof of a film (Fight Club), with friends of Peter depicted as the characters. Only these people and a few other friends in the know were given the website's address. There was a link on the site to a message board on a separate site (belonging to a friend of Adrian's) where comments could be left. All completely above-board and a contribution to staff morale that did not abuse work time.

Out of the blue there was a complaint to management about something someone had posted on the external message board that was seen by the woman complainant to be a physical threat against her personally. Nobody else could see how it could be so construed, being clearly in the spirit of the film which Adrian's website was spoofing. The complainant had a very junior management position and for five months while Adrian had been a lowly admin assistant, she was directly his senior, and her behaviour towards Adrian over this time earned her a rebuke from management for bullying and harassment. On the face of it, the complaint looked like simple revenge for having been found out, and in itself a continuation of the bullying. What's more, Adrian could not possibly have been held responsible for the message board posting.

Home Office Human Resources seniors did not see it this way at all and by their actions showed that they did not even consider it as a possibility. The woman complainant was left in place, and not even interviewed, while Adrian was suspended and an investigation begun. This was little short of an attack, spuriously charging Adrian with various things that clearly he had not done; such as abuse of work time and computer systems. He was being held to account for a bogus chain of 'extended responsibility' that could render liable any of us to be charged and convicted of anything. Adrian's life outside the Home Office was held not to be his own but brought into the domain of his work.

I went with Adrian as his representative for a second interview, where he outlined more than a dozen breaches by the Home Office of disciplinary procedure, some of them very serious, and comprehensively showed he had infringed not a single Home Office rule. I presented a collation of research into false accusation of men by women, making the point that it is quite unfair to presume that a female complainant's case always has substance while a male's does not, quite apart from the obvious history in this instance; not to mention the presumption of innocence in the natural justice that the Home Office owed to one of its employees. Still the woman was not interviewed. Adrian's counter-complaint against her was ignored and he was dismissed for no stated reason. He was to lodge an appeal, followed by bringing an Employment Tribunal if necessary, on the grounds of sex discrimination: the treatment of Adrian being inconceivable if you imagine the sexes reversed. But he decided he was well out of the Home Office and felt he had nothing to prove.

* * *

On a rare occasion when the Home Office invited discussion about equal opportunities it went out of its way to actively suppress debate. After a struggle I was finally allowed to attend a focus group back in October 2003 on 'gender'/flexi working. I was the only male present and several women there complained that men they knew who had e-mailed their desire to attend were never responded to. The only reason I was there was because of my badgering and the intervention of my team leader and even then an invite came only the day before the event. But there was no point in my being there because the points I raised were refused discussion by the facilitators, despite my protests. Of the dozen people present (excluding the two facilitators), no less than three were equal opportunities staff from HR, including one who was clearly steering discussion.

A focus group is a sub-group designed to provide useful and representative feedback from the workforce (in this case), electorate, or whatever. The people evaluating the results — the equal opps staff from HR — should have been the last people present. One of them insulted the Home Office's top man in Sheffield, saying that it would do him good to be forced to attend a full day equal opps course. As if anyone in senior management would not have the innate intelligence and interpersonal skills to be aware of and sensitive to the issues, which are hardly complex.

I complained about the focus group session and met with a senior Sheffield HR manager. She refuted my complaint saying that the focus group was not intended to be representative; but representation was clearly intended because the results of the focus group were to be used as feedback from staff in formulating equal opps policy — otherwise why waste time and money? If Philip Gould was told that all the focus groups New Labour spend so much money on were not meant to be representative, he would go bananas.

The HR manager, now in a bad mood, also said that I had no right to quote anyone present as this was an infringement of their confidentiality. Was she really saying that a session supposedly open to all staff is a forum where anything can be said, however wrong or abusive, without any possibility of comeback? In which case, why was a complaint considered against me in respect of an equal opps day (see below)?

What all this amounted to was contempt for staff and a refusal to listen even when it is obvious that there is something wrong. The focus group appears to have been set up with this contempt in mind, building in assumptions and keeping out participation. Instead of debating 'gender' and flexi-work separately, linking them together presupposes that both are concerns of women where men should have little or no import.

* * *

The classic way to try to fend off a complaint is to turn it round to say that the complaint itself, or something about how it was made, was itself an abuse in the very area complained about. A clear 'shoot the messenger' approach. This is exactly what the HR department tried to pull when I complained about yet another inept training day. This was a one-off, day-long background session on asylum. Because we were handling applications from people who had been refused asylum, management thought it would be useful if we knew about this area of the Immigration Service.

People like training days because it's a break from routine, you start late and finish early, get free coffee and snacks and a chance for a natter and maybe even a bit of a laugh. There may be a downside in the excruciating boredom of a trainer who hasn't been given any instruction in how to lecture. But in this case we could not even evaluate the training skills one of the two facilitators (as trainers are now called in our pseudo-interactive age) as it was hard to understand anything he said. A nice chap to be sure, but clearly he had neither grown up in Britain nor learnt English anywhere in earshot of a native-sounding speaker. That he so clearly was not able to communicate according to the most basic criteria begged the question of how he could be in a job that requires good verbal abilities above all else. How else could this be explained other than by an over-zealous implementation of equal opportunities?

To check that it was not just my ears at fault I asked around of dozens who had been on the same course on other days and there was unanimous agreement that it was, to say the least, hard work trying to follow what on earth this guy was saying. One colleague admitted that although he always took notes in training sessions, in this instance he could not, because it took all his effort just to get a vague understanding of the content.

Now, if you put your ear to the ground in the Home Office you hear some talk about preferential treatment of ethnic minority staff (and women), and this from some staff in HR as well as regular employees. While you can hear it through informal channels you most certainly do not hear it above ground — except in regard of senior positions, where there are actually set 'aspirational targets' for the proportion of people from disadvantaged or supposedly disadvantaged subgroups. These are, of course, quotas in all but name. I thought I would test the water, just to see if the knee-jerk counter-accusation of racism would fly back at me.

I worded my comment/complaint carefully. I used the phrase 'would appear to' (be because of an over-zealous implementation of equal opps) and prefaced with a compliment that the trainer in question was perfectly personable. No doubt wishing not to humour me after past experience, my e-mail was ignored. When I asked why there was no reply (and I told them that no, it was not just a comment but a complaint), then the predictable happened. The words 'inappropriate' and 'offensive' came out of the equal opportunities armoury and they were delivered face-to-face by my team leader. I had 'overstepped the mark', he said. No I had not, I insisted. You are objecting to the equal opportunities policy. No, I am objecting to the implementation of equal opps policy, which in itself infringes the equal opps rules. I pointed out that I had a submission currently with the Cabinet Office on this very issue regarding men–women which clearly demonstrates my support for equal opps principles.

My complaint was offensive to the trainer, it was claimed. Absolutely not: my complaint is not against the man himself — good luck to him if he snaps up a job offered to him — but against the Home Office. Another question: how can you know why he was appointed? — It could be for any of a number of reasons. And not one of them reasonable, I said, because anyone and everyone who is appointed in a teaching role must very first of all be able to communicate clearly in his speech. Otherwise he does not get to first base and no other reason can be good enough to appoint him. We agreed to disagree. My team leader then said it was likely that I would be interviewed by senior HR officials at Liverpool (the HQ of the northern division of the Home Office). Very happy I would be, I told him, to take the opportunity of such an interview to vigorously defend my position and to challenge the Home Office line.

But there was another matter. As everyone had to, at some time or other, I had attended an 'equal opportunities' training day back in November. My contributions on that day were minimal; most concerning factually incorrect information given out by the facilitator, some of which were directly or indirectly from inappropriate sources. (I can support my brief corrections with evidence from highly reputable peer-reviewed sources.) Now, suddenly, this equal opportunities training day was dragged up. So it was indeed going to be 'shoot the messenger' and, just in case once isn't enough, then some spare ammo from elsewhere would be handy — or something that at least made a nice bang if the real stuff couldn't be found.

The equal opps training day was by now months ago, so why was a complaint against me suddenly resurfacing now? My team leader agreed with me that this was interestingly strange. There was more than one complaint, he said. But I knew that there was not. I had found out indirectly from local HR staff that a complaint received at the time was of no consequence, which is why I was not even told about it at the time. It seemed that I had caught the Home Office unscrupulously trying to build a bogus case against me.

I went to see the top line manager (the Grade Six officer in charge of half the teams at Managed Migration in Sheffield) and she came out with exactly the same arguments as my team leader had and I demolished them in the same way. As a parting shot I added that there was also the question of the public interest (or not) of the work we were doing and, although I had signed the Official Secrets Act, a defence against a charge under that Act was to cite public interest. My team leader's boss did not react; quite likely a little stunned. We were leaving the room commandeered for our meeting and spilling on to the main office floor. I thought better of leaving things on such a note, so I changed tack, saying it would be a good idea if I kept my head down for a while and concentrated on getting off probation.

You could say that the Home Office had once again been clearly warned about my concerns about the immigration work we were doing, and quite specifically. I spoke about the general issue of casework by way of putting in context my complaint — that there was generally something awry at the Home Office, not just with regard to meta-issues like equal opps. I did not feel unsafe in saying it because at this time I had no intention of going to a newspaper about ECAA cases, bogus students/colleges and marriages, or anything to do with the casework. In a way it was just another blow of the safety valve; just like joking with junior staff about the absurdities of what we were obliged to do and how there might be people with placards on the pavement outside if what went on here ever got out. On the other hand, was I, almost unbeknown to myself, flashing a warning to lay off building a spurious case with a view possibly to dismissing me? Had I brought about something of a stand-off? In exchange for dealing with me fairly in my battles over equal opps, they may have hoped that I would not throw the whole department over a cliff by shouting over the rooftops about the farce of Managed Migration.

All right, I'm flattering myself that anyone even took me seriously, but the fact is that this was the last I heard of any interview by HR, Liverpool, or of any 'complaints' against me. I even got an e-mail confirming 'no action' from the HR manager when, after several weeks, I queried when HR Liverpool were finally going to get round to trying to grill me — when they would have found themselves on the end of a grilling from me. With the way the rumour mill works it would not surprise me if in retrospect some may now reckon that the thread of equal opps complaints I had made was really a feint to distract attention from my real purpose. The truth is that equal opps re men-women was and remains my hobby horse and served to blind me to the scale of the systematic failure to implement the law in the casework we were doing. Without this complication I think I would have come to a full realisation sooner and thereby have come forward at an earlier date than I did.

When I had more or less decided to whistle-blow, I was holding on to see if I could get anywhere on the equal opps front. I sent an e-mail to the senior staff member in HR on the training side to press for an answer about the asylum trainer, and I got a reply promising a reply, but then silence. So I then wrote a concise history of the string of equal opps matters I had highlighted — plus a couple of paragraphs about the serious problems with casework as a sting at the end — and e-mailed it to the very top man (actually a woman): Paula Higson. This was the same woman who had got the ball rolling for me when I turned up to her 'meet the people' session shortly after she was appointed and, through raising the idea of doing equal opps presentations, got a clear path to go to head office to submit a proposal. This was my paper, 'Equal Opportunities In Reverse', judged to be over their heads and forwarded to the Cabinet Office where, as they promised it would, it has remained for months. An overt kick into the long grass. It turned out that there would be a delay before I got a reply because Paula Higson was off on leave, but when she got back she bounced it back over the fence aiming for my greenhouse, saying that all was in hand with my managers and HR staff.

Well actually the reply was not Higson's at all. It had been drafted by an HR senior at Liverpool. The real reply to me was the one from HR Liverpool to Higson:

> In summary, Steve Moxon is a difficult employee who I feel may now need to be dealt with quite firmly. … there seems to be a particular problem in terms of his attitude and willingness to work by Home Office values. In particular he has strong and unconventional views on certain diversity issues and some of these conflict with the Home Office in a material way. The note from Steve comprehensively misrepresents the issues, and my opinion at this stage is that you should not get involved. There are a number of issues being dealt with separately, and Steven trying to pull these together does not help.

Even by Home Office standards this was an arrogant refusal to address a series of episodes that clearly demonstrated the wilfully ignorant and contemptuous attitude of the Home Office to its own staff. And this note was written by someone whose job supposedly was to champion equal opportunities! Classic 'shoot the messenger'.

This was the final stall I would allow them. I knew that I was not going to get a reply from the minister anytime soon, because I had gone back to the senior in local HR to press for a response and she had agreed to do so, but several weeks had now passed. Either the minister was refusing to reply or the senior in our (Sheffield) HR was blocking it — or on the instructions of someone above her? It was coming up to three months since the minister had visited us here at Aspect Court when I had first tried to raise serious concerns directly with her. Three months seemed a nice long and round timespan. The other significant milestone was that I had by then been in post over six months, and this meant that I was now considered to be an experienced caseworker, so any complaints I had about casework could not be dismissed as the misunderstandings of a novice. It was at last time to strike. The only problem that worried me was that if my computer work was being closely monitored then a pattern would be detected in the e-mails I would have to print off and remove from the office. I decided to leave the gathering of concrete evidence until almost the last moment, so that even if it was picked up I would have what I needed safely at home beyond possible confiscation.

Epilogue

When is a Whistle Not a Whistle?

I have heard it said that 'whistle-blowers' become defined by this one thing they have done, and are then trapped by it. Perhaps this is why Katherine Gunn keeps herself away from the snappers and the scribblers? Well, you could just as easily say that any job anyone happens to do defines and so ensnares them. But usually it doesn't in their own minds, and neither does it in the eyes of the other people in their lives outside of work. I don't feel at all hidebound by the 'whistle-blower' tag, however irksome the epithet. If anything it's liberated me.

People come up to me and wish me luck, as if I hadn't already been blessed with plenty; as if I wanted to continue to work for an organization as bad as the Home Office. I don't at all mind — I am pleased to receive — concern people express on my behalf, but I hope they don't feel sorry for me! It is not something personal. Plenty of other people could find themselves in a not dissimilarly interesting pickle, and anyone can easily imagine themselves where I am. It is the generic 'whistle-blower' that I stand for, and I think that people do see the principle of the thing, except that what I called time on really does grab everyone. I have rarely had to convince somebody that it needed doing. Welcome pats on the back make me feel a bit like the sports club mascot, who leads the team without having to play. All I have to put up with is the unfairness of the bureaucracy, but that's what got me here. It's not hard, because I don't have anything to prove; frequently reminded as I am that 'you told the truth'.

I still haven't met Katherine Gunn, ex of GCHQ, who seems such a retiring girl, with not a murmur since she went to court and the Government failed to show up. But I did meet her fellow intelligence service 'whistle-blower', David Shayler. I was invited to be the centrepiece of an edition of Now You're Talking, the BBC1 morning replacement for Kilroy, with Nicky Campbell standing in for the silver-haired ex-green leather mite who may have long irritated viewers, though not the BBC, until he made a remark that the Big Brother Censor deemed racist (or 'faithist') — the one about Muslims being woman oppressors, limb amputators and suicide bombers, that I cited above. Notwithstanding that the BBC has broadcast worse prejudice against Muslims in the context of women's rights, Kilroy got the sack, or agreed to resign; but as consolation the BBC made a deal for his company to provide the replacement show. Perhaps Kilroy personally had a hand in my selection, thinking it would be a wheeze to have someone else who the BBC had mistakenly seen as a rabid crusader against Islam.

The half-hour show was on 'whistle-blowing'. Not exactly a hard news slot or intellectual debate, but I was up for it. I reckoned any flak would be taken by David Shayler. The format is fairly 'low-brow', you could say, but the level of discussion was surprisingly high, albeit with a few forced oppositional figures. There was an ineffective Labour MP who had drawn the short straw, there to try to contrast my disclosure to those of a couple of doctors (one of whom had been suspended for four years), and some ex-army bloke with nothing to say except that I should have done my duty and not been a 'traitor'. It got feisty at times and easy to forget that it was staged. After an hour-long (or so it seemed) grilling by Simon Mayo on BBC Radio 5 Live, this was water off a duck's back. In fact, since the Mayo encounter, different bits of the BBC have rung me with invites on the strength of having seen him off. Campbell was good. He probed me on being 'David Davis' best friend', and what was I doing hob-nobbing with the Tories? 'So?', I said. Like who else have I got at Westminster? Solid majority support in the studio and nothing to trouble me. It was a good platform to restate that I had taken no money and that I had no connection of any kind with any political party or organization. The whole thing was done straight through with no pauses or re-takes, with me at the start, finish and in much of the middle. I really quite enjoyed myself. A day well spent.

I was right: David Shayler did take almost all the flak, despite elo-quently making the point that he had got IRA terrorists locked up but then drew the line at giving money to al-Qaeda to blow up kids (which is how, perhaps melodramatically, he summed up his case). He defended the allegations that he had taken money: the sixty grand from a newspaper was for expenses to live abroad so he could stay out of jail. I had a long natter with him and his girlfriend afterwards and I now know what he's about. She backs him up well. A really nice couple. He doesn't do himself any favours though with the style rebellion of unkempt long hair and clothes to match. It signals that maybe his 'whistle-blowing' was also a revolt more in appearance than in substance. (I had stuck with my usual white collar worker look sans tie, to click with the more civically engaged older generation who I guessed would be most of those watching, given the transmission time. These are the majority of the people who recognize and come up to me in the street.) Just after I appeared it was announced the show was to be axed. Close to a million was thought not high enough in the ratings. I hope it wasn't partly my fault.

* * *

Question: When is a whistle not a whistle?
Answer: When it's blown at the Home Office.

Late in the afternoon of Monday May 17 a courier showed up at my flat with a very broad and fat brown paper package I had to sign for. It was the report of the investigation by the Home Office HR chief, Rosalind McCool, concluding that what I had done did not fall within the terms of the 'Whistle-blower's Act'.

Expert legal advice, my union and all commentators, were unanimous that broadly I was protected by the Act and I was personally very confident of this. I had been even more confident after McCool interviewed me. I genuinely thought that even the Home Office would not have the sheer brass neck to deny truth so brazenly. Given the pattern of obstruction and unfair treatment by the Home Office, then I should have expected this latest turn, but strangely I didn't. What now dawned on me — in a flashback to a conversation I had with a lawyer friend who had pointed this out — was that not until August 18, the anniversary of my appointment, would I have full employment rights. I was still on 'probation'. Were they moving to dismiss me before this date so I would not be able to claim unfair dismissal? Well, a close look at the Public Interest Disclosure Act confirmed that anyone can claim unfair dismissal under its terms, regardless of how long they have been in tenure. But there was a potential problem in that for anyone in place under twelve months there is a stiffer test of the 'reasonableness' of their coming forward to disclose 'externally'. So there might be something in it for the Home Office. The logic from the Home Office's position would be to leave doing anything until near the last moment so that the maximum time would have elapsed between the start of the immigration furore back in March and any unfair treatment of me, simply so as to limit damage.

The report opened the way for a disciplinary hearing set for June 9, with a deadline of June 2 for my written response to the investigation report. The hearing would be a formality and — unless they sacked me there and then — after several weeks I would be sent a dismissal notice, so from then on I would be appealing from a position of being off the Home Office books. My days of suspension on full pay were numbered. Any Civil Service appeal is bound to fail, so the next port of call would be an Employment Tribunal. Only then would I be able to demolish the Home Office's argument about the application of the Act. In the meantime the Government will be embarrassed that it was having to deny the application of its own Act when it is itself the subject of an instance of its use. But the Government will not have been shown definitively to have complete contempt for public interest and fairness until the outcome of an Employment Tribunal some way down the line.

McCool's argument rests on her unsupportable contention that my warnings to the minister and the Managed Migration senior director were not the same as my disclosure to the Sunday Times. Clearly they were the same, merely differing in detail. There was no need to give detail internally, but every reason to do so in justifying to the general public why I had come forward. McCool also argued that I had subsequently made further disclosures, but of course all I had done was either to clarify aspects of the original disclosure or react to developments; all of which were already in the public domain, so the issue of disclosure by definition simply does not apply.

Given McCool's conclusion, she then goes on about breaches of confidentiality; but of course, these are irrelevant, because issues of contractual confidentiality are superceded in a 'whistle-blowing' case protected by the Act. That's what the Act is for. The breach of confidentiality ruse is then developed into: 'an irretrievable breakdown in the fundamental need for the existence of trust and confidence essential in the relationship between a civil servant and the employer'. This has it backwards. My disclosure and behaviour is a direct consequence of the pattern of obstruction and unfair treatment of me and the refusal by the Home Office to concede that workers were being asked — and continue to be asked — to flout the law by systematically failing to fully implement the immigration rules and so to work against the public interest. It is the Home Office and not myself that has caused an irretrievable breakdown between employee and employer, and on this I reckoned I would be able to argue unfair dismissal.

Other errors were apparent in McCool's report. Although I had complied with the terms of the 'Whistle-blower's Act', the Home Office maintained that I did not follow the internal prescribed rules for escalating my complaint to higher and higher levels within the organization before I went outside of it. McCool is wrong, and she obligingly provided me with the detail, on the last page of the appendix to her report, showing that, however unwittingly, I had followed the rules almost to the letter. This was a copy of a Home Office Notice from May 2003 about 'raising matters of conscience' and 'how to deal with rapidly developing events'. The prescribed procedure to follow is laid down thus:

- carry out the request or instruction
- record your dissent in writing immediately, with reasons
- send the minute to the head of department who will advise the departmental Minister, if applicable, and inform the Head of the Home Civil Service

Although I had not come across this notice, as it turned out I pretty well exactly followed the rules without knowing it. I had written to the head of Managed Migration, Paula Higson and more than just leaving it up to her to advise the minister, I went directly to the minister myself. I followed Home Office rules for internal disclosure and with bells on. This was not so much a lucky accident when you consider that the Government could hardly draw up a 'whistle-blower's Act' and then outline its own departmental 'whistle-blowing' procedures that required that you went beyond anything required in the Act.

Another major error of McCool's was her claim that I could not reasonably have believed that if I had kept everything internal to the Home Office I would have suffered 'detriment' and/or that 'evidence relating to the relevant failure would have been concealed or destroyed'. These are from clauses in the Act that if answered in the affirmative would support my case. The answer is indeed a 'yes' to both of them. There was no maybe about it. I had clear evidence of concealment. My own questions to the minister revealing dire procedural failure were repeatedly obstructed, for God's sake. I also had clear evidence about threats of disciplinary action and even dismissal against me — actually there in black-and-white in some of the interviews with staff and their e-mail chatter about me included in the report itself. Of course, this came to light only now, whereas what is relevant is the basis on which I *believed* I would be blocked and attacked; but I had stacks of evidence that I was fully aware of such back in February and early March. With this ammunition I could hardly fail in the test that it was 'reasonable' to go to the media. At some point down the line I was going to have a field day.

* * *

I have always said in response to media enquiries that I did not expect to get my job back and that I thought some pretext would be found to end my suspension by dismissal. How right I was. My thinking had changed after talking with my union and others: some speculated that the Home Office might offer me a pay-off in exchange for a confidentiality agreement. They might have considered this but reckoned that the damage had already been done. What would be the point in preventing me, for example, from publishing this book when I am only repackaging what is already out in the public domain bar fine detail, structured commentary and personal details? Why risk yet another feather in my cap from the public exposure of the Home Office attempting to do a deal? Given my principled stance on both the tearing up of immigration rules and the abuse of equal opportunities, they would have anticipated a rebuff. Another possible outcome that crossed my mind was that they might find some 'Home Office Siberia' they could shunt me off to. Some might think that Managed Migration Sheffield was already well east of the Urals and the Home Office probably think that I could cause damage just making the tea. Pretty unlikely, this solution, I think you'll agree. No, they will have had a meeting after which Rosalind McCool went off to twist logic and write a suitable report to pave the way for giving me the sack.

I contacted Martin Kelsey, my union rep, who said he couldn't make June 9 for the hearing because he was by the seaside for his union conference, so he would write to get a delay (and we got one: to June 30). He told me what I expected he would say: not to reveal details of the investigation report. He would seek an expert view from Thompsons, the leading employment law specialists. The union were pulling the stops out for me, it seemed. The problem was the same as with my interview with McCool; that is, if I revealed details then it could be construed that I had made an additional disclosure to the one I made originally. But could this be an infringement of the Act? I wanted to argue that my defence required freedom to show a consistent pattern of Home Office unfair treatment of me and that this helped to confirm that the Home Office's way of tackling the serious problems in immigration was cover-up and not action. To reveal this was itself in the public interest and in any case was not further revelation of key aspects of how the Immigration Service worked, but of admin procedures by Human Resources, quite outside my work, that set up fresh legitimate grievances that I should have the right to air. But getting a lawyer to come off the fence and give clear advice on this proved to be impossible.

Still, I was in no hurry, because I thought that it would be best to delay announcing the investigation report's conclusion until the same day as the disciplinary hearing — though if someone could helpfully leak it to the Sunday Times then Leppard could run a piece the Sunday before to flag it up. Making an announcement about McCool's findings without any other context has more of the air of a gratuitous 'disclosure', whereas the hearing is an event and involving other people so I am on safer ground to resist a challenge that I'm making a disclosure. I would come out of the meeting and decline to give details, as I had done after the interview with Rosalind McCool. Immediately outside Apollo House (the Home Office Immigration & Nationality Directorate HQ in the high rise soullessness of central Croydon) is a public place where TV crews and press cameramen could legitimately gather, tipped off by who knows who. Combining the fact that I was now about to lose my job, with the Home Office's contempt for the Public Interest Disclosure Act, and in a situation with the right visuals for a TV news piece: this would make a good item that would guarantee wide coverage. Unfortunately a planned rail strike (that never materialized) forced relocation of the hearing to the middle of nowhere: the Holiday Inn at Bramhope, a village near Leeds/Bradford Airport. They were going to fly the Home Office in. It would likely mean less coverage: some TV crews not bothering to make the journey.

The union was waiting on legal advice, to arrive no later than June 11 on just what the heck a 'disclosure' was. They had given me interim advice that I should not talk to the media, and ticked me off that I had been on a Sky discussion panel on the day the National Audit Office published its nonsense about the fall in asylum figures not being offset by an increase in immigration stats. I was starting to question the point of sticking by the book to fight the Home Office. After all, I had done loads of media, especially at the start. In for a penny, in for a pound.

The question is: in playing carefully by the rules, how would I gain, other than getting a formal censure of the Home Office? If I cannot get much if any compensation then am I not better off bringing everything out into the open: the embarrassment of the Home Office being my reward inasmuch as it further strengthens my position? This was the line taken by the charity Public Interest at Work. I had rung them anonymously before I came forward and now I could ring them and they would know something of my situation. The advice was that compensation, should I receive any at all, would be minimal, so why not simply resign? The thinking here is that I was in a very strong position and it would be public spirited to save the taxpayer the expense of an Employment Tribunal. My instinct though was that some would see it as a retreat and wonder if the Home Office had something which I knew would have undermined me. Nobody else agreed with the suggestion to resign. A few pointed out that under the PID Act there was no limit on damages, but I suspect the Public Interest at Work guy was right that I would get peanuts.

Finally, on June 15, the revised deadline for a reply to be made to the Home Office's report, my union came good with the legal advice they had requested from Thompsons. Martin Kelsey phoned me to say that it wasn't all good — some doubts about 'reasonableness', but some helpful points. I picked up his e-mail and realized that my position was stronger than I had thought. The opinion was that the disclosures to the minister, Paula Higson and the Sunday Times were indeed the same; and that the evidence showed that it was reasonable for me to conclude both that I would suffer detriment if I disclosed internally and also that 'destruction or concealment' would occur. This means that I can argue that the issues I complained of were of an 'exceptionally serious' nature, and this means in turn that it becomes more reasonable for me to have gone to the media. Not that this was pointed out in the advice. On the question of my 'good faith', which McCool also cast spurious doubt on, the advice was that the issue was an irrelevance given that the Act does not address mixed motives. Still though, no ruling on what was and what was not a 'disclosure'.

* * *

As if I needed any indication of how I would be treated by the Home Office, on June 14 James Cameron, the Romanian consul who had 'blown the whistle' in my wake, had a four-hour disciplinary hearing at the Foreign Office. They threw every nonsense at him: that he hadn't followed internal procedures; that his motives were not to uncover wrongdoing but because of what he had seen on TV; that he had gone to David Davis after going to the Foreign Office; and that the Sutton investigation was already underway. I should stress that this information comes not from James Cameron himself, you understand, but from 'friends of James Cameron'. Bugger me if that Foreign Office is nearly as leaky as my place. On the previous day the Sunday Times had run a front page story on his framing by the Government. Despite full support from diplomats, all the staff in Romania and a positive vetting earlier in the year, the Government were now smearing him with the bizarre charge that as the head of the visa section at Bucharest he had improperly processed visa applications in exchange for sexual favours and money. They had done exactly the same to the ambassador to Uzbekistan, Craig Murray. That the Government was now resorting to criminal accusation against Cameron was a depth it had indeed previously fathomed.

Cameron's disciplinary hearing was only in respect of the disclosure, but for his public spirit he was put on a 'final warning', removed permanently from Romania, denied the current year's pay rise and barred from promotion for three years. The Government punished him in every way it could under the terms of the Act — which protects employees from dismissal, demotion, and pay cuts. So it was a victory for Cameron in the sense that the Government did not contest that he had the right to 'blow the whistle' in the situation in which he found himself. Obviously, the criminal charges will now be used as a pretext to dismiss him. Scandal or what?

I phoned Leppard and he said that Cameron was absolutely furious and was not going to go without making a lot of noise. He joked about putting the two of us on an open-topped bus to wend its way through Whitehall. 'We can have a lot of fun with this', he chuckled. Cameron had been cagey thus far and I doubted he would ever be up for such a stunt, but for the two of us to meet looked as though it could be on the cards.

Two days after Cameron's hearing the National Audit Office came out with a supremely damning report about the ECAA fiasco. This was the report that generated the headlines about nine in ten applications should never have been granted. The BBC's home affairs co-ordinator, Brian Ging, rang to alert me, followed by GMTV and Radio 5 Live. At first I said that I had been instructed not to talk to the media, but when I found out what was in the report — and after the appalling treatment of James Cameron — I relented and did a media blitz: GMTV, BBC TV One O'clock News, Radio 5 … and appearance number four on Sky News' Littlejohn show. The PCS Union would not be amused. Even so, I didn't tell anyone about the Home Office report: just that I was soon to have a disciplinary hearing.

Leppard had somehow managed to get hold of the investigation report. That leaky Home Office again. He was going to run a story on that Sunday ahead of my disciplinary hearing the following Wednesday. I provided him with a quote: 'the Act is not worth the paper it is written on.' A cliché I concede, but sometimes a cliché is just the succinct turn of phrase required. Still with no legal guidance on 'disclosure', he promised to get an unofficial ruling from the Sunday Times' legal team later that week. This was increasingly looking 'academic', however; I had already decided that come what may I would go down the media path. After all, I had broken with the advice from my union. I gathered that the Foreign Office seemed to be back-tracking and it now looked like Cameron would not lose his job: they were shelving the bogus charges. In other words, they were not sending him back to where he could cause more damage, but would go down the Siberia route instead.

I asked if a meeting of Cameron and myself would be possible: Leppard thought that would be a good idea and that Cameron would be up for it. Next thing I knew we were communicating by e-mail and then I got a phone call from Cameron inviting me down to his place in the West Country for a long chat. We met on his home turf — the garden of his local pub. Cameron came across as much less cagey than I thought he would be. I am not going to quote him or say much about what we talked about, because I don't want to compromise his position, which is different to mine, he being a career civil servant. Cameron does expect to lose his job, but he also thinks he can move sideways in the civil service. A self-imposed comfortable Siberia, if you will. We found that the procedures he faced under the Foreign Office were quite different to what I would have to contend with, so our cases could not illuminate each other very much. We agreed that both our departments were trying to make the PID Act unusable. Like me he couldn't find in the Act any stuff about not making further disclosures. The big surprise was that they had told him that they were not competent to deal with the situation under the Act — 'friends of James Cameron' later told me. The buggers had simply side-stepped it! Well they won't be able to get away with that in a Tribunal.

As June drew to a close and my hearing loomed, there was silence from my union. I suppose that with my continued media presence they saw no point in having a meeting between me and their rep to discuss the case. As for the Home Office, they were embroiled in the strange debacle between the Home Secretary and the Chief Constable of Humberside Police, David Westwood, who refused to suspend himself over the report into the Ian Huntley affair. His Police Authority backed him and asked Blunkett to reconsider. This was rebuffed and on June 28 Blunkett lodged papers with the High Court to force the Police Authority to bend to his will. Commentators made the point that the Home Office was at fault in not having identified failings much sooner and not providing the money for a national police computer system enabling forces to share information on suspected serial offenders such as Ian Huntley. I was waiting for someone to suggest that never mind his showdown with David Westwood, David Blunkett should suspend himself for the gross incompetence and deception regarding immigration that he presided over. Perhaps that someone should be me: I was booked for both the GMTV and BBC Breakfast sofa on the morning of my hearing.

Having done the breakfast media round I got back to Leeds in plenty of time and arrived at the hearing venue courtesy of the BBC. All the other TV guys were there. The hearing lasted well over four hours. Steve Barnett, the Home Office IND head HR guy, was adamant that contrary to press reports and what I had said, no decision had been made. I stifled a guffaw, very effectively under the circumstances. We went over the same ground in several different ways. Barnett made a strange admission: he read McCool's report as having the underlying assumption that a disclosure meant any and every media contact. In other words, merely repeating the same thing to a different outlet amounted to an additional disclosure. This was a startling admission. It was not an interpretation that could stand up. Discussion turned to what is and what is not a disclosure. No firm conclusion. They had transcripts of what I had said, including that morning's breakfast TV appearances. Barnett pulled me up on my description of Beverley Hughes as a serial liar. I stood firm, pointing out that this was not my opinion but fact, and could be proved according to a criminal standard with evidence fully in the public domain. My 'extremist' epithet regarding Blunkett was pulled out of context, so I put it back in: 'a ridiculous thing for a home Secretary to say', I said, of Blunkett's claim that there was no ceiling on levels of immigration. Virtually nobody other than a few Labour politicians think, let alone publicly pronounce, such a self-evidently unsustainable position.

I actually repeated what I had said to the media: that the situation was surreal. I didn't want to go back to work and they didn't want me back at work, so the exercise was simply one of ascribing blame.

The TV guys would be used to hanging around half the day for a non-story and that is what they got. I apologized to them for the 'no verdict' outcome. Actually I had known this would almost certainly be the case: I had rung Barnett's secretary to ask what would happen, and she said that no decision would be made on the day. Of course, I wouldn't tell the media this, otherwise they would never have taken an interest in the first place. I did say that I thought 'no verdict' would be the more likely outcome. The thing is that the Home Office are only going through a disciplinary procedure because of the publicity glare and the PID Act. They could surely get round the Act — something along the lines of not behaving according to the standards of a civil servant (using the 'serial liar' and 'extremist' stuff) — and simply dismiss me without a reason if they wanted to, because I was still on 'probation'. So if the media were thin on the ground and the buggers thought their interest had sufficiently died down, then they might just revert to form.

Just as I was about to go back to Leeds with the BBC, a Yorkshire TV guy came up to me to tell me that he had overheard the two Home Office HR men. Barnett had said to his scribe something about it being 'unacceptable in the current climate'. Mr Yorkshire TV thought they were talking about whether they could sack me. Or were they talking about my on-record comments about ministers? Could it be that they would simply keep me on suspension? For how long? Might I have to resign? If they didn't sack me, on the grounds that my disclosure was protected by the PID Act, then I would have proved my point, so then I could resign without anyone wondering if it was because I wasn't confident about my position. But I suppose I might be able to bring a case to an Employment Tribunal of unfair suspension from work, so the Home Office wouldn't necessarily get themselves off the hook. I recalled the Now You're Talking TV show on 'whistle-blowing' on which I had appeared; the two women doctors who had been suspended for years. Why had they not got redress through a Tribunal? Maybe things were to be more up-in-the-air than I had supposed.

* * *

The Home Office then changed tack. On July 8 I received a letter from the Treasury Solicitor (TS) — the Government's lawyers – requesting a copy of the manuscript of this book within seven days and an undertaking not to publish or to seek to publish without permission. The letter ended with the comment that the Home Office would not unreasonably withhold permission. Come again?!

The TS guy must have found it hard to keep a straight face about the idea that the Home Office would be in any way other than totally unreasonable about any of this. 'They're gonna try and get yer, boy!' Leppard quipped. I e-mailed back to tell them that the book was still work-in-progress — which it was — and that the scheduled publication date was one picked out of the air — which it also was; and suggested he go and see Steve Barnett to gen up on the Public Interest Disclosure Act. This latest move gave me some ammunition, because by getting its solicitors involved it seemed to show that the Home Office was admitting that it was not competent to deal with me under the PIDA. The TS followed up with another letter, again asking for an assurance that I would seek permission before publishing. And again I just tossed it back at them, making the same points but adding that I was under no obligation to answer hypothetical questions.

This may have got the faceless ones around some committee table snapping their pencils: a few days later another courier courtesy of the Home Office arrived at my flat, this time very late in the day — almost eleven o'clock at night (this was Monday July 26). Obviously — I knew — it must be my dismissal notice. After twenty weeks of suspension while they faffed about, boy are they all of a sudden in a rush: they were not going to give me until the end of the month, but 'with immediate effect' it said. Guilty as charged: of 'gross misconduct', which meant they would not pay me in lieu of notice, so I was from now on without any income. I had already reckoned that if they hadn't long ago decided to get shot of me, then the promise of the book would have spurred them to put maximum distance between my sacking and publication.

Popping open some celebratory wine in anticipation of my impending release, I opened and read the miserable five-page document. HR head Steve Barnett had simply endorsed all of the non-sense that Rosalind McCool had put forward. Clearly the decision must have been made before the disciplinary hearing and Barnett's assurances to the contrary deserved the guffaw that I had half stifled. For once somebody in HR could claim to have earned his salary: as recompense for causing his own personal embarrassment.

I rang Leppard and we agreed I would keep quiet about my sacking for a few days, until the following Sunday (August 1), so as to give him another front page exclusive. Well, for my own credibility I had better demonstrate loyalty to *somebody*! (The ST rewarded this on the day with a front-page scoop and leading article calling for my re-instatement. They quoted David Davis's claim that 'it was outrageous that the man who is primarily responsible for the government having to take a grip of our failing immigration policy has been punished for so doing.')

The Sunday Times had become the whistle-blower's home, consistently supporting James Cameron as well as myself, and the previous day the paper had run a front page story on John Morrison — the chief investigator for the parliamentary intelligence and security committee, who was sacked for the high crime of criticizing Blair on TV after the Butler inquiry supposedly cleared him over Iraq. The ST was still talking of some kind of job for me hauling in would-be Whitehall whistle-blowers, and I had an agreement with them that should I ever be without any income as a result of all this — no job and no Job Seeker's Allowance because of disqualification on the grounds of dismissal for gross misconduct — that they would cover me. Certainly they would save me from having to sign on the dole from the day after the courier landed, because going down the dole queue obviously would have given the game away.

My publisher had already decided to bring the book forward to more like mid-August than August end in anticipation of my getting the order of the boot at the end of July, so delaying announcing my dismissal would cut the lead time to the book hitting the shelves to just a fortnight; perfect timing for maximum publicity ahead of any launch. And the perfect clip for the TV news on the day after the Sunday Times front page would be me turning up at the Job Centre. I might even do a Boys from the Blackstuff 'gissa job?!' cameo:

> I need a job: any offers?! Excellent written communication, interviewing and research skills; good verbal and inter-personal ability; some experience of campaigning work with a degree of political nous; fully computer and internet literate; relishes challenge; has integrity.

* * *

With obvious parallels to the fate of Andrew Gilligan and John Morrison, I will leave the last words on my case to the Independent's Simon Carr:

> The practice he exposed was unconstitutional, contrary to the Civil Service charter, and possibly illegal — and yet it was he who'd been suspended!... Anyway: the department will hold its enquiry. No one will be blamed — not ministers, not department heads, not the senior managers.
>
> The whistle-blower, of course, has had it.

Further Reading

Angrist, J.D. & Kugler, A.D., 'Protective or Counter-productive? Labour Market Institutions and the Effect of Immigration on EU Natives' (2003), *Economic Journal*, vol. 113 no. 488.

Borjas, George, *Heaven's Door: Immigration Policy and the American Economy* (1999) Princeton University Press.

Borjas, George, *The Labor Demand Curve Is Downward Sloping: Re-examining the Impact of Immigration on the Labor Market* (2002) Harvard University Press.

Browne, Anthony, *Do We Need Mass Immigration?* (2002), Civitas (published online at www.civitas.org.uk/pdf/cs23.pdf).

Browne, Anthony, 'Some Truths About Immigration', *The Spectator*, 2 August 2003.

Cavanagh, Matt *Against Equality of Opportunity* (2002), Oxford University Press.

Coleman, David, 'Demographic, Economic and Social Consequences of UK Migration, in *Work In Progress: Migration and Integration in the European Labour Market*, ed. Helen Disney (2003), Civitas.

Collins, Michael *The Likes of Us: a Biography of the White Working Class* (2004), Granta.

Donnison, David, *Policies for a Just Society* (1998), MacMillan.

Dustmann, Christian et al., *The Local Labour Market Effects of Immigration in the UK* (2003) Home Office Report (published on-line at: www.homeoffice.gov.uk/rds/pdfs2/rdsolr0603.pdf).

Eatwell, Roger, *Fascism: A History* (2003), Pimlico.

Epstein, Y.M. 'Crowding Stress in Human Behaviour' *The Journal of Social Issues*, vol. 37, no. 1, Spring 1981.

Ferguson, Niall, *Empire: How Britain Made the Modern World* (2003), Allen Lane.

Ferguson, Niall, *Colossus: The Rise and Fall of the American Empire* (2004), Allen Lane.

Fukuyama, Francis, *Trust: the Social Virtues and the Creation of Prosperity* (1995), Hamish Hamilton.

Goodhart, David, 'Too Diverse?', *Prospect*, no.95, Feburary 2004.

Gregor, James A., *The Faces of Janus: Marxism and Fascism in the Twentieth Century* (2000) Yale University Press.

Hatton, T. & Tani, M., *Immigration and Inter-regional Mobility in the UK* (2000), CEPR.

Home Office, *Statistics on Race and the Criminal Justice System 1999* (on-line at: www.homeoffice.gov.uk/rds/pdfs/s95race99.pdf).

Morrison, Reg, *The Spirit of the Gene: Humanity's Proud Illusion and the Laws of Nature* (1999), Cornell University Press.

Mullan, Phil, *The Imaginary Time Bomb: Why an Ageing Population is Not a Social Problem* (2000), I.B. Tauris.

National Audit Office, *Visa Entry to the United Kingdom: the Entry Clearance Operation*, 17 June 2004 (published online at: www.ukcosa.org.uk/conference/images/E9Informationsheet.doc).

National Audit Office, *Asylum and Migration: A Review of Home Office Statistics*, 25 May 2004 (published on-line at: www.nao.org.uk/publications/nao_reports/03-04/0304625.pdf).

New Century Foundation, *The Color of Crime: Race, Crime and Violence in America* (1999) (online at: www.amren.com/color.pdf).

Pannell, Norman *Immigration, What is the Answer?* (1965), Routledge & Kegan Paul.

Putnam, Robert, *Bowling Alone* (2000), Simon & Schuster.

Ray, John J., *Modern Leftism as Recycled Fascism* (2004) (published on-line at members.optusnet.com.au/~jonjayray/musso.html).

Rowthorn, Robert, *The Economic Impact of Immigration* (2004) Civitas (online at: www.civitas.org.uk/pdf/Rowthorn_Immigration.pdf).

Roy, Olivier and Volk, Carol, *The Failure of Political Islam* (1994), Harvard University Press.

Ruthven, Malise, *A Fury For God* (2002), Granta.

Sergeant, Harriet, *Welcome to the Asylum* (2001), Centre for Policy Studies.

Sergeant, Harriet, *No System to Abuse: Immigration and Health Care in the UK* (2003) Centre for Policy Studies.

Sternhell, Zeev, *The Birth of Fascist Ideology: From Cultural Rebellion to Political Revolution* (1995), Princeton University Press.

essays in political and cultural criticism

Contemporary public debate has been impoverished by two competing trends. On the one hand the increasing commercialization of the media has meant that in-depth commentary has given way to the ten-second soundbite. On the other hand the explosion of scholarly knowledge has led to such a degree of specialization that academic discourse has ceased to be comprehensible. As a result writing on politics and culture tends to be either superficial or baffling.

This was not always so—especially for politics. The high point of the English political pamphlet was the seventeenth century, when a number of small printer-publishers responded to the political ferment of the age with an outpouring of widely-accessible pamphlets and tracts. Indeed Imprint Academic publishes a facsimile reprints under the banner 'The Rota'.

In recent years the tradition of the political pamphlet has declined—with most publishers rejecting anything under 100,000 words. The result is that many a good idea ends up drowning in a sea of verbosity. However the digital press makes it possible to re-create a more exciting age of publishing. *Societas* authors are all experts in their own field, but the essays are for a general audience. Each book can be read in an evening.

The books are available retail at the price of £8.95/$17.90 each, or on bi-monthly subscription for only £5.00/$10.50.Full details:

www.imprint-academic.com/societas

EDITORIAL ADVISORY BOARD

IMPRINT ACADEMIC, PO Box 200, Exeter, EX5 5YX, UK
Tel: (0)1392 841600   Fax: (0)1392 841478   sandra@imprint.co.uk

SOCIETAS

essays in political and cultural criticism

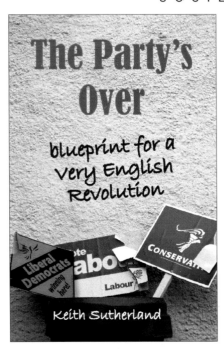

The Party's Over
Keith Sutherland
200 pp., £8.95/$17.90, 0907845517

- 'This timely book examines why British politics has descended into the quagmire in which it now squirms.' **The Ecologist**

- 'An extremely valuable contribution – a subversive and necessary read.' **Graham Allen MP**, *Tribune*

- 'His analysis of what is wrong is superb … No one can read this book without realising that something radical, even revolutionary must be done.' **Sir Richard Body**, *Salisbury Review*

- 'Pithy, pungent, provocative — Keith Sutherland is becoming the Hazlitt of our age.' **Professor Robert Hazell**, Director, The Constitution Unit, UCL

- 'Anyone who is concerned about the serious lack of interest in the parliamentary system should read this book.' **Lord Weatherill**, Speaker of the House of Commons (1983–1992)

Consider the following paradox: As the leaders of both of the main British political parties subscribed to the neoconservative doctrine on Iraq, everybody else in the birthplace of parliamentary democracy was effectively disenfranchised. Yet one of the rationales supporting the deployment of UK forces in Iraq was the wish to export democracy to the Middle East. The Emperor would appear to have mislaid his clothes.

Judging by the lack of ministerial resignations in the wake of the Butler enquiry, Britain is no longer a *parliamentary* democracy. The classical doctrine of joint and several ministerial responsibility is revealed to be a fiction, and Lord Hailsham's verdict of 'elective dictatorship' is a better assessment of the British constitution. By contrast unelected bodies like the BBC are now far more accountable for their actions. The reason of this paradox is the monopoly power of the ruling party, controlled by the Prime Minister.

The UK political party started off as a loose association of like-minded MPs. However, in recent years the tail has been firmly wagging the dog— politicians now have no alternative but to choose and then fall in line behind a strong leader with the charisma to win elections. This book examines the historical forces that gave rise to the modern political party and questions its role in the post- ideological age. If we all now share the liberal market consensus, then what is the function of the party?

The book argues that the tyranny of the modern political party should be replaced by a mixed constitution (*politeia*) in which the phrase 'Her Majesty's Government' is restored to its original meaning, advocacy is entrusted to a true aristocracy of merit, and democratic representation is achieved via a (selective) jury-style lottery. Keith Sutherland is publisher, *History of Political Thought*; his previous books include *The Rape of the Constitution?* (2000).

sample chapters, reviews and TOCs: **www.imprint-academic.com/societas**

SOCIETAS

The Case Against the Democratic State
Gordon Graham

We are now so used to the state's pre-eminence in all things that few think to question it. This essay contends that the gross imbalance of power in the modern state is in need of justification, and that democracy simply masks this need with an illusion of popular sovereignty. Although the arguments are accessible to all, it is written within the European philosophical tradition. The author is Professor of Moral Philosophy at the Uniiversity of Aberdeen. 96 p., £8.95/$17.90

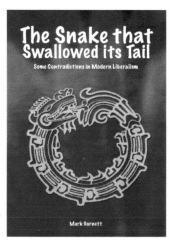

The Snake that Swallowed its Tail
Mark Garnett

Liberal values are the hallmark of a civilised society. Yet they depend on an optimistic view of the human condition, Stripped of this essential ingredient, liberalism has become a hollowed-out abstraction. Tracing its effects through the media, politics and the public services, the author argues that hollowed-out liberalism has helped to produce our present discontent. Unless we stop boasting about our values and try to recover their essence, liberal society will be crushed in the coils of its own contradictions. 96 pp., £8.95/$17.90

The Modernization Imperative
Bruce Charlton & Peter Andras

Modernisation gets a bad press in the UK, and is blamed for the dumbing down of public life. But modernisation is preferable to lapsing back towards a static, hierarchical society. This book explains the importance of modernisation to all societies and analyses anti-modernisation in the UK—especially such problems as class divisions, political short-termism and the culture of spin.

96 pp., £8.95/$17.90

sample chapters, reviews and TOCs: **www.imprint-academic.com/societas**

SOCIETAS

Democracy, Fascism and the New World Order
Ivo Mosley

Growing up as the grandson of the 1930s blackshirt leader, made Ivo Mosley consider fascism with a deep interest. Whereas conventional wisdom sets up democracy and fascism as opposites, to ancient political theorists democracy had an innate tendency to lead to extreme populist government, and provided demagogues with the opportunity to seize power. This book argues that totalitarian regimes can be the outcome of unfettered mass democracy. 96 pp., £8.95/$17.90

The Liberty Option
Tibor R. Machan

This book advances the idea that for compelling moral and practical reasons it is the society organised on classical liberal principles that serves justice best, leads to prosperity and encourages the greatest measure of individual virtue. The book contrasts the Lockean ideal with the various statist alternatives, defends it against its communitarian critics and lays out some of its policy implications. Machan is a research fellow at Stanford University. His books include *Classical Individualism* (Routledge, 1998). 104 pp., £8.95/$17.90

The Last Prime Minister
Graham Allen MP

Echoing Gandhi, Graham Allen thinks the British constitution would be a very good idea. In *The Last Prime Minister* he showed the British people how they had acquired an executive presidency by stealth. This timely new edition takes in new issues, including Parliament's constitutional impotence over Iraq.

'Well-informed and truly alarming.' **Peter Hennessy**

'Iconoclastic, and well-argued, it's publication could hardly be more timely.' **Vernon Bogdanor, THES**

96 pp. £8.95/$17.90

sample chapters, reviews and TOCs: **www.imprint-academic.com/societas**